10-12-92

GV
865
H 68
A 3
1989

BETWEEN ·T·H·E· LINES

One Athlete's Struggle to Escape the Nightmare of Addiction

STEVE HOWE
with Jim Greenfield

SOUTHWESTERN
COLLEGE
Library
CHULA VISTA
CALIFORNIA

MASTERS PRESS

Published by Masters Press, 5025 28th Street, S.E., Grand Rapids, Michigan 49508

© Copyright 1989 by Steve Howe and Jim Greenfield

All rights reserved

No part of this publication may be reproduced, stored in a retrieval system, or transmitted, in any form or by any means, electronic, mechanical, photocopying, recording, or otherwise, without the prior permission of Masters Press.

Distributed by Little, Brown, & Company

Printed in the United States of America

Library of Congress Cataloging-in-Publication Data

Howe, Steve, 1958–
  Between the lines : One Athlete's Struggle to Escape the Nightmare of Addiction / Steve Howe with Jim Greenfield.
    p.   cm.
  ISBN 0-940279-25-8 : $17.95
  1. Howe, Steve, 1958– . 2. Baseball players—United States—Biography. 3. Narcotic addicts—United States—Biography. 4. Cocaine habit—United States—Case studies. I. Greenfield, Jim, 1951– . II. Title.
GV865.H68A3 1989
796.357′092′4—dc19
[B]   89-2795
                                                                              CIP

Dedication

To my wife Cindy and my children Chelsi and Brian, for the happiness and love they've given me.

—S. R. H.

To Dorothy Weisler Greenfield, who led me to books, and who would have derived more pleasure than anyone from this book; and to Albert Greenfield, the "Silver Eagle," a warrior with consummate grace on and off the court, my earliest and most enduring inspiration as an athlete and a man. With all my love.

—J. J. G.

Acknowledgments

I am grateful to all my Christian friends and the people in AA who did not give up on me, and to Jim Greenfield for working so hard to make this book a reality.

—Steve Howe

Contents

Foreword

The phone rang, and Steve was on the line. "Pastor Jack, my book will be out in a few weeks, and I want to ask you to write the foreword."

Nobody'd be interested, I thought to myself. Who cares what a *preacher* thinks about a *ballplayer's* story? But I didn't say that to Steve. Instead, I paused a few seconds, and wanting to assure him of my trust in what's happening in his life, I said, "Sure, Steve, I'll write it if you want me to."

I wasn't patronizing him. Steve Howe is no baby, and he's certainly not a dummy who wouldn't recognize he was being "shined on." In fact, Steve is a strong, maturing guy who has begun to learn the difference between trying to prove his manhood by playing the macho-athlete and becoming a solid citizen who knows who he really is, and who he can become.

As true as that is, I still didn't want to risk hurting Steve. Most of us get our feelings walked on enough to build defenses against letting anybody know we care when we're hurt. A lifetime of that can create a monster instead of a man, and when hope and healing are getting a start in a person, the last thing that person needs is a turnoff from someone he respects. My willingness to stand by a friend outweighed my hesitation over writing an opening for this book, something people might think outside my line of work as a pastor.

However, people *are* my line. And this book is as much about all of us—you, me, *people*—as it is about baseball. As fast-moving and exciting as its sports drama is, it's penetrating and insightful in another way. It has something for us all to learn about the way people miss their greatest successes because they get sucked under in the quicksand of their worst tendencies.

That's what happened to Steve Howe.

A great pitcher lost his shot at athletic immortality, swallowed up in a cocaine habit that fed on his deep insecurities and the arrogant excesses he used trying to mask his fears. He lost.

He didn't strike out. He was kicked out of the game.

Still, I've come to judge Steve Howe a winner. I think by the time you finish these pages, you'll feel the same way.

— **He's won at self discovery.**   He's risen above the idea that traps so many of us; the idea that our identity is the sum total of our accomplishments, victories, and possessions—what we did, won and got. He's learned instead that true identity is in your person, not your performance; what you are inside, and what you are becoming.

— **He's won at marriage.**   He's survived a slugfest with hell and come out with a strong union with Cindy; able now to enjoy a pair of growing kids who love their Dad. A family that should have crashed on the rocks is settled on the Rock, and the Howes are happy people deepening family roots in a day when domestic tragedies are a way of life.

— **He's won the battle with addiction too!**   This, because he'll tell you he knows this victory isn't decided by one pitch steamed by the batter in the bottom of the ninth. It's won day by day; gained by keeping honest with his weakness and keeping dependent upon God for grace and power to stay clean, to keep free, to overcome.

I'm writing this because I welcome the chance to walk right beside Steve as he continues a steady stride forward in becoming the truly great man he was made to be. That's no cheap "puff" job of flattery on him: I believe God created you—all of us—with a potential for special greatness. Few of us will be celebrities, but all of us were intended in his plan for high destiny and real significance.

Read these pages. You'll get to watch the change happening: a smart-faced wiseguy with one of the finest pitching arms ever swims through a sewer of failure and begins to become a genuine-article man. I don't expect a sports biography to spend a lot of time on a theme few think is relevant to life. In fact, who anywhere can touch the depths of the reality occurring when God reaches in and rescues a person from hopelessness?

But when you hear Steve describe how he fouled it all up on the brink of becoming one of baseball's brightest stars, listen well. You and I are candidates for the same failure if we miss the lessons Steve learned the hard way. And when Steve, in a few well-chosen words, tells us that Jesus Christ turned the key that unlocked him from the feelings of low self-esteem that pushed him to cockiness and cocaine, listen again. This isn't religious bilge: It's worthwhile stuff you and I can use. Today.

So, I've done it. Steve, here's that foreword. And to you, dear reader, I present a "hot" book.

It's exciting baseball action. It stirred the juices of my own lifelong athletic interest. It gives an inside look at people who make the game—the good guys and otherwise; draw your own conclusions.

But for my part, I'm slow to make negative judgments on people. I'm a shepherd of souls, and every one of them is too precious to "put down" or to count out—even when you've counted way past ten. The Good Shepherd never counts anyone out. A very athletic guy who "failed" wrote a song about him nearly three thousand years ago, describing him this way:

> Even when I'm struggling like a sheep sur-
> rounded by wolves at the edge of a cliff—in
> the very shadow of death, you'll be there
> with me!   (Psalm 23:4)

I got involved with Steve Howe because another pastor called him a "loser" and seemed to give up on him. Anna and I chose to love Steve and Cindy, not because we're better people, but because we knew a better Shepherd. He's the one who brought Steve this far.

I think you'll like the story of Steve's journey. I think it will give a lot of people hope.

Jack W. Hayford
Pastor, The Church On The Way
Van Nuys, California

> Hope makes us able to hold our heads high
> no matter what happens . . . for we know
> how dearly God loves us, and we feel this
> warm love everywhere within us because
> God has given us the Holy Spirit to fill our
> hearts with His love.
>   (Romans 5:5)

BETWEEN

T·H·E

LINES

1

Looking Over the Edge

The fat guy had a gun, a .44 Magnum hand cannon. Between tokes of freebased cocaine, he waved it threateningly and told me it would be a bad idea for me to leave his house. He was mad because I wouldn't smoke with him, although I'd snorted quite a few of the lines he'd laid out for me. I didn't want to test his breaking point by standing up and walking out. I knew if the gun went off at the wrong time, accidentally or intentionally, they'd find pieces of me all over his den.

I was suffocating in paranoia caused by the coke and the weirdo who was force-feeding it to me. I worried that this was the end of my uneven path of addiction and athletic stardom, of broken promises and half-fulfilled potential. I wondered if my violent death at the home of a dirtball dealer would be the last of many insults to my wife, Cindy, and 20-month-old daughter, Chelsi Leigh. Maybe the Los Angeles Dodgers would be secretly relieved that they would no longer have to babysit their talented but troublesome left-handed relief pitcher.

It was late January 1985. In less than 27 years of life, I'd covered a lot of ground. Some baseball authorities—including Bill James in the *Baseball Abstract*—thought I was the best left-handed reliever alive. In a little less than four full major league seasons, I'd been Rookie of the Year, a world champion and an All-Star, and I'd compiled some impressive career statistics. I was also a cocaine addict who'd never

3

met a party I didn't like and wasn't interested in a cure. I'd been through three rehabilitation programs and had started snorting again shortly after completing each one. At one point I was inhaling nearly $1,500 worth of coke a week. I spent so much on drugs and toys that I had to declare bankruptcy in late 1983.

Cocaine was slowly destroying my marriage. It was amazing that Cindy had stayed with me. Considering all the times I'd walked out on Cindy so I could get high without interference, and all the times I'd stayed out for days on wild binges without even calling her, it was guaranteed that heaven wouldn't be my destination if Porky got trigger-happy.

The drug had also poisoned my relationships with my parents, brothers and sister, who were tired of explaining to their friends and co-workers every time I screwed up and caused embarassing headlines. I'd become a person my family didn't know. They no longer looked forward to my visits to Clarkston, Michigan, where I grew up.

My habit had even cost me a full season of baseball. Commissioner Bowie Kuhn suspended me for 1984 because of repeated relapses. Even though I'd just had surgery to repair a ruptured ulnar nerve in my pitching elbow, I was planning a comeback in 1985. This was a hell of a way to begin it, wired on coke and staring down the barrel of another addict's gun in Sherman Oaks, California.

The fat guy was like a lot of people who wanted to tell their friends they'd gotten high with Steve Howe, baseball's favorite junkie. He was just a little extreme about it. For two nights I'd been his prisoner. Trying to keep my head so I could plot an escape, I snorted just as much coke as was necessary to satisfy his demands that I get high.

I saw my chance when he answered nature's call and forgot to take me with him. I leaped for the door and found it secured by four locks. I struggled frantically for seconds that seemed like half an hour. I was sweating buckets from coke and panic. Finally, I turned the knob and the door swung toward me. As I pushed the screen door open and hurried out, I tore my shirt on the handle. I dashed into the path of a car and almost got killed. The car banged my left knee, the bad one. I ignored the driver's shouts and ran, head down, eyes forward, afraid to look back. What was left of my brain guided me to my car.

It wasn't over. There would be more drugs, more baseball and more questions. But when I found the answers, I was too far into denial of my disease to pay attention to them.

As the 1988 baseball season drew near, the fat man seemed so far away that he could have been a fossil from a lost civilization. Since that day in January 1985, I had pitched for three major league and three minor league teams in three different countries, used more cocaine, been suspended or released by four teams and one entire league, urinated in hundreds of specimen containers to prove I was (or wasn't) clean and waged a successful two-year war of words and threats against the commissioner of baseball so that I could reclaim my livelihood. I made it back to the majors with the Texas Rangers in 1987 and earned a lucrative two-year contract that guaranteed me a total of $925,000 for 1988–89. All I had to do to collect the money was stay away from chemicals and follow an aftercare program designed to ward off relapses. But I couldn't handle that simple assignment or the prosperity that would have followed.

The Rangers went out on a limb for me in 1987 when they signed me. Even though at that point I'd snorted no cocaine for almost a year, Commissioner of Baseball Peter Ueberroth advised the Rangers against signing me, telling them that I was a good bet to break their hearts. Then, when the Rangers brought me up from the minors without Ueberroth's approval, he fined the team $250,000. I wanted to prove Ueberroth wrong. It didn't work out that way.

On Monday, January 11, 1988, the Rangers began three days of winter workouts for pitchers and catchers at Arlington Stadium in Texas. I was excited and eager to show the Rangers that I was in good shape from a rigorous winter training program. I was determined to use the workouts and spring training to claim the role of bullpen stopper, the guy who closes out enemy threats in the late innings and wraps up the victories.

That Monday, I threw hard for a while to catcher Geno Petralli. My fastball was good, and my breaking pitches would have been nasty surprises for any hitter. Geno told Rangers General Manager Tom Grieve that I was throwing better than at any time during my two months with the Rangers in 1987. I could tell that Grieve and Rangers Manager Bobby Valentine were impressed.

Looking back, I can see now that I had been planning my next bender for weeks. I had stopped going to AA and NA meetings, and I was determined to cut loose in Texas, figuring that a lost night or two wouldn't ruin my progress toward recovery. Simply put, I was in total denial of my disease once again, and I was going to use drugs if the opportunity arose. It did.

I was staying at the Sheraton, about 100 yards from the ballpark, and rooming with Brad Arnsberg, a young right-hander the Rangers had just acquired from the Yankees. Brad—like every breathing American who played or followed baseball—knew I was a cocaine addict, but he didn't know I wasn't supposed to drink, and I didn't tell him. That Monday evening, he offered me a hit from his bottle of Jack Daniels. It was exactly the kind of situation I needed to avoid in order to beat chemical dependency, and I knew it. But I accepted Brad's offer—several times.

Brad and I were joined by another ballplayer in our room, where we watched a basketball game on television. Somebody suggested going to Lace, a bar in Arlington, and by this time the chemical nature of my disease had produced a change in me that made it impossible to decline the invitation.

I had a few more drinks at Lace, and then I did something I hadn't done in over a year and certainly hadn't planned on doing that night—I started looking for cocaine. If that's not an example of powerlessness in trying to control addiction, I don't know what is.

For the next three days, I went into hiding. I disappeared and missed two days of workouts because I thought I'd been snorting cocaine. Actually, I'd been using "crank," a homemade substitute for speed, but whatever it was, I was definitely blasted. Once again, I had to try to manufacture a story to cover myself.

When confronted by Tom Grieve, Bobby Valentine and Sam McDowell, the Rangers' substance abuse advisor, I tried out a story, which at the time I was pretty proud of. It went like this: I had a couple of drinks in the room, and then we went to Lace. I met some people, and we all went to a party. At the party, a wild dancer from the club must have slipped something into my drink because I was suddenly so whacked out that I decided I couldn't return to the camp and take the urine test.

Sounds pretty convincing, doesn't it? If I had indeed only been drinking, I would have contacted McDowell immediately, told him the truth and accepted the consequences. I now realize that it was only the denial of my disease that made me so desperately afraid of getting caught. I wasn't nearly as clever under the influence of drugs as I thought I was.

While I was in hiding, the Rangers had half the law enforcement agencies in the Dallas-Fort Worth metroplex searching for me, but I was well hidden. When I finally surfaced on Friday, I had to admit I'd been drinking. They gave me a urine test (negative for cocaine and positive for both amphetamines and alcohol) and sent me home to Montana. That Sunday, January 17, the Rangers called a press conference and announced they had terminated my contract for violation of my aftercare program. The career I'd worked so hard to restore was gone again, as if I'd flushed it down the toilet. Whoever said that each life is a work of art obviously never stood in my shoes.

Deceived by my denial, I thought I was doing so well. My family was happily intact and had a new addition, Brian Steven Raphael Howe, born June 25, 1987. I'd found a wonderful home in White-fish, a beautiful, friendly town surrounded by mountains in north-western Montana, only half an hour from Glacier National Park. It's also 1,400 miles and a world away from Los Angeles, which turned out to be a bad place for me. In Montana I could take advantage of the cold, snowy winters to go ice fishing and run my high-powered snowmobile up and down mountains and enter it in races. I'd have driven it almost anywhere to escape from a disease that followed me relentlessly.

Before I screwed up in Texas, I'd avoided cocaine since January 1987, although I was still drinking at times. My struggle to stay clean continued every day, but I still felt like a loser, and I wasn't dealing with my disease. I was trying to live the rest of my life with the same control and confidence that I'd brought to baseball. It didn't work.

I wasn't ready to live without baseball. My life didn't feel normal or complete without it. It's my gift and my greatest obsession. On the mound, I'm in a world in which I'm a master. But today I'm totally at peace with myself, and I'm content with my family. Baseball has taken its rightful place in my life. God and sobriety are most important.

Because my self-worth had been totally tied to my performance on the baseball field, I had to preserve my career so I could prove I was a good person. In my sickness I thought that if the fans clapped and cheered for me, I was a worthwhile human being. Now, because of the forgiveness I have found in Jesus Christ, who died for all my sins, I no longer have to prove myself. Today I believe that if I ask God for strength, there is nothing I cannot conquer through him. As I write this, I am asking that the Lord never let me forget my disease and my powerlessness against chemicals, whether or not I ever play baseball again.

I'll always regret that I've already let drugs wipe out four baseball seasons that should have been among the best of my career. Coke got me suspended for the entire 1984 season. Drugs, alcohol and a bad elbow shortened and ruined 1985. The commissioner's relentless obstruction and one night of weakness sabotaged my bid to reach the majors in 1986. It took me half of 1987 to prove I was clean and deserved another chance, but I barely got to enjoy another taste of the big time before I threw away 1988. I also missed seven weeks of the 1983 season and the playoffs because of relapses into cocaine dependency. I'm still on the sidelines while others are playing. What a waste. That's why I feel so strongly that I must keep trying to make the most of my gift before time takes it away.

If it had been up to Peter Ueberroth, my career would have died in September 1985, when Minnesota released me. Rumors say the commissioner is interested in national elective office, and he campaigns hard against drugs. After the Pittsburgh drug trials ended in late 1985, Uebie announced to the world that he had saved baseball from drugs. No one believed him—especially not major league players, who knew better—but that didn't stop him from trying to make it come true. Part of his plan was to keep me away from the game so I wouldn't relapse, stain the national pastime and, most important, leave a mess all over his campaign platform. I believe he worked overtime to poison my prospects.

For a while, the owners and executives of major league teams went along with the commissioner and denied me a job, although known drug users, former rehab cases and ex-cons were playing for several teams. Addiction starts as a mistake and becomes a disease, not a crime, but most of baseball doesn't see it that way. If you get cancer or have a nervous breakdown, you can go back to your job when you recover. If you're a ballplayer with a drug problem, you face not only the personal pain that results from addiction, but punitive action from the commissioner as well. Each relapse counts as a strike against you. When you run out of strikes, you're history. Unfortunately, Uebie has never told anyone how many strikes a player is allowed. He makes up the rules as he goes along. *Der Fuhrer* of baseball figured I'd had enough strikes—I was going to be "The Example."

For most of 1987, I was the boy who cried wolf. In the past, I'd often claimed I was clean when I wasn't. When I put the drugs away for a while, no one would believe it. I wasn't surprised. In fact, it made sense that baseball executives wanted something more than my word before they'd take another chance on me. No problem. If the baseball world needed proof, I'd supply it. I was determined to do whatever it took to return to the majors. Anything except admit I was powerless against the chemicals that still controlled me.

In mid-March, after the Japanese commissioner of baseball decided I couldn't sign a contract with the Seibu Lions, I returned to California from Tokyo and set up a drug testing and consultation program for myself. I contacted Joan Elvidge, a therapist with whom I'd always felt comfortable, and her boss, Dr. Forest Tennant, a drug-abuse expert who'd treated me when I was a Dodger and who also serves as drug advisor to the National Football League.

Three or four times a week, at my expense, I visited Dr. Tennant's clinic in West Covina and gave a urine sample for testing. In early April Dodgers Vice President Fred Claire suggested that I test every day for a month. Daily testing was unnecessary because Dr. Tennant's equipment could detect cocaine traces up to four or five days after use. But I wanted to please anyone who might offer me a job. That meant I'd sometimes drive an hour out of my way for a test after a grueling workout. I had to stop at the clinic to pee in a cup every Sunday morning before church. Under the same circumstances, I'd do it again.

On June 1, 1987, Dr. Tennant issued a report that said he'd tested me about 50 times in two and a half months and I was off cocaine. He went even further, recommending me as a good candidate for a job on someone's pitching staff. Dr. Tennant wrote, "I never get the opportunity to see a person who appears in a better recovery state and able to resume employment than Steve now appears." Boy, did I fake him out. It's not something I'm proud of.

My Montana lawyer and agent, John Lence, immediately sent copies of the report to all 26 major league teams. Within days, the

Rangers called and expressed interest. It wasn't long before I had a job.

But I wasn't able to put on a Rangers uniform without a fight. For weeks we struggled to get the commissioner and Johnny Johnson, the late president of the National Association of Minor Leagues, to clear me to sign a minor league contract. Then, when the Rangers wanted to bring me up from their Oklahoma City farm club, Ueberroth put his boot down. He urged the Rangers to consider "the best interests of baseball" and keep me in the minors for another four weeks, and he threatened to slap a six-figure fine on them.

The Rangers stood their ground. In early August, Rangers owner Eddie Chiles and Rangers President Mike Stone flew to New York, confronted Uebie and told him in strong language that they didn't need his advice on how to run their ballclub. The Rangers were penalized for their independence and compassion. A month after they brought me up, Ueberroth fined them $250,000. These days they must be wondering about the wisdom of their investment.

Although I'm no longer a Ranger, I have a lot of admiration for Chiles, Stone, Tom Grieve and Bobby Valentine. They had the guts to "just say no" to the commissioner. Later on, they had the courage to say no to Steve Howe. By doing so, they may have saved my life.

I've wished many times that when I was first offered cocaine during my sophomore year at the University of Michigan, I'd had the sense to refuse. There may be people who are able to use the drug socially, in moderate amounts, but I've never met any and I wasn't so fortunate. Coke gained increasing domination over my life until, in 1981, I became obsessed, living primarily for that next snort. I was addicted.

The reasons for my inability to control my use have been explored by several rehabilitation clinics, and I've heard all kinds of theories. Whether the real reasons were genetic or psychological— and I'm still not sure what they were—I know I was a prime candidate for dependency from the moment I snorted my first line or drank my first drink.

My session with the fat guy began with an innocent visit to my barbershop. A guy there had some coke and offered it to me, and we got high. Then he suggested we go see his source, who turned out to be Dirty Harry.

The binges began that way. Friends or acquaintances, sometimes teammates, would propose we have a party or go to one. Sometimes, though, people I'd never met offered me coke, and I rarely hesitated. It seemed like everyone in L.A. was snorting the stuff, and I was right in the middle of it, happier than a lottery winner.

Apart from my addiction, everything in my life was going my way. While proving myself on the playing fields of Alaska one summer, I courted and won the hand of a cute little blond named Cindy Holliday. Our daughter, born during the height of my addiction in May 1983, is a beautiful, precocious child, the apple of her daddy's eye.

I was a desired commodity in Major League Baseball: a left-handed relief pitcher who could throw the ball 95 miles per hour with pinpoint control. In 1980, as a 22-year-old rookie with only 13 games of minor league experience, I earned a job on the Dodgers' pitching staff, stepping into the unfamiliar role of reliever. Immediately I established myself as the closer, the guy Tommy Lasorda could rely on to squelch late-inning rallies, preserve leads and earn saves. I performed my job well enough to be named the National League's Rookie of the Year for 1980.

In 1981 I helped the Dodgers reach the World Series, then got the win in the fourth game and saved the decisive sixth game. I experienced the thrill of being on the mound in Yankee Stadium when the Dodgers became world champions. In 1982 I pitched for the National League in the All-Star Game. In 1983 my efforts helped the Dodgers reach the playoffs again. We lost to the Phillies, possibly because I was in my third rehab program instead of the bullpen when Tommy needed me.

In my first four full seasons, when I was physically (if not psychologically) sound, my earned run average declined every year, from a high of 2.65 in 1980 to 1.44 in 1983. During that period, I averaged 14 saves a year. I was improving with age and experience.

But when you're an addict, you can't live outside the context of your habit. Sooner or later, addiction affects every aspect of your life, especially when you're snorting as much as I was.

As my control over chemicals vanished, my priorities changed completely. When my professional career began, my priorities were, in order: family, career and self-gratification. By the beginning of the 1982 baseball season, I was most concerned about getting and using chemicals. Next in importance was my career. My family finished out of the running.

In retrospect, it seems I was last on my list of priorities. I never acted in my own best interest. I've paid a greater price than anyone else for my drug lust.

Remarkably, with the possible exception of 1982, drugs did not seem to affect my performance on the field. In fact, 1983 probably was my best season, although my brain was so fried that I can scarcely recall events that had a profound impact on my life that year. If I hadn't been young and physically strong, I never would have been able to keep pitching as well as I did. I wonder if cocaine will take its revenge by cutting some years off the end of my career. If I still have a career.

Despite my accomplishments, I learned that pitching success didn't guarantee that my career wouldn't be affected by what I did off the field. I learned the hard way.

At the end of 1982, I became a drug abuse pioneer. I was one of the first major league baseball players to step forward, admit chemical dependency and ask for help in the form of rehabilitation.

At first my problem was treated as an illness, in accordance with generally accepted medical and legal practice. But after my relapse in June 1983, the baseball powers, groping for a solution to a problem they've never understood, decided that repeat offenders should be treated differently. Fines, the 1984 suspension and the 1986–87 blacklist followed.

It still works that way. If drug rehabilitation centers offered foolproof cures, there would be justification for baseball's attitude. Unfortunately, rehab programs sometimes don't work when the disease hasn't run its course.

In the fall of 1985, when I'd found a permanent spot at the bottom looking up, two events set me on the slow, uphill road to recovery: I underwent rehab therapy at St. Mary's Hospital Rehabilitation Center in Minneapolis, and I moved to Whitefish.

My treatment at St. Mary's, under the direction of Dr. George A. Mann, finally helped me deal with my feelings of inadequacy, anger and resentment that may have contributed to my chemical abuse. It may also be true that my addiction was starting to run out of steam, because I was beginning to recognize that I was not going to beat the problem with my own program.

I'd first seen Whitefish from the inside of a rented motor home during the summer of 1984. Cindy and I followed her parents to Montana to visit Cindy's uncle, Ron Holliday, who lives in White-fish and is a developer and Honda dealer. A town of 3,700 people that sits at the foot of the Big Mountain Ski Resort, Whitefish is rimmed on three sides by mountains. I was awed by its beauty.

I love fishing and hunting and winter sports like snowmobiling and ice skating. The outdoor life is popular in northwestern Montana where, as they say, "Men are men, so are women, and sheep are nervous." The people in Whitefish were friendly and genuine. I played golf, fished and relaxed during my visit, and I felt more at ease than at any time since I'd moved to crazy L.A. for the start of the 1980 season.

When I left L.A. to play for the Minnesota Twins in August 1985, we sold our California house and bought one of the townhouses that Cindy's Uncle Ron was building on the Whitefish River. By the time I left St. Mary's in October, we had a new home.

My aftercare program required that I get a job. Ron put me in touch with Benny Bee, who operates the KJJR and B-98 radio stations that broadcast out of Whitefish and nearby Kalispell. Benny became my employer and sort of adopted father as well.

Benny Bee is Mr. Antidrug. If you work for Benny and he finds out you're using drugs, you're past tense at Bee Broadcasting. And Benny's going to find out if you're a druggie because Whitefish and Kalispell aren't very big.

Benny put me to work broadcasting football and basketball games for Whitefish and Columbia Falls high schools. Benny also figured that since I have a natural sales personality (in other words, the gift of con), I could sell advertising. He gave me his worst sales list—the impossibles. Some of the impossibles are now on the air.

Benny took advantage of my mechanical aptitude. I've fixed Benny's snowmobiles and Mama Bee's cars, and I spent several weeks in the fall of 1986 working on improving the quality of the signal that Bee Broadcasting transmits from Big Mountain. Benny has put to good use all of my talents except pitching.

John Lence practices law in Kalispell. Lence sounds like a big, gruff Montana cowboy on the phone, but he's actually a short

Italian with curly hair and a lot to say. His real family name is Licciardoni. John found out from his client, Ron Holliday, that I was in town. I met John in a restaurant, where he walked up and addressed me as "dirtball." I didn't know whether to step on the dwarf or just insult him. If I'd squashed him, I'd have lost a great lawyer, agent, friend and occasional golf partner. John Lence is probably the best tax and business lawyer in Montana, and he knows a lot about baseball. He stayed with me long after other agents would have given up hope and gone looking for more lucrative clients.

The people of Whitefish want and expect nothing from me and don't seem to care that I'm a professional athlete. If you need something in Whitefish, people will lend a hand without asking anything in return. When Charley and Becky Berry, good friends of ours, built their barn, I went over to help out. I know that if I want to build something, Charley and lots of others will be there to help. It was that way in our subdivision in Clarkston when I was growing up. In Los Angeles, many people look at things a little differently—they don't lend a hand without leaving a bill.

The predominant values in L.A. are money and success. When I lived there, I lost my root system of values. Whitefish restored my perspective and sense of what is important in life. I began focusing on watching my children grow up, creating a stable home environment for them, building friendships that aren't dependent on drugs and enjoying the outdoors. Whitefish gave me a second life. If someone will only give me another chance to pitch after all my mistakes, I'll truly be blessed with a perfectly rounded life.

It isn't pleasant for me to tell the story of my descent into addiction and the pain it has created in my life and the lives of those around me. But it's important to me that people understand that drugs are a dead end. Though I didn't pay the ultimate price of addiction—I'm still alive—I've lost so much because of chemical abuse. I hope my story can help others avoid the same mistakes.

2

Wild in Clarkston

He took my truck one time, and we looked for him all night long, and we waited up until he got home and drove the truck in the driveway.

I looked at my truck from the kitchen window, and there was something different about it, you know, and I couldn't really place what was the matter with it. He explained to me that it rained real hard that night, and he drove the truck in a ditch, and it flooded out. Now, this is a four-wheel-drive vehicle. I told him, "You've been driving in a lake."

I kept looking at the truck, and I figured it out. The grill was gone. I hollered at Steve and said, "Steve, where's the grill on the truck?" He came over to me and looked at it. "I don't know what happened. I don't know what happened to it."

I called the police and told them that somebody had stolen my grill. The Oakland County cop told me, "I guess you're going to have to cook inside." I said, "No, you don't understand, I'm talking about the grill on my truck." Well, the officer came over and talked to Steve and made a report on it.

For a long time, this was a big joke with us. I'd say, "Steve, come on now, it's been five or six years, you can tell me. What happened to the grill on the truck?"

When we went to the rehab center with him, we found out Steve had been bothered by the stolen grill all this time. I mean, if I'd known it

*was bothering him like that, I would have never even brought it up
again.*

—Virgil Howe
Clarkston, Michigan
November 1986

I am not descended from generations of losers, con artists and
dirtballs. The truth is that there are some pretty famous and even
respectable folk in my family tree.

I've been told that Lord Howe, the commander of the Redcoat
forces during the early stages of the Revolutionary War, was an
ancestor. Roy Murdoch, my mother's grandfather, was land clerk
of the city of Detroit for more than 40 years and accumulated a
considerable fortune. At one time he owned all the houses and
land on Main Street in Clarkston, which was just a village then. But
none of his wealth sifted down to my parents, Virgil and Barbara
Kay Jones Howe.

I'm Irish and Algonquin Indian on my mother's side, and a mix-
ture of English and Irish on my father's side. When you consider
that I'm part Irish-Indian, it's not surprising that trouble came looking for me, and that I didn't exactly turn tail and run from it either.

My parents were both born and raised in Rochester, Michigan.
Dad was 16 and Mom 15 when they married, and I was born within
a year, on March 10, 1958, in Pontiac. My sister, Kathi, came along
a year later, and she was followed in machine-gun fashion by three
brothers, Chris, Jeff and Mike. There were five kids in about six
years.

My parents had very little chance to enjoy themselves as they
grew up. With five kids to care for by the time they reached their
early twenties, they were children bringing up children. They had
to work hard to hold everything together.

When I was about nine, Mom went back to work. She got a night
job in the machine shop at the Four Star Corporation plant near
Lake Orion, where legend has it that Jimmy Hoffa was killed many
years later. Mom got home at five or six in the morning, and barely
got in an hour of sleep before she had to get up and pack the kids
off to school. We used to call her "Bear in the Morning," all five-

foot-one of her, because we could hear her growling in the kitchen, trying to wake up.

Breakfast every morning was fried eggs with broken yolks and a piece of toast with a big slab of oleo right in the middle. The breakfast of champions. We knew how hard Mom was working for us, so we made a big joke out of it.

Dad had to drop out of high school to provide for his kids, but he soon found a good job. When I was about a year old, he began repairing and constructing diesel engines for trucks at the GMC truck and coach plant in Pontiac. After 25 years of punching a time clock and working on his feet from 6:00 a.m. to 3:00 p.m., he finally got a desk job in the same plant. Dad is about to pass his 30th anniversary at GM, retire and move with Mom to a new house near Cadillac in northern Michigan.

We lived first in a farmhouse in Rochester, then in a little house in the middle of Clarkston. When I was in my teens, Mom and Dad bought a house on Walters Lake, about two miles outside Clarkston, where they lived until Dad's retirement. In 1964, when we moved to Clarkston, Dad bought a brand new Malibu SS. The combined house and car payment was only $84 a month, but scraping together enough money for the payments wasn't easy.

The financial situation improved when Mom started working and bringing home about $250 a week. Eventually she returned to school, got her graduate equivalency degree and went on to Oakland County Community College, where she finished near the top of her class with a degree in tool and die engineering. She then went back to work as an engineer at the Fisher Body division of Pontiac Motors.

Jeff and I were hyperactive children. Jeff was worse than I was, and he spent a lot of his overabundant energy eating. He ate anything, in vast quantity. For breakfast, or whenever he felt like it, Jeff would take half a box of cereal and half a gallon of milk, throw it all into a mixing bowl and go to war. Between meals, which wasn't often, Jeff chewed on Milk Bone dog biscuits. Today he goes six-foot-four, 230 pounds—he's the guy you want on your side in a bar fight.

Jeff and I by ourselves were more than a load for Mom to handle, so she tried to slow us down by putting us on a drug called Ritalin. I must have been nine or ten years old when I started taking it, and I hated what the drug did to me. When it wore off, I was twice as hyper as before and I couldn't sleep.

I agreed, at Mom's insistence, to take my pill, but I'd cup it under my tongue, run outside and spit it out. When I came back in, she'd notice I was still hyper. I'd try to get her to believe I'd taken the pill, but she knew better and would make me take another.

The Food and Drug Administration decided years later that Ritalin could increase hyperactivity in some children. I've often wondered whether my cocaine addiction was related to Ritalin. Maybe it permanently altered my body chemistry in some way, because my reaction to cocaine was unusual. Coke wakes most people up, but it pacified me, at least after I became addicted to it.

I was obsessed with sports as a kid. I usually hung out with kids who were several years older, primarily because I was as good as the older kids at baseball, and they let me play with them. I wanted to fit in, so I tried to emulate the older guys, down to the way they dressed.

So many kids played baseball in Clarkston that subdivision rivalries developed. One subdivision would agree to meet another, and we'd take our fathers' lawnmowers to the chosen field to prepare it. Lots of lawnmowers were destroyed by boulders on the fields of Clarkston.

When we couldn't organize a full-scale game, several of us would go down to a nearby lake and play fast pitch with a rubber ball and plastic bat, using a big shed as a backstop. Trying to make contact with a rubber ball fired at you from 30 feet away is a great way to develop reflexes. In our subdivision I was friendly with the boys from two Williams families and the Lape family. When I was about 12, Dad gave me a full football uniform for Christmas. I was so thrilled that I suited up immediately and went down to David Lape's house. Even though there were a couple of feet of snow on the ground, we played one-on-one tackle in his backyard for five hours.

When I was 12 or 13, Dad bought me a new bat. I took it to the field and left it there. When I remembered it and went back for it, I discovered that my friends had broken it. I started crying and furiously swinging at them, but they were older, bigger and stronger than I. They wrestled me to the ground, and Johnny Forbus twisted my pitching arm almost to the breaking point.

I went home crying and sat in the backyard. When Dad came outside, I reluctantly admitted what had happened. Instead of getting angry at me for leaving the bat at the field, Dad said, "Come on, we're going down to the Williams's house."

Actually, we went to two Williamses' houses, and my grandfather went with us. The message Dad delivered was basically the same at both stops, father to father: "If you want to fight somebody, and if your kids want to gang up on my kid, then you're gonna have to deal with me." I'm sure Dad made his point, because four Williams boys got the hell beaten out of them by their respective fathers that night. Dad had taught me a lesson in intimidation.

Dad's a mere six-footer, but he's all heart and desire. If you want to fight him, you're going to have to kill him. He could brawl with the best, and he looked scary when he got mad. We used to call him "The Thermometer." When the red flush crept up his neck and reached the back of his ears, Mom would say, "It's time for you kids to go outside—immediately!" By then we had usually figured it out and were out the door.

Many of my ballplaying friends were talented, but they gave up sports toward the end of high school. Most of them wound up working in automobile plants. They had things to do that were more important to them than playing ball, like partying and chasing women. But I saw no reason why I couldn't do all of the above.

Tragically, nine of my close friends in high school were killed or disabled in fights or accidents. One friend, Roy, was introverted until he started partying, and then he became boisterous and rowdy. One night, when we were still in high school, Roy got drunk, went home and blew his brains out with a .44. No one knew why.

Another friend got drunk at a party one night and refused to let anyone drive his 455 high-output Trans Am. It was raining hard. No one would ride with him, so he took off by himself. A few miles down the road, traveling at 120 miles per hour, he couldn't avoid a stalled car, wrapped the Trans Am around a tree and died in front of his buddies, who had been following behind him.

The most bizarre accident involved a friend who was sitting on top of a truck at a drive-in movie, drinking beer and smoking pot. While coming down to go to the refreshment stand, he slipped and the truck's radio antenna ran up his nose and into his brain, killing him.

Another friend stepped outside of a bar one night and beat up the leader of a local gang. When my buddy came out of the bar a little later, another gang member shot him three times in the chest and killed him.

One high school buddy is serving a life term for murder. He and two other guys raped, mutilated and murdered a girl who would have graduated with me. Just before the girl's death, her brother had been hit in the head with a hammer in a bar fight, and he's a vegetable today.

The tragedy that struck closest to home involved David, a tall, good-looking guy who was my best friend and my sister's boyfriend. David may have been the wildest of all of us. He would get sloppy drunk, but I could always get him to let me drive him home.

After my second year at college, I played baseball in a summer league in Alaska. I hadn't wanted to go that summer, but my parents insisted. While I was away, David got drunk one night and fell asleep at the wheel of his 454 SS Chevelle. He hit a line of parked cars and a tree, and he was left paralyzed. I felt partly responsible. I knew that if I'd been with him, he wouldn't have been driving.

That was also the summer that Cindy, her parents and I were involved in a serious car accident in Alaska. When I returned to Ann Arbor wearing a cast and a neck brace, David was still in a coma. I went to see him, and I leaned over and whispered in his ear, "David, you've gotta wake up now." Incredibly, he opened his eyes.

To this day, I can hardly stand to see David confined to his wheelchair. I can't help but think of him as he was before the accident, strong and full of life. It was another tragedy that was the result of chemical abuse.

Most of these tragedies occurred within about five years. It seems as though Clarkston was under a curse or hex. Whatever it was, I wasn't spared.

———————

Auto workers in the Detroit area have demanding, physically exhausting jobs. They like to stop at a local pub and let off steam after a hard day's work. My father was part of that culture, and he frequently enjoyed a drink or two on his way home for dinner.

I paid attention to Dad's drinking, because from time to time it affected me. The only time we argued was when he'd been drinking, or when he failed to show up for a scheduled event because he'd been drinking. Dad was a different person when he drank.

Sober, he was passive as a puppy dog, yet calmly assertive when he had to be. When he drank, his inhibitions vanished and his anger surfaced, and then it was best to avoid him.

In my preteen years, I didn't understand why Dad missed a sports banquet or other function that was important to me. He almost always made it to my games, which was a big thrill for me because I played as much for him as for myself. Maybe that's why it hurt so much when Dad didn't show for other events.

Dad was a binge drinker, like I was a binge addict. Usually he just had a drink or two at the bar, or picked up a six-pack on the way home. But once every month to six weeks, he'd go on a one- or two-day bender, and that was hard on the family.

Mom seldom drank. She was home a lot more than Dad, and she assumed the role of enforcer. When Mom and Dad were both out or otherwise occupied, I was responsible for my sister and brothers. I was the oldest, so my parents expected me to fill in for them. When one of the other four kids messed up, I was punished.

The role that Mom and Dad carved out for me should have been reserved for a child who was emotionally strong and mature and able to mask his own feelings in order to set a good example. I didn't have those qualities. I was slow to mature—I'm just now getting there—and I resented having to look after the other kids and answer when they broke the rules. I tried to do what my parents expected, but there were consequences. Sometimes I didn't get the chance to explore my own needs and desires, and that may explain my excessive self-indulgence after I left the nest.

When I was 16, I took my sister, Kathi, to a party and she got drunk. My parents blamed me, which I thought wasn't fair. After all, I didn't tell her to get drunk. My punishment was that I didn't get to go ice racing. Kathi's penalty was less severe: She was sent to her room.

My brother Michael sneaked out the sliding glass doors one night when I was babysitting, and he went to a party and got wasted. Again I got punished. Dad said, "If I let you get away with anything like this, then they're going to try to get away with it. So you set the example."

My parents didn't believe in physical beatings as punishment. I'm thankful for that, because some of my friends—the Williams boys, for example—were beaten when they messed up, and the results weren't pretty. Dad sometimes gave us a whack on the back of the coconut, but that was about it. Mom was a little nastier. She came after us with a wet washcloth or a flyswatter, sometimes raising welts that stung for days. It wouldn't have done her much good to use her bare hands on the four boys, though, because we all quickly grew to be a lot bigger than she was.

By design, I sometimes mediated fights between Mom and Dad. None of the kids wanted to see them fight. Mom and Dad had given their oldest son responsibility, and I suppose that along with that responsibility came some authority as a voice of reason. Most of the time, I was able to deflect some of the anger that passed between them. Unfortunately, I also absorbed some of it.

When Dad was gone and Mom was unable to confront him, she took it out on the guy who was supposed to fix things—me. As a result, I became closer to Mom than to anyone else in the family, but at the same time I resented my role as a lightning rod for her frustrations. If I had told her so, we would have hashed it out immediately and gone on to more constructive matters. But I suppressed my feelings of resentment.

My mother is remarkable and admirable in many ways. She'd lay down her life for her children and grandchildren. Even though she sometimes works 60 hours a week, she finds time to make clothes and dolls for Chelsi. When we visit, Mom takes Chelsi shopping and cooks one great meal after another. She's accomplished a great deal for a woman who, at age 22, had no high school diploma and already had five small children.

If Mom had a failing, it was her tendency to deliver a constructive message in a negative manner. When I was unable to fix strained relationships or straighten out my brothers and sister at home as a teenager, or when my performance fell short of her expectations, Mom came after me. "You aren't worth a damn," she said. "You keep screwing up. You're a screw-up, and you'll never be anything but a screw-up unless you do what I say."

The same message was delivered by telephone long after I left home to go to college and later to pursue my professional baseball career and nurture my drug habit. "You need a keeper," Mom said. "If you make $500,000, you'll need $600,000."

I know that Mom was trying to light a fire under me, to push me to become a better, more responsible person. Her motives were noble, but her negative methods just didn't work on me. Mom probably never realized how sick I was, but I didn't complain or enlighten her because in the society in which I was raised, big boys don't cry.

Because we were so close, Mom's harsh words had the lasting, searing effect of a branding iron. She unintentionally created and then persistently reinforced in my mind the impression that out-side of sports—where my performance was beyond her criticism and drew the reward of her praise—I was good for nothing. Even at a supposedly safe distance of 2,500 miles, that voice of authority on the telephone tore me apart.

When I was first treated at St. Mary's in Minneapolis in Septem-ber and October 1985, I learned that you can program yourself to become the person you think you are. As an adolescent, I wanted to prove Mom wrong, but I heard the same criticism for so long that I came to believe she was right. Instead of challenging her, I became the screw-up she always told me I was. It was my own immaturity and self-indulgence that led me to addiction, but after I became dependent on cocaine, I sometimes fed off Mom's criti-cism, and the low self-esteem it fostered, to get high.

While my emotional development lagged, my worldly experi-ence raced ahead. In Clarkston you learn very quickly what life is all about.

I first got drunk at 15. It was wrestling season, and I was trying to lose enough weight to wrestle at 155 pounds. Dad was buying expensive dietetic fruit cocktail and other exotic substances to help me, so he had a vested interest in my training regimen. That was one reason he didn't want me to go to a party that some of my friends were throwing at a home in the neighborhood. Another reason was that he knew there would be no parental supervision.

But this was an experience I didn't want to miss, because girls were going to be there. My friend Chris and I downed a fifth of Kessler's Smooth as Silk between us during the evening. At one point, Chris walked out of the house and passed out in a snow-bank. I don't remember much of what I did, except that I chased several girls.

Mom found me and dragged me home by the hair. I needed her assistance to stay upright and put one foot in front of the other. At home I headed for the bathroom, where I spent the rest of the night moaning, groaning and throwing up a combination of Kessler's and dietetic fruit cocktail. "Look at that!" Dad raged. "All that expensive stuff."

The next morning, Dad poured a shot of booze and brought it to me, and I threw up again at the sight and thought of it. If that was a joke, it was lost on me.

Throughout high school, I experimented with drugs. I was always looking for new experiences, and I was afraid to miss anything. I smoked marijuana at a party, but it made me sick. I tried mescaline and LSD as well. I liked mescaline because it provided a pleasant, positive, euphoric high.

I was on LSD one night, and I was sure I saw stereo speakers breathing. To get away, I left the house and took off running. I ran right into a split rail fence that looked like it was miles away but was actually ten feet in front of me. The total loss of control frightened me. That was the last time I dropped acid.

Generally, though, alcohol was my drug of choice. Even after my first bad experience with alcohol, I continued to drink a lot. Many times in my senior year, I skipped school with friends just to get drunk.

When I was 16, Dad and I developed a buddy-buddy drinking relationship and I started going to the bars he frequented. I got a fake ID by erasing the birthdate on a duplicate of my birth certificate and typing over it. It was an obvious fake, but I got away with it because the codger at the Christian Literature Center who notarized my bogus ID was about 90 years old and functionally blind. Because the ID was notarized, no bartender ever questioned it.

Dad never knew I had the ID, and I was rarely asked to show it. Dad figured it was better to have his boy along as company than to have me go elsewhere. Mom didn't like it that I drank with Dad, but she also knew that I could keep an eye on him that way, so she only complained about it when she got mad at Dad. After yelling at him, she'd point at me and say, "And you, you're just like your father!"

Not long after I left town for college, my brother Jeff took my place as Dad's drinking partner. By the time Jeff was 15, he stood well over six feet tall and had a mustache. No bartender in Michigan with any respect for his well-being was going to question Jeff's right to a drink.

Dad did most of his drinking in three places: Ron's Roost, a shop bar in Pontiac; the Stein House; and the Wagon Wheel in Lake Orion. We'd tip a few together about once every two or three weeks. When I wasn't drinking with Dad and I needed to find him, I knew he'd be in one of those three bars.

The first time Dad and I went to the Wagon Wheel together, I got into my first bar fight. I had my varsity jacket on, and I was playing pool against three older guys and taking all their money. Dad was nearby playing shuffleboard. All the Howe boys are good at both games, and we learned everything we know from Dad. When Dad was in his early twenties with five small kids, he couldn't afford to drink unless he made enough money playing pool and shuffleboard to pay for it, so he learned to play.

The guys I was playing weren't going to pay me after the last game. I had bet them double or nothing that I could pocket the eight-ball on the break. I made the shot. They began to threaten me, and words were exchanged. Dad heard the commotion and pulled me over to him. When we left the bar, all three of them followed us down the street, throwing insults and challenges our way. Dad put his arm around me and I said, "Aren't you afraid, Dad?"

"Afraid of what?"

"Well, they're gonna kick our ass."

"I doubt that," Dad said. "I don't think that all three of them could kick our ass, do you?"

When we got to the corner, Dad turned and said, "Hey, why don't you guys just go on your way and we'll go on our way, no problem." We tried to walk away, but they persisted.

Dad said, "Let me ask you guys a question. Which one of you is the toughest?" One of them asked why Dad wanted to know. "Whoever's the toughest," Dad said, "why don't you just come with me, and we'll go in that alley and settle it. If you beat my ass, fine, you walk out of there. If I beat yours, then I walk out. It's as simple as that."

"We want to fight him," one of the guys said, pointing to me.

Dad said to me, "Steve, we're not going to get out of here without fighting these guys. Why don't you just kick this guy's ass, and we'll forget about it?"

So I pounded the guy, and Dad took care of the other two. Then, just as the cops were rounding the corner, one of the guys kicked the fender of Mom's new car, which Dad and I used that night. The cops grabbed all three of the guys, loaded them in a cruiser and asked Dad if he wanted to press charges for damage to the car.

Dad said no. "Why don't you take them out of town and drop them off? We'll follow you out there, and I'll get my money's worth out of them," he suggested.

"By the looks of those three guys, you already got your money's worth," said the cop. The fight was over, but we still had to deal with Mom when we got home.

Dad and I were involved in four or five other nasty incidents when we were out drinking. One of them happened at a bar called Scribner's, five years after the Wagon Wheel fight. Scribner's sounds like the name of a bookstore, but it draws a tough crowd. This time my brother Chris, who was then 18 and smaller than Dad and I, and my friend Rob were with us.

We were playing shuffleboard. There was a group of four guys next to us doing some serious drinking. They were a lot further along than we were, but there was no trouble until we got up to leave. On our way out the door, Chris was the tail-dragger. One of the other guys said to him, "See ya later, boy."

Chris caught up with us outside and said, "Hey, that guy in there's calling me 'boy' and stuff."

I said, "Well, go back in there and tell him you aren't a boy."

"I'm not going back in there myself."

"Don't worry," I said, "we'll be right behind you."

I can still see Chris walking back in there with his chest stuck out a mile in front of him, standing in front of the loudmouth and saying, "Who you callin' a boy? Who you callin' a boy?"

This time everybody on both sides got into it except the fool who started it. One of the guys hit me in the head with a beer glass, and he looked pretty surprised when it didn't faze me. After we wiped out the three who fought us, I turned around and drilled the guy who mouthed off to Chris. I know I broke his jaw. At the time, I thought I'd killed him. They took him away in an ambulance. For two weeks afterward, I lived in fear of being arrested.

Fighting was a way of life in Clarkston. The blue-collar families who lived there had their share of frustrations, and drinking and fighting were accepted means of relief. The only people in town who didn't fight were the teachers. Every other day or so, somebody I knew was involved in a fight. Fights weren't limited to bars. They were liable to break out anywhere—school, playground, hockey rink, McDonald's, Burger King, street corner. I never fought anywhere near school, though, because I was afraid of what Dad would do if he found out I'd caused trouble at school.

We even had a rival town, Ortonville (we called it Hooterville), with which we had gang-style rumbles. Once some of the Ortonville guys came to Clarkston looking for trouble. We pushed one guy's car out in the middle of the road, beat the hell out of him and wrecked his car by ramming it with six or seven of our cars.

I fought for the usual macho reasons—to prove myself and to demonstrate my masculinity. All the Howe boys fought, and Dad neither promoted nor discouraged fighting. His credo was, "You don't start nothin', but you don't take nothin' either." Of course, we all had a low threshold of irritation, so Dad's words were like an invitation to war.

I fought often and well enough to build a reputation in town. Guys were ready to test me from time to time, and there were some anxious moments. I was stabbed once on a basketball court. On another occasion, a guy belted me in the back of the coconut with a lead pipe. When the guy looked down, I was staring back up at him and hanging onto his legs. Then he knew he was in big trouble. I wonder how he would have reacted if he could have read my mind.

I've been arrested only once, when I was 17, because of a fight with a gas station attendant. A friend and I pulled up to the pump in Dad's new truck during a downpour. It wasn't a self-service station. The attendant was inside on the phone and made me wait. After ten minutes, I got out and started to pump the gas myself.

The attendant came running out. "Get your hands off the pump," he said.

"Well, come out here and pump the gas," I said.

"I will when I'm ready."

"You will now, or I'll pump the gas. I've been sitting here for ten minutes."

The attendant picked up a squeegee and fired it at our windshield. I grabbed him and began to flog him, just as an Oakland County sheriff's deputy pulled in.

The attendant accused me of taking a swing at him and trying to steal gas, but my story was supported by a witness, so the cops didn't press charges. Nevertheless, I spent a night in jail, which didn't bother me nearly as much as the thought of what Dad would do when he found out his new truck had been towed. Dad worked hard for his few material possessions, and when you borrowed one of them, you'd better be able to account for it on schedule.

I wouldn't even call Dad from jail. I had my buddies bail me out the next morning. When I got home, Dad immediately inspected the truck. He saw that the spare tire had been bent, apparently because someone tried to steal it after it had been towed. "Where were you, and what were you doing?" he wanted to know.

"Well, a cop gave me a ticket and they towed your truck, and I spent all night trying to get the money to get it back, because I was scared you were going to hit me." The story worked pretty well. About five years later, I got up the nerve to tell him that I'd been arrested that night.

I try to avoid fights these days. For one thing, if you walk around thinking you're the toughest and try to prove it, you're eventually going to find out that you're wrong. For another, I'm 31 years old, and I'm not anxious to shorten my career by volunteering for unnecessary wear and tear on my body.

It was in my sophomore year of high school that I first used mood-altering substances for a purpose other than kicks. I was 16, and my 15-year-old girlfriend, Renee, thought she was pregnant. I figured that if she was, the proper thing to do would be to marry her. I knew how my parents had struggled after marrying at the same ages, so I worked my tail off trying to save enough money to get us started. Then I found out that Renee had gone out with a good friend of mine.

I was in love with her, and I was devastated. To chase those feelings away, I dropped mescaline and got drunk. Then I got into fistfights, first with the guy who had dated Renee, then with another close friend who was dating my sister. The arena was the front yard of a friend's house, with his parents in attendance.

I was wasted and didn't know what I was doing, and I was embarrassed when the chemicals wore off. But the experience wasn't unpleasant enough to prevent me from ever again using chemicals to mask or suppress my emotions.

Drinking did a lot for me. I drank because without a chemical, I didn't fit in. Although I thought of myself as a leader—and I still do, as an athlete—I was a follower socially. I did what the others wanted to do, usually on impulse. I decided to go drinking the same way I decided to go on a 200-mile hunting trip. When someone called and said, "Let's do it," I went along without much thought. My impulsiveness always got me into trouble, especially in my sophomore year of college when I first tried cocaine.

3

Expecting to Dominate

There's an anecdote I like to tell about Steve. When he was a sophomore, we were playing Lake Orion, and I had another pitcher who was a senior, a left-hander who I felt was going to be a pretty good ballplayer.

The other kid got out of a jam in the first inning after he gave up two or three runs. Then he walked the bases loaded. I could see I couldn't stay with this guy, so I said to Steve, "Here's your chance to come in. Let's see what you can do."

Steve came in, struck out the side and went on to strike out 14 batters in the ballgame. After the game, the kid who was a senior quit because he could see the writing on the wall. From then on in, Steve played for me.

—Paul Tungate
Athletic Director and former
Baseball Coach
Clarkston High School
November 1986

All the Howe boys were sports crazy, a trait we inherited from Dad. We played baseball, but we also loved contact sports such as wrestling, football and hockey, and I lettered in all four sports at

Clarkston High. None of us cared much for basketball because you're supposed to pretend the collisions are accidental. We preferred authorized mayhem.

Baseball was my serious sport. It was Dad's game and the first sport I ever played, and I recognized that my skills in baseball were exceptional. Next on my list of favorites was wrestling.

I used wrestling to stay in shape for baseball. The conditioning regimen for wrestling was a killer, especially because I was always struggling to make weight. There were weeks when I had to lose 20 pounds to qualify in my weight class. The starvation and self-denial made me mean as well as lean. By the time I got out on the mat with my opponent, he looked like a pork chop.

My brother Michael was the same way, only worse. Michael wouldn't pin anybody. He'd rather beat his opponent 25–1. Dad would ask Michael why he hadn't pinned the guy when he could have done it easily. "Dad," Michael said, "I had to lose weight all week to wrestle that guy for six minutes. I was gonna kill him. I didn't want to pin him and let him go after two minutes."

Michael was good at baseball as well as wrestling, and Chris was a top-notch wrestler. Jeff's size made him a beast on the football field, and he was a wild, hard-throwing, intimidating pitcher in baseball. Kids were so scared of Jeff that when he got the ball over, they wouldn't swing. But Jeff, Chris and Mike paid a price because they followed me. Coaches expected them to live up to my standards, and my brothers tired of hearing the same old tune: "Why can't you do what Steve did? Why can't you be like Steve?"

As I would have done, my brothers retaliated with defiance and confrontation. Their response was usually something like: "Because I'm not Steve, and kiss my butt." That usually got them in trouble.

Jeff actually dropped out of school because the coaches kept hounding him. Of course, denying himself an education wasn't the most effective way for Jeff to send a message to the coaches, but it was true to the Howe tradition of striking back at others by hurting yourself. Mike had a similar problem in baseball. He was cut because the coaches didn't like his friends.

My brothers have since branched out, pursued other interests and done well. Chris is considering a career in law. Jeff now has his own roofing business and a growing family. Michael is a body builder and has a 46-inch chest to go with a 28-inch waist.

I think all my brothers feel a void because they never got the chance to realize their full potential in sports. I feel guilty at times, knowing that my achievements were at least partly responsible for the difficulties they experienced.

In his teens, Dad was a baseball prospect as a pitcher, but a freak injury ended his career. As he rounded third in full stride during a game, he slipped and fell on his pitching arm, suffering a compound fracture. He was never able to pitch again.

Until about 1978, Dad could still hit me. On my trips home, he'd say, "Oh, you think you're good, huh, kid?" Then he'd grab a bat and we'd go to a nearby field and go at it, one on one.

I'm sure Dad, like so many baseball fathers, wanted to live his lost dreams through his sons. From the time I was a toddler, he was my trainer, guru and greatest fan. Dad wasn't one of those fathers who push so hard that their sons learn to despise the game and treat it as a job. Dad's approach was to instill in me his love for the game, then play upon my natural competitive instincts to get me to work at it. He said, "I'm not going to force you to do it, but when you make up your mind that's what you're going to do, you'd better finish it." By then I wanted it more than he did, so he had no problem getting me to run the drills he designed.

When he didn't stop for a drink on the way, Dad got home from work shortly after I got off the bus from school. I waited for him in the driveway, glove on hand. We worked together until Mom called us for dinner.

Dad had me throw baseballs and footballs through a tire hanging from a rope, a time-honored drill that develops control. He thought I had potential as an outfielder or first baseman because I could hit, had a strong arm and could go get the ball. We ran another drill in which I'd turn my back, and Dad would throw the ball in the air and yell, "Ball up!" Then I'd have to find the ball and catch it before it hit the ground. Dad's rule was that if you could touch it, you should catch it. So I did, not because I felt threatened—I never felt that way—but because I wanted to make Dad proud of me.

I wanted to be a big league ballplayer and play for my favorite team, the hometown Tigers. My heroes as a youngster were

Mickey Lolich, Denny McLain and the late Norm Cash. (Interesting choices for a future cocaine addict: Lolich had a beer belly and a reputation as a serious partyer, McLain has served time in federal prison, and Cash died tragically in a boating accident after a drinking bout in October 1986.)

Dad used the Tigers as a training tool. I was allowed to watch Tigers games on TV if I squeezed tennis balls throughout the game. My arms cramped so badly that I couldn't pry my fingers loose from the ball. Toward the end of the games, Dad would say, "Had enough?"

"Yes!"

"You can't do any more?"

"NO!"

"Good. Do four more."

It sounds barbaric, but it strengthened my arms. I never suffered an injury of any kind to my pitching arm until November 1984, when I was pitching winter ball in the Dominican Republic. Dad's training went a long way toward making me a mature, controlled pitcher by the time I reached the Dodgers. I owe Dad a lot for his attention to my career.

Dad came to all my high school games and a lot of my college games, especially the home games in nearby Ann Arbor. Sometimes he made a road trip to see me pitch Big Ten games. It was fun to pitch in front of Dad because winning gave me extra pleasure when he was there to see it.

Dad's attendance was an event in itself. Once I had a one-hitter going against Illinois down in Champaign. Some of the Illinois players began mouthing off at us, and a brawl nearly broke out on the field. Taking their cue from the players, some rowdy Illinois fans began taunting the Michigan supporters.

Dad walked up to one of the Illinois rooters and said, "You'd better shut your mouth, or you won't be around for the second game of the doubleheader." The guy sat down and shut up. Dad commands respect, even on the road. He's sort of like E. F. Hutton claimed to be. When he speaks, people listen.

––––––––––

I first played organized baseball at the age of 12 in the Widget Division of Little League. Our team, H & A Party Store, had been the doormat of the league the year before. Hoping to avoid another season of embarassment, team sponsors Hank and Audrey offered every player on the team a free bottle of pop for every game the team could win consecutively.

I signed up with a friend, Steve Johnson. The two of us rode our bikes back and forth to games, which were played at the high school field seven miles away. If our bikes weren't working, we walked. That's how much we wanted to play.

H & A Party Store was the only team I've ever heard of that had four left-handed infielders and a left-handed catcher, Mike Hooper, who later caught me in high school. The infield didn't turn many double plays, but there aren't that many in Little League anyway.

I've always wondered why there aren't any left-handed catchers in pro ball. A left-hander is in equally good position to throw to any base, and when a left-handed hitter is at the plate—an occasion when managers like to order steals of second base because of the catcher's obstructed view of the runner—a left-handed catcher can throw to second without interference from the hitter.

H & A Party Store stunned everyone by terrorizing the league that year. We went undefeated and beat our principal rival 18–0. After that game, we tramped down to the party store to collect. Dad said, "You can't be doing this to Hank and Audrey. You guys are up to seven or eight pops apiece, and there are 15 kids on the team. That'll break the guy." But we had our hearts set on 16-ounce Faygos, the good stuff, and I don't think Hank and Audrey minded a bit. It was my first competitive payoff.

I won every game I pitched for H & A and hit about .700. I had only two pitches, an overhand fastball and a sidearm fastball, but I threw hard for a 12-year-old and scared a lot of kids.

I beat the odds my sophomore year of high school by making the baseball team and even doing some pitching. I pitched well my first year, and I really began to shine in my junior year.

I looked and acted like anything but a classy ballplayer in those days. I had long, scraggly hair, which I thought was pretty cool, and the cocky side of my personality had taken root. When the football coach told me to cut my hair, I said, "Would you make Jim Thorpe cut his hair?" I don't remember how many additional laps he made me run around the field that day. The coaches in all of my high school sports had remarkable patience with my appearance and attitude, even when I insisted that my team pictures be taken without a hat.

Paul Tungate, my baseball coach at Clarkston, knew how to handle young athletes. He was approachable and easy to talk to, and he always had time for his players. He tried to build our confidence with positive criticism and never chewed us out for mistakes. In fact, he never yelled at us unless he suspected that someone was giving less than his best effort.

I think the coach also did a lot of informal publicity work for his players, although that was something he never would have wanted us to know. I suspect that some of my college scholarship offers resulted from his behind-the-scenes work.

Coach Tungate was there to console me during my sophomore season when I suffered my first loss ever. Waterford Township beat me 1–0 on an unearned run. I gave up six hits, but we got only five. Because our field was wet, we had to play the game on a junior high field with no fences. I hit two balls to deep center that might have gone out of our park, but were just long outs on the junior high field.

Afterward I sat in Coach Tungate's car in a state of shock. "Everybody's gotta lose a game," he told me.

"Not me," I said, and I meant it. Ever since Little League, when I learned I could dominate, I've expected to win or save every game in which I pitched. My confidence has never been shaken by defeats or bad streaks. It may sound like I'm cocky—and I am—but I believe that top-notch athletes must expect to succeed if they hope to make it as professionals. You need that kind of belief in yourself to get through the rough spots.

In my junior season, Clarkston won the Wayne-Oakland League baseball title. My record was 10–0 with an ERA of 1.13, and I was named to several local all-star teams and received honorable mention All-State recognition. The scouts started coming around in my senior year, when I was 13–1 with a 0.37 ERA and led Clarkston to the state Class A championship. This time I made first team Class A All-State.

We had a team built on pitching and defense. The team ERA was only 1.22, and we made only 47 errors in 31 games, remarkable for a high school team. We hit just enough to win. I was third among the regulars with a .302 average.

In the state semifinal game, I threw a one-hitter and struck out 12 to beat Owosso 3–0. I doubled in the only run I'd need in the second inning. In the final, a 2–1 win over Hazel Park, the alma mater of my future Dodger teammate Bob Welch, I came in to get the final out. It was my first save.

In 94 and a third innings that year, I walked only 29 to go with 122 strikeouts. My success was based as much on control as on the intimidating speed of my fastball. I'd proved to myself that Dad had been right when he'd said, "It's not what you throw, it's where you throw it."

The Reds and the Phillies let me know they were watching me during high school, and Phil Sahara of the Dodgers stayed in touch. The Pittsburgh Pirates told Dad they wanted to draft me. Dad told them, "Don't even consider it, because he's already decided he's going to college." So it came as no surprise when no one chose me in the June 1976 free-agent draft.

I did well academically in high school, but not because I was a diligent student. I found out early that I could get A's and B's without busting my tail. When my academic record and baseball achievements were combined, I looked like a good investment to colleges with competitive baseball programs.

During my senior season, I received scholarship offers from Mississippi State, several schools in Florida and Arizona and every major college in Michigan. My choice was easy. The University of Michigan was tops in the state, and that's where I wanted to go. I had visions of Big Ten pageantry, parties everywhere and thousands of gorgeous girls. Ann Arbor was so close that Dad could see a lot of my games, and the baseball program was competitive nationally.

After my graduation from high school in June 1976, I was invited to a Dodger tryout camp run by Phil Sahara and his boss, Dale McReynolds. From the time I was a little kid, the word "Dodgers" was synonymous with "pitching." Every kid who knew anything about baseball in the mid-1960s knew that the Dodgers had three of the greatest pitchers in the game—starters Sandy Koufax and Don Drysdale and reliever Ron Perranoski. I wanted to find out what the Dodger organization was all about.

I was impressed with Dale McReynolds, the calm, knowledgeable, fatherly man who ran the tryout camp. He gave me a lot of attention, seemed genuinely interested in my future and told me I was doing the right thing by going to college.

Years later, during the height of my struggle with cocaine, Mac's letters and phone calls were a constant source of encouragement to me. I didn't always respond favorably, but it was nice to know someone cared. He stuck with me after others had written me off as a washout. I still hear from Mac a lot.

At the tryout camp, I formed a bond with Mac and the Dodgers. I decided that if the Tigers didn't want me, I'd like to play for the Dodgers.

4

Seduction

I had a camp in Grand Ledge, over Lansing area, not too far from Steve. Well, it was a decent drive at that. I invited him and he came. It was in the latter part of June of that year.

We had 25, 30 kids. Not much else there. He stood out like a sore thumb. I remember the day quite well. He was crude. He stood on top of the rubber and did more things wrong than he did right. But there was something about him; he just fascinated you.

It was a very hot, muggy day, and most of the kids and my helper wanted to get out of there and get in the shower and relax. He didn't want to go; he wanted to stay and work out more. So we kept a catcher there, and he worked out.

I can still see my part-time man up on top of a hill by the clubhouse, where he'd cleaned up after camp. He was all showered and in his civilian clothes, ready to go, and I'm still down there on the field, working with Steve. Or watching him work. I wasn't helping him that much. I'd give him a few tips, but he just wanted me to see him throw more. He was trying to sell me. That's Steve.

He has to be a boy that has great aptitude, because all those rough, crude little flaws just vanished in no time, and he'd become a hot item at the end of his first year [at Michigan].

—Dale McReynolds
Scout, Los Angeles Dodgers
October 1986

38

College was everything my overactive imagination had expected. I was never the shy, retiring type, and I rapidly discovered that sharp college women were friendly and plentiful, especially in a playpen the size of the University of Michigan. I loved the excitement of Big Ten football on autumn weekends, the competitive challenge of Big Ten baseball in the spring and plenty of partying all year long. No one had to twist my arm to get me to join in. When I wasn't screwing around, I was getting an excellent education in the field of exercise physiology.

I lived in the dorms my freshman year. I did the usual drinking scene, featuring keg parties on weekends. Almost always I went overboard and got sloppy drunk. I smoked grass now and then, although I didn't really enjoy it. I'd take a few tokes, get real mellow and quiet, giggle for a while, throw up and go to sleep. My body just didn't respond well to marijuana. That was established once and for all by an incident that happened during my sophomore year.

In the fall of 1977, I moved into a three-story apartment with Rex from Bad Axe, Michigan, Sam from East Lansing and Pete from Pittsburgh. A U of M baseball teammate moved in later. Rex was premed, the only serious student among us.

Sam and Pete enjoyed smoking pot. One afternoon, when Pete and Rex were out, Sam thought up a devious trick to play on his smoking buddy. Sam had saved a lot of marijuana seeds, and he'd heard that if you boiled down the seeds, you'd have a very potent residue. Knowing that Pete loved cookies as much as he did the evil weed, we whipped up a batch of the nastiest cookies ever to hit Ann Arbor.

All went according to plan until curiosity got the better of us. We had to find out how good a job we had done. My teammate, Pete and I each ate one. Hmmm, these aren't bad. Let's see what two will do. How about three? We had to be pigs and test the extent of our warranties, so to speak.

Not long after we ate number three, my teammate stepped out the back door and threw up. The sound from our stereo seemed to be coming out in slow motion, so we tried TV and got "Happy Days." The Fonz crashed his motorcycle when he tried to jump some garbage cans. We started crying.

Pete and Rex came back shortly before dinner time, took one look at us and started laughing. It didn't take them long to figure out what had happened. Pete ate a cookie, but he didn't react. The guy was a human garbage disposal.

Pete and Rex had bought a cabbage that was too big to fit into the refrigerator. Howe to the rescue. I started punching the cabbage, and I must have nailed it ten times before they threw me out of the kitchen. When they finished cooking dinner, we were too brain-damaged to eat. We just sat there and stared at each other.

What scared me more than anything was that the high was totally out of control and threatened to consume me. I kept getting higher and higher, and I was sure that any minute I was going to explode. The next morning I was still in the ozone. It was one of the most unpleasant experiences I've ever had.

Shortly after the cookie affair, I went to a jock party thrown by some friends. It was winter and most of the guests were idle football and baseball players. I was offered cocaine. I was very much into expanding my experience on all fronts, so I inhaled two or three lines without thinking. I had no reason to think the stuff was harmful or addictive, and even if someone had told me it was, I would have proceeded under the assumption that I was immune to the consequences.

After a few minutes, I experienced a sensation of mild euphoria. My whole body felt good and I seemed to have renewed energy. The euphoria lasted only a few minutes, but my energy level stayed up for hours. I walked around the party, rapping with friends and watching a dice game. I felt great. I stayed several hours, went home and went to sleep.

I thought I'd discovered something pretty good, especially when I awoke the next morning with no hangover and no physical indication that I had taken a drug. I compared the high and aftereffects of a few lines of coke with those of eight or ten beers, and coke won easily on both counts. I was sure I was more pleasant company when I was on coke. Liquor made me aggressive, unpredictable, obnoxious and inconsiderate. Coke seemed to make me passive and even-tempered, yet talkative and more conscious of what was going on around me. I liked the positive feeling coke gave me. It seemed like a miracle drug.

Coke was an occasional treat for me during my three remaining semesters at Michigan. I didn't use it often because I couldn't afford it. Almost always, I took it in the same limited, social dose I'd taken it the first time. I could put it down whenever I wanted. On the other hand, coke gave me the ability to stay out all night without getting tired. I snorted without anxiety, guilt or compulsion. It was fun.

On my 21st birthday in my junior year, when I was living with Cindy, some friends threw a small party for me. Four couples were there, and we drank moderately and sniffed small amounts of coke. Then everyone went home and went to sleep. No muss, no fuss, no overpowering urge to keep snorting until I was wacko.

That's what's so baffling about the drug. For several years, I was able to use it socially. Then it seemed to reach out, grab me and take control. There came a time when I envied the weekend warrior, the guy who could snort lots of coke on Friday and Saturday nights, then recuperate Sunday and stay straight all week for work. By 1981 I couldn't walk away like that.

When and why did I cross the line from use to abuse? I've tried to figure that out, and the only conclusion I can draw is that I never should have tried any drugs. Perhaps some people can handle chemicals indefinitely in moderate amounts, but I'm not one of them. Maybe, given my personality and background, I never was. Once my control over chemicals was lost, it was gone forever.

Dozens of college baseball teams from California, Arizona, Florida and the Deep South begin their seasons in February each year. If you want to play baseball in Ann Arbor in February, you'd better have a domed stadium, or at least a fleet of snowplows and a couple of heaters the size of the World Trade Center towers. The University of Michigan began its baseball season in Florida, which helped us maintain competitive parity with southern schools.

It was against Stetson in De Land, Florida that I pitched my first college game as part of a doubleheader. In college baseball, both games of a doubleheader are seven innings long. With two outs in the seventh, I was pitching a no-hitter when someone named Colin Leisher hit a two-run homer. We won the game, though, 3–2.

My first Big Ten start was against Minnesota in the second game of a doubleheader. Our coach, Milbry "Moby" Benedict, wanted to use his two best starters, and by then I was number two.

Minnesota's star was a masher named Paul Molitor, then a junior and the best player in the Big Ten. Later the same Paul Molitor hit in 39 straight games for the Milwaukee Brewers in July and August 1987, the sixth longest batting streak of all time. It was my first conference game, and I was about to face the nastiest hitter in the conference. I felt like I was carrying the weight of the entire state of Michigan on my back. Watching Molitor crunch two homers off Billy Stennett in an 8–0 Gopher win in the opener, I got so nervous I couldn't spit.

I got over it. I threw a six-hitter and we won 3–2. I fanned Molitor three times on nine fastballs. I never had Big Ten butterflies after that, and I never lost a Big Ten game until my junior and final year. I finished my freshman year with a 9–3 record and an ERA of 1.87.

My sophomore season was my personal best for the Wolverines and the team's most successful while I was there. We made it all the way to the College World Series, where we won a game before losing two straight and getting bounced from the double-elimination tournament. We were 30–17 that season, 13–3 in the Big Ten and 4–2 in the NCAA tournament.

I almost wasn't around for the ride, though. I spent most of the first semester of my sophomore year partying. I nearly flunked out, and I lost my scholarship for a semester. If I had appreciated not only the value of my education, but also how much I could have accomplished as a student with reasonable effort, disaster wouldn't have come so near. I was still a hard case at times. You couldn't tell me anything.

That was the only time Coach Benedict got on my case, and he really aired me out. He was a strict disciplinarian whose philosophy was that if you didn't make decent grades, you didn't play— no exceptions. Michigan wasn't like some schools where all you had to do was show up with your glove and get somebody to take your exams for you. Coach Benedict was also the best teacher of baseball fundamentals I've ever known. He was a baseball addict who loved the game so much that he even cleaned the field. When Rick Leach, Steve Perry and I took off for pro ball after the 1979 season, Coach Benedict went to work in the Montreal Expos farm system.

The Big Ten race in 1978, my sophomore year, came down to the final game of the season. As usual, we were finishing against archrival Michigan State. Kirk Gibson, who now gets paid megabucks to launch balls out of Dodger Stadium, was Michigan State's star. Kirk and I were well acquainted. He'd played high school ball for Waterford-Kettering, Clarkston's chief rival, and his mom taught at Clarkston. After our college careers were over, we became good friends, but friendship was forgotten when Michigan met Michigan State with the Big Ten title on the line.

The media don't usually pay enough attention to college baseball, but this game was a natural and got a big buildup in Michigan. Kirk was asked about his previous duels against me, and he was quoted as saying, "This isn't high school anymore. Let's see what he can do now." Coach Benedict and the rest of the Michigan team made sure I saw Gibson's quotes in print.

For several days before the game, I had a good chance to sit back and think about my plans for Kirk and Michigan State. I was in the hospital with a wicked intestinal virus or infection of some kind. Doctors were shooting dye through me and telling me I wasn't going anywhere. I had other ideas.

Coach Benedict showed up the day before the game and told me I wasn't pitching because I was too weak. "The hell I'm not," I said. "I've got a bone to pick with this guy."

When I got to the ballpark the next day, Coach Benedict said, "Just keep it in the ballpark." I answered, "They won't even hit it."

In typical cocky Howe fashion, I decided to strike out Gibson with a high school pitch. He was the third man to face me in the first inning. I got two quick strikes on him with overhand fastballs. Then I threw a sidearm fastball, a pitch I'd kept in the closet since Clarkston. Kirk's heart was in it, but his ass wound up in the seats along the first baseline. Strike three, end of inning. As I was walking off the field, I said loudly, "Hey, that was a high school pitch. I haven't thrown one of them since high school."

Kirk was breathing fire the rest of the day. He got a little revenge, breaking up my perfect game by singling with two outs in the fourth. But he and his teammates did nothing else. I finished with a four-hit, 3–0 win.

We sailed through the regional tournament. Coach Benedict chose me to pitch the first game of the 1978 College World Series in Omaha against Baylor. It was Michigan's first trip to the World Series in 16 years.

I really had it going against Baylor. I pitched a one-hitter, only the eighth time that had been done in the history of the College

World Series, and we won 4–0. I permitted only five baserunners: an infield single in the second inning, two walks, an error and a hit batsman. No Baylor runner advanced beyond first. Scouts were crawling all over the ballpark during the World Series, so it was an important showcase performance for me.

Unfortunately, the rest of the series didn't go as well. Southern California beat us, and then we had to beat North Carolina to stay in the hunt. I had only had about a day's rest, so Coach Benedict didn't want to use me at all against UNC. But he called on me in relief in the eighth inning, and I gave up a three-run homer to Greg Robinson. We lost 7–6 and finished in a tie for fifth in the tournament.

In 1978 I finished all 12 of my starts for Michigan and pitched in 15 games overall. My record was 11--3, and my win total set a Michigan single-season record. In the conference I was 6–0 with a 1.17 ERA, and I shared the team MVP award with Rick Leach. Through two seasons I was 20–6 with a 1.80 ERA against top college competition. By now all the scouts knew who I was. All I had to do to ensure a shot at pro ball was continue along the same course.

Although I was pleased with my accomplishments during my first two years at Michigan, I recognized that I needed more work on my skills. When you pitch only 12 to 15 games a year, you have to extend your season in order to get the experience you'll need to succeed as a pro. I joined the Glacier Pilots, a team based in Anchorage in the Alaska League, for the summers after the 1977 and 1978 college seasons.

A lot of top college players, some of whom later became successful major leaguers, were my teammates and opponents in Alaska. Tim Wallach, now the Expos' third baseman, and reliever Ed VandeBerg played for Fairbanks. One of my Glacier teammates was Marty Barrett, now the second baseman for the Boston Red Sox and the Most Valuable Player in the 1986 American League Championship Series against the Angels. Our manager was Marcel Lachemann, now the Angels' pitching coach.

I pitched fairly well in Alaska, compiling a record of 10–5 over two seasons. In the 1978 postseason World Crown Tournament, I threw a six-hit shutout with no walks against Kenai, a city about

165 miles from Anchorage. The competition was excellent and the experience was invaluable, but I had expected all that before I went to Alaska. What I didn't expect to find was a wife.

Most of the players who came up from colleges in the lower 48 stayed with families who were gracious enough to offer us lodging for the summer. In 1978 I lived with Emmett Wilson, head of the Teamsters Credit Union in Anchorage. On June 24 I went with the Wilsons to a party at the home of their friend Paula Beltz. Emmett introduced me to Cynthia Ann Holliday, whose mother, Marianne, was branch manager at Alaska National Bank, where Emmett did business.

I had seen Cindy for the first time the night before Paula's party. The Pilots had flown back to Anchorage from Kenai, and when I got off the plane I saw a little blond teenybopper in jeans who looked like she was maybe 16 years old. I thought she was cute but too young for me. Besides, I was already dating someone in Alaska, a girl named Linda.

At Paula's party, most of us were drinking beer and playing pool, but Cindy was bouncing around drinking Kool-Aid all night. I thought that was corny, but her bubbly innocence was also appealing. We spent a lot of time talking and joking. I was surprised to find that I wasn't interested in hanging around with anyone else that night.

Late in the evening, a group of us went to a place called The Cattle Company to dance. By then I'd grown protective of Cindy and responsive to her interests for some reason. I pulled out a pack of cigarettes and Cindy said immediately, "I don't date anybody who smokes." Uh, sorry. I put the cigarettes away and didn't pick them up again for the rest of the summer (except when Cindy wasn't around).

We began dating almost daily. After we'd gone out a couple of times, she was with me at the ballpark one night when Linda pulled up. My heart sank, because it was instant decision time. I really liked Linda, but the choice wasn't hard. I told Linda in the parking lot that it was all over.

I couldn't put my finger on what it was about Cindy that overwhelmed me. It helped that she was a feisty little blond like my mother. She was kind and polite, but she spoke her mind and was quick with a response when someone started talking trash to her. I also noticed that, aside from her disinterest in liquor and drugs, she seemed as rambunctious as I was, especially on the highway.

The Teamsters Credit Union repossessed plenty of cars from Anchorage deadbeats, and all summer Emmett let me choose which ones I wanted to drive. I was motoring around on some of the hottest wheels in Anchorage.

One of my favorites was a Datsun 280 ZX with pink flames painted on it. One day Cindy's mom asked me, "What are you doing driving that car?" I told her it was one of Emmett's repo specials. "That was a pimp's car," she said, "and that guy owed a lot of people a lot of money. They'll shoot you if they see you in that car." I found out how fast the Z would go when I took it straight back to Emmett.

Then Emmett got me a real screamer, a 454 high-output Trans Am that was the fastest car in town. I ran a few drag matches in it, and I never lost. Once Cindy tried to race me with her new Firebird, which resulted in a mishap that has been a family secret until now. Cindy was lagging behind, so she floored the Firebird, lost control for an instant and hit a curb. Her rear axle was bent, and her dad had to buy her a new one. I don't remember what Cindy told her dad about the axle, but it was pure baloney.

Three and a half weeks after we began dating, Cindy and I had our first argument. I told her I'd be over to pick her up after dinner, which was to be served at the Wilsons' after Emmett and Sue got home. I watched the Wilsons' kids while they were out. Emmett and Sue were late getting home, dinner was late, and of course I was a late arrival at the Hollidays'. I was ticked off because in those days I was Mr. Punctuality, at least where Cindy was concerned.

Cindy got into the car and immediately began airing me out, big time. She paused just long enough to give me a chance to defend myself. I said, "Look, are you going to make it that difficult for me to ask you to marry me?"

Cindy gurgled and then shut up, probably for the first time in her life. And the last. But she didn't say no.

At the end of the evening when we got back to her house, as Cindy was putting her car away for the evening, she ran into the side of her parents' garage. She was suffering from massive shock.

Cindy and I decided she'd enroll at Michigan and we'd get married the following summer. We planned to break the news to her parents the next evening, so we invited them out for dinner at a restaurant called Tiki Cove. They must have suspected something was up, but I'm sure they didn't know what. Dick Holliday had been telling Cindy to watch out for those ballplayers because they'd love her and leave her.

We ordered drinks. I figured I'd better get it over with before dinner, in case one or both of the Hollidays were going to get sick when they heard the news. I said, "We were talking about school and stuff, and Cindy says she wants to go to school."

Dick Holliday turned to Cindy and opened his mouth. I thought Dick might not approve of that, so before he could say anything, I continued, "I asked her to marry me, and she accepted."

Marianne Holliday grabbed her huge margarita and chugged it down. Dick was speechless, another first.

There was an engagement party, primarily for Cindy's friends and my Glacier Pilot teammates. Some of the women were envious of Cindy because they were hoping to land a ballplayer. Many of the families that housed the players had eligible daughters, and some of them wanted the same kind of matchup. I don't think Cindy had any such intention.

After the Alaska League season, the three Hollidays and I drove to Fairbanks, Cindy's birthplace, to make wedding arrangements. We returned on the two-lane Alaskan Highway, the only major road between the two cities, the day before I was scheduled to fly back to Michigan.

We stopped along the road to watch salmon swimming upriver to spawn. They were running so thick that if you stepped into the river, you'd have a chance to catch one with your bare hands. I tried to grab one. No luck. When we got back to the Lincoln Town Car, I replaced Dick at the wheel. Cindy sat in front, right next to me.

I set the cruise control at 58 miles per hour, a crawl for me, but I was in no hurry and didn't want to upset the Hollidays by driving like Steve Howe. None of us was wearing a seat belt.

As we moved into a large, sweeping curve, I saw the Cadillac Coupe de Ville firing out of the far end of the curve, heading toward us at high speed. Its driver was drunk and going between 90 and 110 miles per hour, the police said later. The crash happened in an instant, although what I'd heard about accidents is true: Everything is in slow motion for those who survive.

The Caddy's speed took it just off the edge of the road, and as the driver struggled to bring it back, its tires caught the gravel and shot it right into us. It happened so fast that I didn't have time to hit the brakes.

I remember the cars' frames buckling and chrome flying in slow motion. My right arm slid off the steering wheel and punched a perfect hole through the windshield. My head, neck and chest surged forward, crushing the steering wheel and then snapping it off at the column. I cracked my first and fourth cervical vertebrae, and a piece of metal sliced into my left knee underneath the kneecap.

Dick Holliday lurched from the back seat through the front passenger seat, crushed the family dog to death, and rammed his left arm through the windshield, suffering more than a dozen fractures between his wrist and elbow. Dick's face was so severely cut that he required plastic surgery.

I was lucky to have traded positions in the car with Dick just before the accident. If I'd been in his place and suffered the same kind of injury to my left arm, I definitely wouldn't have pitched again. And if Dick would have been driving, he might have been killed, because his neck and esophagus might not have withstood the impact with the steering wheel.

Marianne Holliday was the most gravely injured. She flew up and crashed into the Lincoln's internal wraparound lights, crushing the side of her skull. When we came to rest, Marianne was having seizures and was suffocating on her vomit. Fortunately, an off-duty paramedic was traveling behind us, and he managed to clear her airway. Marianne later underwent hundreds of thousands of dollars worth of brain surgery. Surgeons removed one side of her skull, froze it and replaced it after the swelling in her brain had subsided.

If Cindy had been sitting in the normal front-seat passenger's position instead of right next to me, she probably would have been crushed to death. As it was, she cracked four ribs and her tailbone, and a piece of glass left a perfect slice on the bottom part of one of her eyelids, coming within a fraction of an inch of cutting her eyeball in half.

The driver of the Caddy survived, but a passenger, his brother-in-law, was dismembered and killed. We hit so hard that the Lincoln's sunroof blew out and was never found, and its rear axle snapped in half. The front end was demolished.

In the eerie post-collision silence, I looked first at Cindy and noticed that she was trapped between the seat and the middle part of the console, but otherwise she didn't appear to be seriously hurt. I decided to get out of the car for two reasons: I smelled gas, and I wanted to finish off the guy who had hit us, if he was still breathing. I could hear Dick moaning, "Marianne, don't leave me."

I don't know how I got out of the Lincoln, and I don't remember much of what happened after that. They found me wandering around trying to get into the Caddy. Cindy had to be cut out of the Lincoln with emergency equipment.

The closest treatment facility was Palmer Hospital, 60 miles away. Palmer wasn't equipped to treat Marianne's injuries, so she and Dick were ferried to Anchorage hospitals by helicopter. Cindy and I remained at Palmer. I had surgery on my right arm to repair severe cuts, and on my left knee for the removal of embedded steel. I was hospitalized for a couple of weeks and lost 20 pounds.

As I lay in my hospital bed, I fell apart emotionally. Even though I knew I couldn't have avoided the accident, I felt responsible. It looked like Cindy's mother might not survive, and I'd grown close to her during the summer. Once again I'd fulfilled my mother's prophecy that I'd always screw things up. I'd done it royally. I began to cry uncontrollably.

Life in the hospital in Palmer wasn't a total disaster. By the second week, Cindy and I were placed in adjoining rooms that shared a bathroom. A night nurse was nice enough to let us sleep together in Cindy's room. The nurse woke us at 6:00 a.m. so I could return to my room and avoid detection and swift punishment by the day nurse. Cindy wasn't very mobile. She needed my assistance even to go to the toilet. We got to know each other on a very intimate and personal basis.

Marianne Holliday was in grave condition for weeks. Her friends set up a prayer chain that extended from Fairbanks to Anchorage. Most of us thought she wasn't going to live. Only Cindy knew her mother would make it.

Marianne retired early because of her injuries. Dick turned his business over to his son, and Dick and Marianne later moved to California.

When I left the hospital, I drove up to a service station where Dick Holliday's Lincoln had been towed. I wanted to retrieve some things from the trunk. The sight of the crumpled wreckage made me sick and thankful at the same time. Blood was everywhere, and the smell of death made my skin crawl. For some reason, we had all lived to tell about it.

A gas station attendant saw me taking it all in, and he said to me, "The sucker who drove that car is dead."

"No he's not," I said. "I'm him."

"You're crazy. No way," said the guy, and he walked off.

Dad sent Mom to Alaska to fly back to Michigan with me because they thought I shouldn't make the trip alone. I was glad to see her, but our trip wasn't the most amicable.

Mom and Dad began campaigning against my marriage to Cindy as soon as they learned of our engagement. Their pitch played upon my position of responsibility in the family and my sense of guilt: "You're betraying your family. You're going to have to struggle just to make it on your own, let alone support a wife. You don't care about helping your family." (I know now that my parents always meant well—they just had a hard time making their point in a positive way.)

Quite a blessing, eh? I was so mad at my parents that if I hadn't been in the accident, I would have gone directly from Anchorage to Ann Arbor without stopping to say hello.

Cindy wasn't strong enough to leave Alaska by the time I flew out, so I had time to scheme. Even though I was late getting to Ann Arbor, I found and leased a convenient one-bedroom apartment above a travel agency. Then I had to convince Cindy that she had no alternative but to live with me. I lied about the availability of other housing and told her how economically sensible it was for us to be together. It worked.

When Cindy first saw our pad, she nearly broke into tears. The place was dirty and in disrepair. It had an ancient, decaying, turquoise linoleum floor, ragged drapes, chipping paint and a red, white and blue bathroom with American eagle decals all over the walls. We didn't have much money because I'd spent my summer earnings of $3,800 wooing Miss Cindy and paying for her flight to Michigan. But with the help of the landlords, we were able to make our nest look respectable.

My first stay-out-all-night cocaine bash happened during the year Cindy and I lived together at Michigan. I went to a bachelor party, where there was enough whiff to take us through the night, so we did it all. There were times when I wanted to leave the party and go home, but a little voice inside me kept saying, "They're just gonna call you a wimp."

I wandered in at about seven the next morning. Cindy was fuming, not because I'd been snorting, but because I'd been out all night.

In those days, Cindy would sniff a little coke with me now and then. The first time she tried it, we were one of three couples out on the town, and Cindy succumbed to peer pressure from me and the others and nervously took a snort in a nearby phone booth. I saw coke as an expensive but otherwise harmless party drug. Cindy, whose upbringing had been conservative and sheltered, didn't think any drug was harmless, but she tolerated coke at that time, probably because we weren't snorting it much.

When I was able, in the fall of 1978, I began daily workouts with Gus Crouch, the head of Michigan's physical therapy department. The coaches said they thought my accident injuries would keep me from pitching during the 1979 season, and I was out to prove them wrong.

I could barely walk when Gus took me under his wing, but in a month he had me ready to play. I was in condition to get the job done, if not at full strength.

There was one more obstacle to be cleared before I could pitch. Shortly after the season started, I was accused of retaining an agent in violation of NCAA rules. The alleged agent was Bob Fenton, a Detroit lawyer who later represented me. I don't know who made the allegations, but I heard a rumor that the Detroit Tigers blew the whistle, hoping I'd be declared ineligible so they could sign me as a free agent without waiting for the draft.

My only contacts with Fenton before the investigation were a phone call or two, which Fenton initiated. He was only one of about 50 agents who had called from as far away as Seattle and asked to represent me. I knew the rules, and I knew I couldn't hire an agent without jeopardizing my eligibility.

During Michigan's investigation, I was interviewed by Marcus Platt, dean of the law school. I told him that I didn't have an agent, had never had one and didn't plan on retaining one in the near future. The university decided I hadn't done anything wrong. The whole incident left a sour taste in my mouth, my only negative memory from my Michigan days.

I finished the season with a 7–2 record and a 1.78 ERA, not bad considering the distraction of the investigation and the questions about my physical well-being. My career record at Michigan was 27–8, and I still hold the school record for wins.

Despite the presence of some pro-caliber talent on our team, Michigan couldn't duplicate its 1978 achievements, and we finished third in the Big Ten behind Michigan State and Wisconsin. My last Big Ten start against Michigan State was my first and only conference defeat after 15 straight wins.

The major league draft of free-agent amateur players took place on Tuesday, June 5, 1979. With the 16th pick in the first round, the Los Angeles Dodgers chose me. Two of my Michigan teammates also went in the first round—Rick Leach to the Tigers on the 13th pick, and pitcher Steve Perry to the Dodgers on the 25th selection.

I was elated. Dale McReynolds had encouraged me all along, telling me the Dodgers were interested. After the draft, he told me the Dodgers hadn't expected me to last until the 16th pick. The only reason the Dodgers drafted that early was that they had been awarded Pittsburgh's pick as compensation for the Pirates' signing of free agent Lee Lacy before the 1979 season.

I was the first such compensation award under an agreement negotiated by the owners and players, and I would soon become Exhibit A in support of the players' argument that the system worked. In 1978 the owners had reluctantly agreed to accept draft choices as compensation when one of their players was signed by another team as a free agent. The owners continued to gripe that such compensation would never be fair, because in exchange for the loss of an established player, they would receive an untested young player who might not be able to contribute at the major league level for years, if ever.

"Compensation Award" Howe made it to the majors after only half a season in the Class AA Texas League and immediately became the Dodgers' bullpen ace for four years. Lee Lacy was a good ballplayer and an excellent hitter, although he never got to play as regularly as he probably deserved. It seems that the system compensated the Dodgers fairly for the loss of Lee Lacy.

I was anxious to sign with the Dodgers. I also knew that first-round draft choices could command considerable bonuses, and I didn't want to be cheated. Bob Fenton and I talked it over and decided we could get a signing bonus of $100,000, and we would ask for $120,000.

When we sat down with Dale McReynolds for negotiations, he offered something like $60,000 at first. But it was obvious that Mac had authorization to go higher, and we soon reached $75,000 as a compromise figure. It was less than I wanted, but I've never let money stand in the way when I really cared about something.

Mac typed up the contract and I signed on the spot. The Dodgers assigned me to San Antonio of the Texas League, and they wanted me to report as soon as possible.

5

Blasting Off

He seemed like a young all-American type. Very competitive, a little bit on the cocky side, but you like that in an individual, especially in someone who was gonna be one of my pitchers.

He did not take any bullshit on the field. Off the field, as far as in the clubhouse or whatever, he was just a lot of fun. But if there was anything happening on the field, he stuck up for his teammates and he was one heck of a competitor.

Even in the Instructional League, the atmosphere is obviously a bit looser than it is in big league games, but there were times when you wanted to knock some people down because you thought they were throwing at some of our people, and he would go right at them. He wouldn't hold back. I kind of liked that in an individual.

Personally, we were real close. He was like one of my sons. A lot of pitchers were, but he was one of my favorites.

—Ron Perranoski
Pitching Coach, Los Angeles
Dodgers
October 1986

I had some important business to take care of before I could begin my professional career in San Antonio. Cindy and I were getting married.

My itinerary for one week in June 1979 went like this: fly from Detroit to Fairbanks for wedding preparations, fly from Fairbanks to Detroit to await results of the draft, fly from Detroit to Los Angeles to negotiate and sign, fly from L.A. to Fairbanks to get married, fly from Fairbanks to San Antonio and pitch the night after my arrival. Single-handedly, I probably saved several airlines from bankruptcy.

The bachelor party in Fairbanks was a big-time blowout. I had never done any coke while I was playing summer ball in Alaska, but the white carpet was rolled out for the main event. There was an ounce available for 30 guys. The party continued for a solid 24 hours.

First there was a cocktail party at my brother-in-law Don's house. Don is a very straight guy. He might drink a beer, but that's his limit, so we couldn't get too crazy at his house. We set up the bachelor party at a hotel, then went and picked up the stuff. I was the man of the hour, as apprehensive as any man in my position should be, and I grabbed more than my fair share of available treats. It was my second major binge.

In midparty, my attorney called from Detroit to discuss business. I said, "Just a minute, Bob," and I turned and threw up in a wastebasket. "Okay, Bob, what's up?" I had full control of the situation.

Meanwhile, my parents were still trying to talk me out of marriage. In whispered conversations before and during the cocktail party, I kept hearing, "Don't do this. You can still get out of it." I was resentful and hurt that they were withholding approval.

A cold war raged between the in-laws. Mom and Dad weren't getting along with the Hollidays, and hostility soon took the form of open confrontation. At the cocktail party, Dad and Dick Holliday both had a few extra drinks and began arguing over how our marriage was going to start. Dad didn't want Cindy to join me in San Antonio right away because he wanted me to begin my career free of interference and distraction. Dick and almost everyone else thought Cindy and I should decide for ourselves.

Dad was outvoted. Score it Love 1, Parents 0.

I was under pressure from within as well as without when I went to get blasted. Although I wanted to be with Cindy, I began to get a little queasy at the prospect of marriage. It would have relieved the pressure if I could have discussed with someone my inner fears of marriage and responsibility and the trouble I was having with my parents. But I couldn't turn to my family, and there was no one else around with whom I was comfortable enough to have such a personal and revealing conversation.

Don't get the idea that inner turmoil drove me to bury my snout in a pile of coke. I figured I was entitled to a good party. What I needed was an excuse so I could rationalize my use of drugs and alcohol.

The morning after the party died of exhaustion, Cindy and I got married. Most of my relatives missed all but the last minute or so of the wedding. They said they were out shopping and lost track of the time.

On our way to the hotel after the wedding, a close friend of Cindy's gave us a gram of coke. We killed it that night. The next morning we flew to Texas.

When we arrived in San Antonio, I was able to put behind me the alternating tugs of revelry and discord that had ripped my head apart in Alaska. I began a two-year period in which I concentrated almost exclusively on my baseball career. That doesn't mean I quit using. My nose found the way to fun and adventure with increasing frequency, but I thought for that period that my wife and my game were what really mattered.

Considering that I was spent from arguing, partying and loving, my starting assignment in AA ball was an unqualified success. I went eight innings and gave up only three hits, a walk and an earned run. I got no decision.

I continued to pitch well for San Antonio. My third win was a five-hit shutout against Midland in which I struck out 13. In my next start against Amarillo, I had a no-hitter in the fourth when a brawl broke out on the field.

For once I wanted to avoid a fight (baseball fights are rarely much fun anyway). But our manager, Ducky LeJohn, had a rule that the last guy on the team to leave the bench during a fight would be fined $25. So I went out there and pretended to be fully involved. I finished with a four-hitter and a 6–3 win.

For my half season, I was 6–2 with a 3.13 ERA, and I allowed only 22 walks in 95 innings. People I talked to in the Dodger organization told me I'd move up to AAA Albuquerque in 1980, but I had my eye on making the big club.

One of the reasons I was so anxious to pitch for the Dodgers in 1980 was the bane of every minor leaguer's existence: bus trips. It was on my first trip to Jackson, Mississippi, a 16-hour haul each way, that I vowed not to spend another year in the minors. Those bus seats are hard and you can't sleep. When a trip like that is over, you feel like you've just played back-to-back doubleheaders.

In San Antonio I discovered and rejected another drug. Some of the ballplayers were using an antihistamine-decongestant you could purchase over the counter. They called it "poor man's speed." Players used the drug the same way they used amphetamines (also known as "greenies") to give them that extra competitive edge on the field. I had no interest in using the drug while I was pitching—for one thing, I didn't need the edge—so I ate two or three of them as an experiment on a day I wasn't going to pitch. I got really wired for a long time, and I was very uncomfortable. I never did the drug again.

Not long after Cindy and I moved to San Antonio, cocaine interfered with our marriage for the first time. We lived in a large apartment complex that was home for most of the players. One night I went out to snort with some teammates.

Cindy didn't want me to go out that night, and, when I insisted, she let me know she wanted me home early. I stayed out half the night. When I got back, Cindy was gone, and she didn't come back for a couple of days. She never left the complex, but I didn't know that. I thought she'd gone home to Alaska. By leaving she was sending a message that she expected me to come home on schedule at night. That sounded reasonable, but it didn't mean I was going to comply.

So began the war for control. It soon became clear to me that Cindy had been Daddy's little girl and was used to getting what she wanted, and that she was tough enough to go after it if it wasn't handed to her. I was surprised and a little remorseful to find she'd followed through on her threat to walk out if I didn't come home. She had won round one. But I think Cindy will admit that in the following years, as my drug use accelerated, she lost the war.

I behaved myself for the rest of the season. I did nothing more adventurous than drink a few beers. I continued to be a model of sobriety in the Arizona Instructional League, where the Dodgers sent me in the fall of 1979 for a longer, closer look than they had gotten in San Antonio. I wasn't about to do anything that would slow the progress of my career.

Arizona was exactly what it was supposed to be—an opportunity for me to learn and grow as a pitcher. Immediately after I got there, I came face to face with two of the pitching gods of my universe, Sandy Koufax and Ron Perranoski. Sandy was a roving pitching instructor in the Dodger organization, and Perry was the minor league pitching coach.

Sandy Koufax. The best left-handed pitcher of his era, maybe of all time. The Dodgers waited patiently through the late fifties while Sandy struggled to gain control over his overpowering stuff. Control arrived in 1961, and for the five seasons that followed, he was untouchable. He retired at the age of 30, after the 1966 season, because of an arthritic condition in his pitching elbow. I was learning from a genuine living legend.

Koufax taught me intimidation and mental toughness. Intimidation doesn't necessarily mean pitching a hitter uncomfortably high and tight to keep him from digging in against you, although that's part of it. Intimidation is achieved by using your pitches and location to make a hitter flinch, hesitate and back off. I'm not going to say exactly what Koufax and Perranoski told me, because I'm working on another comeback and there are plenty of major league hitters who would love to know the way Steve Howe is going to pitch them.

Koufax also gave me some sage advice that sounds simple but is frequently ignored by even the best pitchers. "Kid," Koufax said, "you've got a live fastball. You throw as hard as anybody. Go after their ass. If you come into a ballgame, and you get beat with your second or third best pitch, it's nobody's fault but yours, and you should kick yourself in the ass."

To this day, I don't care if the guy with the bat in his hands is a fastball hitter. If the game is on the line, I'm going to bring the gas. If I set him up properly and put it in the right place, and I usually do, he's mine. When in doubt, air it out.

Perranoski was the game's best left-handed reliever in the sixties. He didn't have the arm and stuff of a Koufax, so he learned to do the job with his head and pinpoint control.

Perry taught me the fundamentals of how to pitch and how to set hitters up and get them to hit the pitch they really don't want to swing at. The location of each pitch was of vital importance in his scheme. You needed good control to execute Perry's lessons properly, and that's one of the reasons we got along so well. I learned quickly that if you were thinking along the same lines as Perry, you won. I became his disciple.

Perranoski's pet peeve was two-strike hits. He figured that when you got ahead of a guy 0-and-2 or 1-and-2, there's no way the guy should see a hittable pitch. He reamed me out several times for giving up hits in that situation, and I'm glad he did because it helped me concentrate. I wish he would have known as much about chemical addiction as he did about pitching.

"If you throw a guy a good oh-2 pitch," Perry said, "it had better be your paint pitch, and you'd better strike him out. You'd better stick the bat up his ass."

In the spring of 1980, Perry and Red Adams, who was then the Dodgers' pitching coach, suggested that I learn to throw a slow curve. They told me I'd need something besides a fastball and a slider to survive in the majors. A slow curve would be especially effective because its pace would tie up hitters who were looking for my hard stuff. I had trouble learning the pitch at first. It required wrist action that was completely different from the fastball and slider. I never had complete confidence in the curve.

I also proved during my first four years in L.A. that I could survive as a two-pitch pitcher, because I almost never used the curve. There were no secrets when I went to the mound. Here it is, and you might as well swing because I'm not going to walk you.

Once in a while, I dusted off the curve in a game. One such instance that happened in 1983 illustrates the almost psychic understanding that Perranoski and I had developed. We were playing Atlanta, and I was pitching to Bruce Benedict, a light-hitting catcher who had been ordered to bunt. With the count 0-and-1, Benedict offered at a slider and fouled it off his kneecap. Benedict claimed he was directly hit by the pitch, and he got into a shouting match with the plate umpire, Dick Stello. Benedict called Stello a posterior orifice and Stello ejected him.

The Braves sent up Terry Harper, a dead fastball hitter who had some success against me, to complete Benedict's turn at bat. Harper inherited the 0-and-2 count. As Harper stepped in, I looked into the dugout, where Perranoski was standing with an otherwise inscrutable expression that screamed to me, "Hook! Hook!"

I knew Harper would be overly anxious, sent up cold with only one strike left, and I knew I could freeze him with the curve, a pitch he would never expect from me. I threw the curve—it was a beauty—and Harper just dropped the bat and walked away. I looked over at Perry and winked, and he grinned and began to stroll to the other end of the dugout.

Cindy and I spent the 1979–80 off-season before and after the Instructional League in Saline, Michigan, near Ann Arbor. I used coke, but there were no major blowouts until just before we left for Arizona. Then Cindy and I had another tussle about my partying. She almost left me again, but I covered my butt by minimizing the severity of my use and making another false promise that I wouldn't do it again.

When spring training rolled around, I put the drug away and devoted full attention to the task of making the Dodger pitching staff. I had a mission. The Dodgers took me to camp as a nonroster player, meaning they hadn't included me on their 40-man spring training roster because I was likely to be farmed out to Albuquerque. I had a feeling the Dodgers were going to be making a roster adjustment.

Before I left for Vero Beach, Florida, the Dodgers' spring training home, Cindy asked me if she should go to Albuquerque and rent an apartment for us.

"No," I said. "I'm going to make the club."

"Oh, yeah," said Cindy, baiting me. "OK. Call me and let me know."

My prophecy was based on something more than the blind brashness of a cocky, not-yet-22-year-old left-hander. I had done some thinking about the Dodgers' needs for 1980. I guessed there would be no room for me as a starter, but the Dodgers had problems in the bullpen. Terry Forster had just had arm surgery, and Ken Brett had a sore elbow. The Dodgers had spent a lot of money to sign free agent right-hander Don Stanhouse, but there was still no left-hander in sight who could provide relief—other than Steve Howe. I had always been a starter, but I was willing to try relief for a chance to make the team.

Before camp opened, I went to Florida with Doug Harrison, a San Antonio teammate whose father had a home in Florida. Doug was also a pitcher, and we took turns catching each other. We lifted weights, ran and tried to get into prime shape to get the jump on the other players.

Dodgertown in Vero Beach was Disneyland for ballplayers: the most modern and complete athletic and residential facilities, a marvelous assortment of the finest food and amusements for the whole family.

Let's start with the food, always a great place to start. Never in my life had I seen spreads like those the Dodgers laid out for the players every day. There were four or five entrees—and I'm not talking ground beef—lobster, shrimp, New York steak, fresh fish, pasta, whatever you wanted. There were five different salads, four or five different vegetables, potatoes fixed every way imaginable, different kinds of milk, fruit punch, soda. You name it, you had it. It was so tasty and plentiful that it seemed Tommy Lasorda himself had done the catering.

Peter O'Malley, the president and owner of the Dodgers, threw parties for the players and their families. There was a game room in the complex and a movie theater that ran a different new release every night. For the kids there were barbecues, horse rides and Christmas at Dodgertown. About halfway through camp, Peter O'Malley actually imported snow so that a hill could be created for the kids to sled on.

One of the reasons the Dodgers were so successful on the field and at the gate for years was because the organization had class. Success, in turn, gave the Dodgers the resources to maintain their image. It was a cycle that paid off for everyone in the organization. It also paid off for dozens of charities to which the Dodgers generously contributed in the Los Angeles area.

Credit must go to Branch Rickey, who built the Dodgers' image more than 40 years ago, and the O'Malley family, who moved the team from Brooklyn. Every worker in the organization, right down to the grounds crew and usherettes, was treated as a member of the Dodger family. As a result, Dodger employees were intensely loyal. Many of those who followed the team from Brooklyn in 1959 are still in the Dodger organization.

The organization took a personal interest in the members of its family. When I got hit by a line drive during spring training in 1985, Peter O'Malley personally visited Cindy to tell her. Annette O'Malley, Peter's wife, went to Cindy's baby shower in 1983.

The Dodgers' family approach was not their only old-fashioned method of dealing with employees. The Dodgers offered their players only straight performance contracts. No incentive clauses were permitted. Their theory was that a player is paid to perform a job, and he should perform to the best of his ability without incentives. That policy cost the Dodgers a few good players, like Steve Garvey, who left after 1982.

It was sad to see what happened to the Dodgers in the mid-eighties. The team wasn't competitive in 1986 or 1987. The starting pitching remained strong, but otherwise the Dodgers fielded a team that had difficulty with the worst major league clubs. The Al Campanis racial scandal in April 1987, followed by public disclosure of the struggle for control between Tommy Lasorda and Dodgers Vice President Fred Claire, tarnished the Dodgers' image as a happy, progressive family. Their fortunes revived in 1988 with their World Series victory, but over the years I had learned that the Dodger image was makeup that concealed a lot of blemishes. In the spring of 1980, however, I was still an innocent rookie, awed by the Dodgers and the daily spectacle of Vero Beach.

I began the spring in the minor league clubhouse. One day I sneaked into the major league clubhouse just to see what it looked like, and while I was there I ripped off a cup of orange juice. Some of the Dodger players looked at me, wondering who I was. They'd soon find out.

The Dodgers always gave uniform numbers above 50 to batting practice pitchers and early camp arrivals they didn't expect to stick around. I was assigned number 57. Later, after I made the team, I asked to keep that number. I liked it, and I also wanted to remind myself that if I worked hard, I could accomplish things that people thought were impossible for me.

Perranoski and Koufax were in camp, and they continued the lessons they had begun in the Instructional League. Red Adams didn't tutor me because I hadn't yet made the team.

My first spring training game appearance was against St. Louis in St. Petersburg, Florida. Bobby Bonds, who was then 34 and nearing the end of a distinguished career, was the first major league hitter I ever faced. My first or second pitch, a slider, got away and caught Bonds flush on the kneecap. He grimaced, limped down to first and muttered, "Goddamn rookies." Bobby hit only .203 in 231 at-bats for the Cardinals that year, no thanks to me.

I believe that my third appearance, on March 26 against the Reds at Holman Stadium, Vero Beach, was the one that earned me a spot on the team. I blew away Cesar Geronimo and Ken Griffey on strikes and got George Foster to ground out. Several members of the Dodgers' top brass were in the stands. They clocked me at up to 96 miles per hour on the radar gun, my best clocking ever.

After that, the Dodger coaching staff seemed to be talking to me more and teaching me more about the way the organization operated. Red Adams took me under his wing. He came up to me one day after the Reds game and said, in his homespun California twang, "What do you think about relief pitching?"

"Red dog," I told him, "I'd carry the water bucket if it's my ticket to the big leagues."

"I thought you'd say that, you little shit."

I'd relieved only in emergencies, like my high school state championship game and the College World Series. I saw myself as a guy who started things and finished them. But I also wanted to pitch in the majors right away. I figured I'd grab a relief job first, and when Terry Forster came back from surgery and the bullpen crisis was over, I might get a chance to start.

Red and Betty Adams are two of the most wonderful people I've ever met. They went out of their way to offer help and encouragement to Cindy and me during our first year in L.A. Red had a wry sense of humor and a disarming manner that could relieve an embattled pitcher's anxiety in seconds.

During the 1980 season, when I pitched myself into trouble or made bad situations worse, and Tommy Lasorda was hysterical in the dugout, Red took the long stroll out to the mound. The broadcasters probably played up the drama, speculating on the strategic importance of our conferences.

I clearly remember one of our typical mound discussions. "Young-ster," said Red, "would you get somebody out? I'm tired of that sonofabitch yellin' at me in the dugout."

"OK."

"Yep, that's all I had to say." We both chuckled and Red ambled off.

Red believed that if a pitcher's style and mechanics were success-ful, he should be left alone. Other than a few minor adjustments to the mechanics of my delivery, he made no changes in my approach to the craft. "How the hell am I going to tell you how to do some-thing?" Red once said to me. "You throw the ball 93 miles an hour; you put it where you want to. My job's easy. I could sit in there and eat peanuts."

I guess the Dodgers were convinced by the Reds game, because they called on me only twice more before the season started. On Easter Sunday Al Campanis and Lasorda told me I was going west with the team for the Freeway Series with the Angels, the final set of exhibition games before the regular season. Pitchers Ken Brett and Doug Rau and catcher Johnny Oates were gone; Steve Howe stayed. I signed my first contract for the major league minimum of $35,900. It seemed like a million.

It was a great feeling to be able to call Cindy with some unex-pected news. "Do you want me to go to Albuquerque?" she asked again when she heard my voice.

"No, I made the club. So go to L.A. and find us an apartment." I could see jaws dropping all over Michigan.

Because of a strike action by the players, the Freeway Series never happened. For a while it looked like the season wouldn't start on time. My new teammate and buddy, Bobby Castillo, lined me up for a job parking cars at Little Joe's in Chinatown in case we couldn't play. As it turned out, the dispute was resolved, and the season opened on schedule. I sure was happy about that. I hadn't planned on moving to L.A. to park cars.

6

Relief, for a Change

It's amazing. He went out there and he performed extremely well. Left-handed relief pitchers are usually noted for movement of the ball and a good arm, but they're wild. This young man, he had all of the qualities to be one of the best relief pitchers in baseball.

He had at least four things: He had a great arm that could come back every day. He had great control for a left-handed pitcher. He was a great competitor. And he just thrived on coming into tight situations. This is what you're after out of a relief pitcher.

He wasn't a selfish type of individual when it came to wins and losses. He wanted a save, knowing that the starting pitcher would get a win and the team would get a win.

As a matter of fact, a lot of times he would be in a save situation and we would take him out and bring a right-hander in, and the right-hander would get the save. It never really fazed him. He wasn't a selfish individual when it came to his business. A lot of relief pitchers, when they're in there for that period of time, they want at least to pick up the save. It didn't matter to him.

—Ron Perranoski
October 1986

The 1980 Dodgers were a tough team to play for if you were a rookie, if you were unusually sensitive or if you couldn't tolerate verbal abuse. That's because Tommy Lasorda, hoping to loosen up his team, had imported Jay Johnstone, signed by the Dodgers as a free agent, to be a spare outfielder, pinch hitter and clubhouse prankster. Lasorda might have reconsidered if he'd known he would be the butt of most of Johnstone's humor.

Johnstone teamed up with Jerry Reuss, a clown in search of a circus, and the two of them terrorized the clubhouse. Pretty soon almost everyone got into the act. You had to be ready and respond in kind, otherwise you'd keep suffering. The atmosphere Johnstone and Reuss created made it especially difficult for rookies to get away with anything.

Rookies are the lowest-paid major leaguers, and they earn even less in the minors, so they don't come equipped with fashionable wardrobes. When I joined the Dodgers, I owned two pastel suits, one blue and one white. I caught constant abuse for both of them. When I wore the white one, they called me "The Good Humor Man."

Catcher Mike Scioscia, also a rookie in 1980, wore shoes that looked like they were borrowed from a derelict, even when he had on a classy suit. When Scioscia walked onto a plane, Mark Cresse, our bullpen coach, would yell, "Kiwi! Kiwi!" The veterans would grab Scioscia's shoes, someone would produce shoe polish, and they'd rip the shoes apart or polish them a different color, all to shame Scioscia into buying new ones.

Any veteran could fine a rookie for an offense, real or imagined. There was a kangaroo court to hear cases and assess penalties. They got me more than once.

Rookies could pocket a little cash on the side by taking advantage of fringe benefits. On the road, we received $42 a day meal money. Sometimes we cut corners so we could save the meal money for life's essentials, which, in my case, meant drugs.

One night Scioscia and I went out and got $10 worth of food from Burger King. He was holding three bags and I had two when outfielder Dusty Baker caught us in the hotel elevator. "That's a crime," Dusty said. "You get $42 a day and you guys are sneaking over to Burger King." He fined us $20 apiece and took half our food.

Players were penalized for offenses committed on and off the field. The most serious offense was appearing in public with an ugly woman. If you were caught with a "mud turtle" before midnight, you were fined. One player was nabbed repeatedly.

Then there were the pranks. Almost every day something happened that was funny or outrageous.

One night my butt made a brief appearance on Diamond Vision, the candid camera that entertains fans on the big screen at Dodger Stadium. Baker had performed some miracle with the bat in the previous half-inning, and as he took his position in left field, the guys in the bullpen just behind him saluted him with a group moon against the Plexiglas. We forgot that Diamond Vision also focuses on the previous inning's offensive hero when he trots onto the field.

Early one morning in Montreal, a couple of days after I'd played an especially offensive trick on Reuss, room service knocked on my door with $100 worth of coffee, champagne, eggs Benedict, New York steak and fresh roses, all billed to me. There I was, dressed in my underwear in the hallway, caught in a tug-of-war with a French waiter.

Steve Garvey was a perfect target because of his carefully cultivated straight image. We got his MasterCard number and used it to send pornographic material to his house.

Johnstone and Rick Monday once sent an elephant over to Reuss's house. The pachyderm trampled Jerry's shrubs and left droppings in his swimming pool.

Reuss returned the favor when Johnstone threw a christening party for his new pool. As everyone stood by the pool, beers in hand, Reuss intoned solemnly, "God, it's a great pool." Then he unzipped his fly and urinated in it.

I was drinking a beer with Reuss in a public bar once when I made the mistake of taking a rest break. While I was gone, Jerry whipped out his schwantz and stirred my brew with it. After I had returned and taken a big swig, he told me all about it.

Jay Johnstone wasn't always the one pulling the pranks. We did several classic numbers on Jay. Once we put his house up for sale, and another time Reuss and I had him arrested. We conned someone we knew from the Los Angeles Police Department to draw a sketch of Jay, the type of sketch police produce and circulate as a composite picture of a suspect after interviewing witnesses to a

crime. Then we had two officers come to the stadium during batting practice, flourish the drawing as evidence and arrest Johnstone for armed robbery.

The cops slapped the cuffs on a stunned Johnstone and began to
lead him out. We played it up, telling the cops they must have made
a mistake and assuring Jay that we'd have the team spring him from
jail right away. All the way out of the stadium, Jay protested his
innocence and begged to be released. When they reached the police
cruiser, the cops took the cuffs off and told Johnstone, "This one was
on Howe and Reuss."

There were also plenty of the usual garden-variety stunts. Guys
who left their pants out found the legs sewed, glued or taped
together. Rick Sutcliffe was always in a hurry to get out of the
locker room, so we cut the crotch out of his underwear. Someone
ordered a Rolls Royce delivered to Rick Monday's house, COD.

One of the players got the key to a mansion owned by an attorney for one of the other players, and while the lawyer was out of
town, some players ordered $15,000 worth of air conditioning in-
stalled at his expense. People were always catching shaving cream
pies in the face. They got me several times, once during a live
interview and once after a skit the team put on at a multiple sclero-
sis benefit after the 1980 season.

At the same benefit, we proved that the world outside the Dodgers was not safe. We were dressed for our skit in Mexican versions
of our uniforms, but we had forgotten our socks. So we used that
as an excuse to make alterations to everyone else's outfits. We cut
the crotches out of the Los Angeles Rams' tutus, which caused a
sensation when they bent over at the end of their skit. We tied the
soccer team's shoes in knots. We put a turd in a cowboy hat worn
by one of the California Angels, and when the guy flipped his hat,
the turd hit another guy on the shoulder.

When possible, we involved the fans. Sometimes we went into
the stands during a game. We were fined when we got caught, but
it was fun to go up and watch the game with the spectators. Once
Reuss and I spotted Burt Reynolds in the stands. We put a six-pack
on a tray, draped a towel over it and delivered it to Burt as though
we were waiters. Burt and the fans got a kick out of it.

There is no question that most of the abuse was directed at
Tommy Lasorda. It may have been his appearance or his nonstop,
gung-ho Dodgerism that caused it. Whatever it was, Tommy was a
magnet.

Tommy's appetite is legendary, and all the legends are true. If you were eating something, Tommy wanted a bite. "Here, let me try that," he always said.

One day, as we sat in the bullpen, Dave Goltz came up with an idea that would play on Tommy's gluttony. Goltz wasn't feeling well. He had an intestinal flu and was making frequent trips to the restroom. He hailed a vendor and bought a barbecued beef sandwich. Then he scraped off the beef and took a duke right on the bottom half of the bun. We put the sandwich back together and wrapped it up perfectly.

Sure enough, Tommy spotted all the activity and rang us up on the bullpen phone. "What are you guys eating down there?" he asked.

"Barbecued beef. We're hungry."

"Bull. No eating during the game. Send that over here."

The first guy who got his hands on the sandwich in the dugout was Reggie Smith. We frantically signaled for Reggie to pass it on. Reggie would have come down to the bullpen and maimed every one of us.

Then we saw Tommy grab it and open the wrapper. Almost immediately, he bolted for the corner of the dugout, where he vomited. Then he dialed the bullpen. "You sonsofbitches," he gagged. "I ought to kill you."

Tommy's a fantastic competitor. His objective is to win at any cost except starvation. In his zeal Tommy sometimes became overly critical of his players. When I was in the dugout—where I often hung out until the late innings—I used to get mad at him for his criticism of the others.

One day, in a nationally televised game, one of our guys took a futile cut and Tommy got on him. "Come on," he yelled. "Can you believe that swing? How can you be a professional ballplayer and take a swing like that?"

"Tommy," I said, "leave the ballplayers alone."

"Shut up, would you?"

Just as the TV camera at the end of the dugout turned its attention to Tommy, I leaned over and bit him on the nose. "Are you gonna stop?" I said to him through jaws locked in a death grip.

"Are you gonna leave them alone?" Tommy agreed, just in time to save his beak. Then he threw me out of the dugout for two weeks.

Tommy yelled at Jerry Reuss for chewing tobacco in the dugout and spitting it next to Tommy. Tommy couldn't stand it because he was a reformed chewer, the worst kind of fanatic. "I don't want you chewing that stuff around me anymore," he told Jerry.

Moments later, when Tommy leaped off the bench to salute a great play, Jerry obliged. He dropped his chew in Tommy's coffee cup. Tommy sat down and took a big slug of coffee. Then he hurried down to the end of the dugout to vomit.

A couple of the guys brought some dog dung to the ballpark one day and rubbed it around the sweatband inside Tommy's cap. For the entire game, Tommy accused Monty Basgall and some of the other coaches of passing gas in the dugout.

I had my own way of torturing Tommy. For a couple of years, I cut the toes out of his dress socks every time we went on a road trip. Tommy would get on the plane and steam would be coming out of his ears. He would pick up his pants legs and only his ankles would be covered.

Tommy figured out who the culprit was in 1984, after I was suspended. A couple of months into the season, he realized that not once had his dress socks been mutilated. I answered the phone one day at home and Tommy said, "You sonofabitch. You owe me about 30 pairs of dress socks."

Of course, Tommy never paid for his socks. He seldom paid for anything. He was the only guy on the team who could come home from a road trip with his meal money envelope still sealed. Friends and admirers in every town took care of him.

Tommy exploited a lot of that goodwill to help his players. In my rookie year, he took me on shopping trips for jackets, slacks, suits, shoes, whatever I needed to improve my sorry wardrobe. He was very generous, and he was also tired of seeing my two pastel ice cream suits.

The Dodgers of the early eighties were also a good-timing, partying bunch. I had many adventures with another relief pitcher who became my best partying buddy. We used to low-ride in his Mercedes around Garvey Avenue and New Avenue in East L.A. That was his turf and no one hassled us, even though I spoke the worst Spanish you've ever heard.

In Montreal in August of my rookie year, the same teammate and I went out in the middle of the night to a club called The Gatsby. We sneaked out of the hotel at two in the morning and came back at five. My teammate's room was on the same floor as Lasorda's, and he was captured. I made it in safely by using the service elevator, and once I was in my room, I unplugged my phone, put cotton in my ears, closed the shades and slept until two the next afternoon.

I arrived at the ballpark on schedule at 4:00 p.m. for a night game against the Expos. I didn't know that my buddy had been caught. Lasorda pulled me into his office in the visitors' clubhouse at Olympic Stadium and asked, "How much sleep did you get last night?"

"Quite a bit."

"I'll see how much rest you got."

In the visitor's bullpen in Montreal, there was an enclosure that looked like half a trailer sitting up against the Plexiglas window. My buddy and I gathered all the big, hooded jackets we could find, made a bed in the enclosure and went to sleep.

But I couldn't hide from Tommy. He brought me to the mound in the eighth after Don Stanhouse had created a mess. Andre Dawson stood at third, representing the tying run, and there was a man on first with no one out. Dawson scored on an infield out, but no further damage was done.

Darned if the game didn't go into extra innings. I was dying out there, since I'd been up half the morning using drugs, but I couldn't let Tommy know it. Fortunately, Garvey homered in the tenth and I got a win. I'd allowed only one infield hit to Gary Carter and a walk in three innings.

Between innings I was getting the gaggies on the bench. My buddy called me up from the bullpen and said, "Hey, man, how you feeling?" After I cussed him out, he hung up and went back to sleep.

When it was over, I strutted into the clubhouse, stuck my face in Lasorda's door and said, "Gotcha!"

My teammate and I instigated the great pizza fight in Chicago. It began with a fifth of tequila, which we drained in short order. Then we ran into some sportswriters in the pizza place, and a good-natured exchange of insults led to flying pies. I barely made it back to my friend's room, did a 360, threw up in the wastebasket and passed out on the floor.

———————

We opened the 1980 season in Houston. The Astros had lost the Western Division by only a game and a half the previous season, and they were ready for another run in 1980. I watched James Rodney Richard blow our guys away in the opener, but I got my first chance to pitch in the major leagues in the second game of the season.

Don Stanhouse was trying to protect a 6–5 lead as the Astros came to bat in the eighth. The Dodgers had awarded Stanhouse a $2.1 million contract and appointed him bullpen savior. But Don had a bad back that drove him out of baseball in 1982, and he wasn't the same pitcher who had saved 45 games during the previous two seasons for Baltimore. He pitched only 25 innings for the Dodgers in 1980.

Craig Reynolds, never known for his power, led off the Astro eighth with a homer to tie the game. Stanhouse then loaded the bases on a walk and two singles with one out. Lasorda waved me in to pitch to Denny Walling, a left-handed hitter who was batting for reliever Dave Smith.

I was nervous until I got to the mound. Then I just concentrated on doing what had gotten me to the Astrodome: going after the hitters with hard stuff.

I shattered Walling's bat, and he lined softly to short for the second out. Luis Pujols, a weak-hitting backup catcher and a right-handed hitter, was next. I got ahead of Pujols before disaster struck. I threw him a nasty 1-and-2 fastball on the outside part of the plate, and he barely got around on it. Catcher Steve Yeager later told me, "He hit the thing out of my glove." The ball hit first base and caromed into right field, scoring all three runners. Art Howe then scored Pujols with a single and we lost 10–6.

I was angry and depressed. I'd had good stuff and the Astros were lucky. Pujols's double, the big hit off me, was a joke. My only concern was that Tommy Lasorda and Red Adams might think I'd need a couple of days to recover psychologically from the misfortune. I wanted to pitch again as soon as possible.

If Tommy and Red doubted my ability to bounce back, they disguised it well. I was back in there the next night against Houston. I came on in the 12th and preserved a 5–5 tie for five innings, during which I surrendered only one hit and two walks. Mickey Hatcher singled in the lead run for us in the top of the 17th, and when Burt Hooton shut down the Astros in the bottom half of the inning, I had my first major league win.

My only strikeout victim was Jose Cruz, one of the best hitters in the National League. I'd been told that Cruz was a great bad-ball hitter and would kill you if you got the ball up around his eyes. I threw him three fastballs right down the middle. I was beginning to learn about the preferences of hitters, and I realized I could learn a lot more by studying hitters on my own.

I even swung the bat well against Houston. In my one plate appearance, I lined to short, the first time I'd made decent contact with a hardball in a real game in about four years. Still, there was no danger that I was going to make a significant contribution at the plate.

Now I was certain that I belonged in the majors and could get good hitters out under pressure. Although I was a little sore from nearly six innings of work, plus warm-ups, within 27 hours I was beginning to think I might like the pressurized spotlight in which a bullpen closer stands. But I would rather have been starting.

It was during that opening series against Houston that I began to distrust many of the sportswriters and broadcasters who covered the Dodgers. There were dozens of them competing for readers and viewers, and they seemed to think that coming up with unique negative angles was the way to get the edge.

After my first appearance, the headline in the Los Angeles Times read, "Dodger Bullpen Fails First Test." The story by Mike Littwin made it sound like I'd blown the game.

When I haven't had good stuff or I've gotten hammered, I've always admitted it. Even if I'd wanted to deny it, there were too many witnesses. But the Times headline and Littwin's story made me wonder if Littwin had been in the Astrodome that night, or if he had even watched the game on TV. Anyone who saw the game had to conclude that the Astros won on breaks.

I will give the L.A. media credit for being consistent. From the first, they wrote consistent garbage. If you think that media organizations pick people who know something about baseball to cover the game, return to square one and start over.

As 1980 wore on, I copped an attitude toward the L.A. writers. It was not a friendly or completely cooperative attitude, although I never stopped talking to them. My attitude developed because at midseason we were getting beat up on the road and my self-esteem was low. The writers placed all the blame on the bullpen for what was a true team effort.

When we asked the writers how they could crank out such trash, they usually said, "Oh, that's just the way it was edited." Right. Ballplayers aren't as dumb as sportswriters would like the public to believe. Players know writers are lying when they blame their amateur couch-potato analyses on editors. Writers should have the guts to stand up for what they write, even when it's based on nothing more than their fantasies.

Although the scribblers were often wrong when they tried to explain the misfortunes of the Dodgers, sometimes they were quite correct in their portrayal of personalities. Like mine. I often demonstrated my immaturity by mouthing off to anyone and everyone, and the press was often there to record it.

One reporter wrote an accurate story in 1982 titled "Cocky." The title could have been "Smartass" if it had appeared in *Rolling Stone* instead of a family newspaper. The story recounted an incident during my rookie year when I walked through a crowd of reporters who were interviewing Steve Garvey, put my hand on Garvey's forehead and said, "Ah shut up, sheepdip, they've heard that crap before." He also wrote about the time in 1981 when I responded to criticism of my attire at a public function by Al Campanis, the Dodgers' director of player personnel, by saying, "Play clam, Chief." And the time during 1982 spring training when I said of Lasorda, "He'd give wrong directions to an ambulance."

I know now that I said those things to mask my low self-esteem. Instead of telling people about things that bothered me, I either attacked others or made a joke out of everything.

Some fans, I'm sure, read that stuff and concluded that I was a disrespectful, egotistical dork. But I know that others found my wise-guy image attractive.

Early in the 1980 season, Stanhouse's back began to act up. He couldn't bend while delivering the ball, and his inability to throw with natural motion limited his effectiveness. Lasorda began using me in save situations because I was getting the job done and could throw strikes.

I got my first save on April 21 against San Francisco, pitching a shutout eighth and ninth behind Burt Hooton. The intensity of the Dodger-Giant rivalry, a throwback to the days when both teams played in New York, was immediately obvious to me. The Giants seemed willing to accept their persistent mediocrity if they could get the better of the Dodgers, but that never happened in the early eighties.

The Dodgers started slowly, but beginning in late April we won ten in a row to move into contention. I got my second and third saves, against San Diego and San Francisco, during that streak. My third save on April 30 was my fifth straight scoreless appearance.

I didn't pitch well in early May. The Phillies roughed me up in Philadelphia, and I lost my first game on May 6 in Pittsburgh. I entered the game in the eighth and stopped the Pirates by striking out Willie Stargell with a man on, but they got me in the ninth.

Bill Robinson began the inning with a high bouncer that I should have shagged, but it rolled into center field instead. Bill Madlock singled, and I walked Lee Lacy intentionally to create a force situation at any base. Lasorda replaced me with Joe Beckwith. With the infield drawn in, Phil Garner bounced one over shortstop Bill Russell's head to score the winning run.

A disturbing trend was developing. I seemed to have trouble getting the first hitter. It might have happened because I was challenging the first hitter by throwing the ball down the middle. You certainly don't want to fall into a pattern like that. Word circulates fast, and soon the opposition is looking for that first fat fastball.

Because I usually came into a game with runners on base, my inability to retire the first hitter was also "painting" the pitchers I was replacing by permitting their baserunners to score, charging them with earned runs. If a relief pitcher paints his starters too often, he won't be very popular in the clubhouse.

I was also giving up two-strike hits—a sin among those who follow the teachings of Perranoski—and generally making bad pitches. So after my defeat in Pittsburgh, I sat down for a talk with Red Adams.

"Just keep doing the same thing you're doing," Red said. "You're throwing the ball hard and you're throwing it well, but you're just not making good pitches. Everybody goes through it, and you're no different from anybody else. I want you to just keep throwing. You're gonna beat a hell of a lot more people than are gonna beat you."

After that, my performance improved in every way but one. I continued to have trouble with first hitters for the rest of the season.

On May 11 Lasorda replaced me with Reuss, another lefty, to retire a right-handed hitter and close out a win over the Cardinals. When Lasorda played percentages by replacing me with a right-hander to retire a righty hitter, it didn't bother me. But this time Lasorda hadn't replaced me to play percentages, and I was throwing well, so I was mad. I didn't say anything about it to anybody, but I was afraid I was losing my role as closer only because Reuss was a veteran. My ego was wounded a bit too.

I shouldn't have worried. Reuss immediately rejoined Don Sutton, Bob Welch, Burt Hooton and Dave Goltz in the starting rotation, where Reuss pitched brilliantly for the rest of the season (18–6, 2.52 ERA). I was again the stopper without question.

On May 17 I saved one against the Pirates for Sutton, who was then 35 and in his final season with the Dodgers. Sutton was a great guy, a veteran who didn't feel threatened by young players and went out of his way to educate inexperienced pitchers like me on the habits of National League hitters. Sutton was always taking us out for dinner or a few beers. Don called me the "arrogant young ass" and I called him the "arrogant old ass."

Sutton was in the midst of a superb season (13–5, league-leading 2.21 ERA), and I saved several of his wins. I got save opportunities because Sutton no longer had the stamina to complete games, and he knew it.

Sometimes in the middle of a game he would say to me, "Get ready, youngster. Seven and one, on the run. Seven and two, that's you." That meant he expected to lose his stuff after seven and a third innings and I should relieve him an out later.

Sutton always complained that he was getting too old to pitch, and the deep thinkers in the Dodgers' front office must have been listening. Don was only 35 after the 1980 season, but the Dodgers apparently decided he was on his last legs and wasn't worth the big contract he wanted. I was sorry to see him choose free agency and leave the team. Seven seasons and more than 90 wins later, the Dodgers signed him again on his way to the Hall of Fame. He's a great competitor.

Through the first half of the season, I pitched in nearly half the Dodgers' games. This was a totally foreign experience for me. I was learning not only the hitters and the science of pitching in the majors, but also such elementary reliever's tools as how to warm up and how to pace myself.

When something amusing happens on the field, the players refer to it as a "big league chuckle." We all got a good one at the expense of Willie Stargell on May 18.

Bob Welch started for us and took a two-hit shutout into the top of the ninth. Welchie was always either on or off; there was no in-between for him. One minute he was brilliant, and the next he was giving up rockets to all corners of the stadium. With two outs Dave Parker singled and Willie Stargell came up, representing the tying run.

Stargell had hit some monster shots off Welch. Some of them left the park with the distance and trajectory of golf drives. Tommy went to the mound to yank Welch and bring me in, and the fans booed.

Welch generously offered to share Tommy's boos by waiting and walking off the mound with him, but Tommy chose to take his medicine. When I got to the mound, Tommy said, "Howzer, you better get this guy out because they're gonna run me out of town for pulling Bobby."

Stargell cranked his bat with extra vigor when he planned to go deep, and he was really windmilling it this time. Steve Yeager came to the mound and said, "Look, man, this guy is looking for one heater, and he's going downtown. He's looking for something down and in."

"Well, I'm throwing it up and in," I said. I knew Stargell would swing at the first one, as he'd done before against me. In fact, I'd struck him out in Pittsburgh by climbing the ladder: Willie had fouled off the first low fastball, then had waved at two more that were progressively higher in the strike zone. This time I wasn't going to give him a swing at a low one.

My first fastball was up and so far in that it might have hit Willie if he hadn't been swinging. He tried to check, but the ball hit the knob of his bat, shot down and hit home plate, and then bounced straight up in the air. Yeager grabbed it and tagged Stargell before he could move out of the box. The game was over.

Willie looked at me, then at Yeager, then back at me. "You little shit," he said.

Even though I was throwing my hard one in the nineties, I was really a finesse pitcher. I won by pitching to spots and letting my fielders do the work, not by striking people out. When I tried to be a power pitcher and go for the strikeout, I got hurt. It was part of my education.

At the All-Star break, I was 2–3 with a 2.19 ERA and seven saves. During the second half, I was 5–6 with ten saves. The statistics suggest that I was thrown into more do-or-die situations in the second half, and this time the stats do not lie.

Just before the break, I sensed that the Dodgers had settled upon me as the present and future closer. I was getting better press, and Campanis was quoted as saying I had ice water in my veins. Lasorda began comparing me to my mentor, Perranoski. It was pretty heady stuff.

Then in June the Cubs offered to deal Bruce Sutter to the Dodgers for Rudy Law, Mickey Hatcher and me. Sutter at that time was the most successful reliever in the league and maybe in the game. He'd had 105 saves between 1976 and 1979, and at the age of only 27 was still at the height of his considerable powers. The trade talk shook me. I had swallowed the Dodgers' "family" propaganda, and I couldn't believe they were callous enough to consider trading a loyal son. Besides, I had no interest in playing for the Cubs, a perennial joke around the league.

The Dodgers turned down the deal. They decided to go with their Kiddie Corps bullpen of Beckwith, Castillo, Sutcliffe and Howe, with its average age of about 23. I felt a surge of confidence and extra motivation. I wanted to prove to the Dodgers that they'd acted wisely. I was hoping to have such a good season that they would never again consider trading me. Of course, they would consider it, but I never accepted the insecurity of trade talk as part of my job.

We seesawed in and out of first place for the last two months of the season. We led by two games when we hit Houston on September 9 for two games, and we promptly blew it. In the first game, we made six errors and lost 5–4. I took the loss. We weren't a great fielding team, and it seemed that the most aggravating and costly errors were made behind me.

On September 17 I picked up my 17th (and last) save behind Sutton in a 2–1 win over the Padres. Houston was shut out by the Reds, and we had a one-game lead.

But on September 21 the Reds beat us 7–2 to knock us out of first place. I relieved in the top of the tenth with the score tied 2–2, and I pitched a perfect inning to preserve the tie. If we could have scored in the bottom half, I would have been spared considerable embarrassment, but we left the bases loaded.

Joe Nolan singled for the Reds to start the 11th. Ron Oester popped up a bunt. I had my hands on it twice before dropping it, and they called it a hit. Reds pitcher Tom Hume was allowed to hit and forced Paul Householder, who was running for Nolan, at third. Then I hit Johnny Bench, and the bases were loaded.

We pulled the infield in. Ken Griffey bounced one that Pepe Frias, who was filling in for the injured Bill Russell at short, probably should have had. It went off his glove and was ruled a hit. More important, it scored Oester and Hume. I threw up my hands, signaling frustration and maybe surrender.

Davey Concepcion singled to score Bench. Lasorda came out and took the ball away, a couple of hitters too late. Nothing I was serving up there was working. Joe Beckwith came in and allowed both inherited baserunners to score. I'd failed in an important game in my first pennant race.

I had given up five runs in the 11th. If performances can be compared in terms of sheer competence or incompetence, this game was the worst of my career. I really stunk it up. The entire Chavez Ravine region was putrid when I finished.

I had two more foul outings against the Padres, but only one cost us a game. The other game was salvaged by a stocky young lefty from Mexico named Fernando Valenzuela.

Fernando was called up in September for the first time, and all he did was throw the hell out of the ball all month as a reliever. He spoke no English, but nobody cared, because he was baffling the rest of the league. He was throwing four different pitches that were shearing off corners of the plate. For the season, he surrendered no earned runs in 18 innings. As far as I was concerned, Fernando was a godsend. I was tired—at one point, I had at least warmed up and sometimes pitched in 26 consecutive games—and I appreciated the help.

On October 2 we led the Giants 2–1 when I was called in with the bases loaded and two out in the eighth. Derrel Thomas was playing second, and I was thinking about waving him deeper as Darrell Evans stepped in to hit, but I said nothing to Thomas. Sure enough, Evans blooped a two-run single just over Thomas's head and we lost 3–2.

Now we were three games behind Houston with three to go. Fortunately, all three games were against Houston in our park, so we could control our own fate. The media turned up the pressure, wanting to know whether we could handle it. We felt pretty good about our chances because we'd whipped Houston all year at Dodger Stadium.

In the first game, on Friday night, we trailed by a run in the ninth and fought back to win in ten. We won again on Saturday.

We began Sunday's game in a hole, down 3–0 in the fourth. We clawed back with a run in the fifth and another in the seventh. I relieved in the top of the eighth, following Hooton, Castillo and Valenzuela, and I held the Astros. Then third baseman Ron Cey slammed a two-run homer off Frank LaCorte in the bottom of the eighth, and I had a chance for my biggest win yet.

In the ninth, I retired Jeff Leonard on a long foul fly to right that Jay Johnstone caught while falling into the stands. After Gary Woods singled to right, Davey Lopes made a fine play on Terry Puhl's slow bouncer to get a force at second. Enos Cabell singled, sending Puhl to third, and Lasorda came to get me.

In a reversal of roles, it was Don Sutton's turn to save me. He was making only his fourth relief appearance in 11 years, but Tommy wanted his best out there with the division title on the line. It took Sutton only two pitches to retire Denny Walling on a grounder to second.

We had won all three games, and it was one of the most exciting series I've ever played in. The electricity generated by more than 50,000 fans who packed the park for each game was overwhelming.

Now we had to beat the Astros once more, in a one-game playoff on our field. We were out of starting pitchers who were rested, so every healthy arm was considered available for at least limited service.

I went to Tommy and volunteered to start. I was beat, but I'd pitched well against Houston all year, and I figured if I could go four or five good innings, we'd win.

Instead, Tommy selected Dave Goltz, who hadn't pitched well most of the year and had been sent to the bullpen late in the season. Goltz was ineffective, as was Rick Sutcliffe right behind him, and the Astros led 7–0 after three and a half. They won 7–1.

I pitched two meaningless but perfect innings for us at the end and had good stuff. I still believe we would have won if I had started. But it was over. The Astros were going to the playoffs against the Phillies, and we were going on vacation. After the high of winning three straight to earn a playoff chance, our sudden burial was painful. That night I got loaded.

I was pleased with my individual performance in 1980. I was 7–9 with a 2.65 ERA and a Dodger-rookie-record 17 saves, breaking Joe Black's 28-year-old mark. At Dodger Stadium, I was 5–3 with 12 saves and an ERA of 1.93. And in 63 and a third innings between May 6 and September 20, I allowed only seven earned runs, an ERA of 1.00.

I believed I'd carved a niche for myself in the Dodger bullpen. I liked the feeling that I was an important, if not indispensable, part of the team.

It didn't take long in 1980 for me to find out which Dodger players were using cocaine. On a spring training road trip, I unintentionally sat in another player's seat. When he came over to eject me, I noticed a little, white, powdery ring around his nose.

I said, "Do you, uh . . . ?"

"What? What? What are you talking about?"

"Hey, man, I've done the scene, and I indulge a little bit."

"What is that?"

I didn't exactly expect the guy to say, "Yes, Steve, you've caught me. In fact, I do snort cocaine regularly. Here, would you like some?" But I was street-smart and experienced, and it was easy to spot other users. From then on, in bits and pieces, I learned which of the players were partyers.

The list of nonpartyers on the 1980 Dodgers would be much shorter than the list of partyers. Not all of the partyers did lots of coke. Some drank heavily, and some smoked a lot of pot. Then there was a group of social users. I'm not going to name any names. I don't want to expose other athletes to the same kind of treatment I've received.

During the season, one of the players began to supply me with cocaine. He was getting it for other players as well. At some point in 1980, he stopped doing that. I think there were two reasons he stopped dealing: He was afraid of getting caught, and he wanted more for himself because he was using quite a bit.

Even though I knew which players were snorting, I didn't join any of them until after the 1980 season. The ice had to be broken, and trust had to be established on both sides. I was not yet willing to snort with anyone who offered me a whiff. I was using two or three times a week, half a dozen lines at a time. I was getting high often enough to mess up my sleep habits, marriage and job performance.

The first apartment Cindy found for us was in Marina del Rey. Later we moved a short distance toward Culver City, into a townhouse. We became friends with neighbors Terry and Sally Mink and another couple named James and Charlene. We partied together and decided to go into the jewelry business together.

Howe's Fine Jewelry was born after the end of the 1980 baseball season. At the beginning, the business was enormously successful. We produced a lot of custom-made pieces, some of them for my teammates, and our prices were about as close as you could get to wholesale.

But problems developed toward the middle of 1981. Terry and I discovered that James, who'd been buying our gold, had apparently embezzled about $15,000. When we questioned him, James produced invoices that appeared to be bogus. We didn't know why he had taken the money, but we knew we could no longer trust him as a partner. When he had drugs, though, he was my best friend.

We demanded that James get a partner and buy us out, which he did in mid-1981. I retained the corporate name, and Terry and I wholesaled diamonds for a while. We later learned that, six months after the buyout, James and his new partner declared bankruptcy. There were also rumors of an insurance investigation of a robbery at the store that had allegedly been staged.

In November the Baseball Writers Association of America voted me the National League Rookie of the Year for 1980. I won over Bill Gullickson of the Expos and Lonnie Smith of the Phillies. It was the second of four straight Rookie of the Year awards for the Dodgers. Rick Sutcliffe had won in 1979, and Fernando Valenzuela (1981) and Steve Sax (1982) would follow me.

The Dodgers' publicity office called that morning with the news and instructed me to appear at the stadium with Cindy in about an hour for a press conference and reception.

When I got there, cameras and lights were everywhere and I started to get nervous. I was used to talking with small knots of reporters in the clubhouse, but I had never faced dozens of them at once in a staged extravaganza like this. As far as that stuff went, I was fresh off the banana boat. I had no idea what to say or how to say it. Cindy was so nervous that she drove me crazy.

At the reception, one of my teammates noticed my discomfort. He handed me one of those familiar little vials and said, "Here, kid, try this." I went into the bathroom and hoovered it.

My nervousness and fears vanished immediately, and I rapped my way right through the press conference. I was answering as fast or faster than they could fire the questions. My mind was focused on the proceedings. I thought I was in complete control.

I snorted more later that day at a party with my friends, but it was not a major blowout. From that point on, my use began to increase, although I hardly noticed it at the time. The Rookie of the Year could do no wrong. I was entitled to more frequent celebrations.

Within weeks after the press conference, trade stories began to surface again. This time they were more than just rumors. I was actually traded to the Boston Red Sox for about four hours. The Dodgers agreed to send Joe Beckwith, Mike Marshall and me to the

Sox for Fred Lynn. But Lynn and the Dodgers couldn't agree on contract terms, so the deal was called off. I first heard about it when I read the papers the next day.

I couldn't believe it. I had done everything they'd asked of me, including stepping into an unfamiliar role as closer and doing it so well that the Dodgers almost won a division title. Now it seemed like they couldn't wait to trade me. I felt insecure, hurt and betrayed. I thought of the time my girlfriend went out on me when I was considering marrying her in high school. The feeling was much the same: This is my reward for loyalty. I was amazed that the Dodgers hadn't even phoned me to tell me what was going on. I responded by getting totally wiped out on coke that day. Once again, I hid my feelings by using drugs.

As it turned out, the Sutter trade, which the Dodgers refused to make, would have been much better for the team than the Lynn deal they were so anxious to complete. During the period 1981–85, Sutter averaged nearly 30 saves a year for the Cardinals and the Braves. During the same time, Lynn was playing an average of only 119 games a year for California and Baltimore, hitting .269 and averaging 19 homers and 68 RBI a year. Marshall became one of the most feared power hitters in the National League, but he has also been hurt frequently.

While the aborted Lynn trade was still a hot topic in L.A., Cindy and I slipped away for a long-delayed honeymoon at Pocono Palace near Echo Lake in northeastern Pennsylvania. The retreat from L.A. was good for both of us. For the first time in months, I could relax free from the pressure to party that is so much a part of the California social scene.

At this time in my life, I accepted Jesus into my heart with John Werhas at Baseball Chapel. I recited the sinners' prayer and felt good about my newfound faith, although I didn't experience the spiritual flash that some people describe. I went to weekly Bible studies and prayed for strength, but I never prayed for deliverance from chemical abuse. I know now that I was in full-blown denial even then.

On December 19, 1980, Clarkston High School honored me on Steve Howe Night. The ceremonies took place at halftime of a basketball game against Waterford-Kettering. Programs were distributed which detailed my accomplishments and said that I'd "achieved success in athletics beyond any other previous graduate."

Coach Paul Tungate and others associated with the school spoke briefly and said wonderful things about my athletic talent and personal qualities. I was moved and filled with pride.

In recent years, I've wondered whether Clarkston High would have held a special night for me if they'd known what everyone knows about me today. I doubt it.

7

Hitting the High Notes

—

I think I found out about it in 1981 when Steve came visiting here with his wife, you know, spending some time. I noticed some guy, I didn't know what his name was, Jose or something, hanging around. I got a feeling that you sometimes get about people. You know, I'm from the ghetto, that's my neighborhood. I grew up here, and I was raised here, and I've got my business here. So I knew the guy right away. I said, "This guy's bad news."

I immediately told him to get rid of that guy. And I noticed that his wife was upset and crying because I said, "There's no way I want this guy to be around Steve or you or anything. This guy's bad news." Steve just said, "This is the guy who sells jewelry to me."

The guy's trying to bribe me with a pen with lights that go on and off. I said, "Get the hell out of here, man, I don't want you here ever." And that's when, by fortune, by accident, I learned from my own son that this guy was a pusher.

—Mike Hernandez, Sr.
President, Camino Real Chevrolet
Monterey Park, California
September 1986

My first major league contract was for only one year, so during the 1980–81 off-season, it was time to negotiate a new one. I wound up signing a two-year contract for less money than I thought I deserved. In my opinion, my agent sold me out.

I had retained Bob Fenton at about the time I was drafted in 1979. I liked him when I met him, and I knew he represented Bobby Welch, who had also come out of the Detroit area and signed with the Dodgers.

I expected to have some leverage in negotiations for a new contract. I had been Rookie of the Year and the Dodgers would not have been contenders without me. But Fenton convinced me that $65,000 for 1981 and $100,000 for 1982 was a good deal, and I thought I would be greedy if I asked for any more than that. I later learned that it was not only a lot less than other front-line relievers were getting, but it was also a lot less than some mediocre long relievers and mop-up men commanded.

For all my aggressiveness on the mound, it sometimes surprises me that I have not been a fierce battler at contract time. To a kid who grew up without much spending money in Clarkston, the numbers on the Dodgers' contract offer looked good. I didn't want to seem greedy, but I guess I should have grabbed for more because no one was going to hand it to me.

I think Bob Fenton probably went to the Dodgers and offered them a package deal. He may have told them that he could deliver Howe and Bobby Castillo for reasonable numbers if they would take good care of Welch, who had the edge on me in experience and had won 14 games in '80 after a troubled '79. Fenton knew such a ploy would work because I wasn't a money-grubber and neither was Bobbo. All three of us signed on the same day. No matter what Fenton worked out with the Dodgers, he wasn't entirely to blame. I'm the one who signed the contract.

I wasn't happy about other things Fenton was doing either. I seemed to be paying a lot in taxes. When I asked him to turn over some of my money, he acted like I was asking for a personal loan. In 1981 I dumped him and retained Tony Attanasio.

Tony was a good agent and represented a lot of ballplayers, but he was expensive. I had to pay him 12 or 13 percent of my gross salary for his basic package of services. There were other services for which I had to pay separately. A lot of agents are bloodsuckers, but you don't mind as much when they do good work, and Tony usually did.

A few things bothered me about Tony. He was tough to get in touch with, and he deserted me when my addiction brought the baseball world down on my head. In good times and bad, I talked mostly with Peter Ciccarelli, who was associated with Tony then but has since opened his own practice.

I wasn't satisfied with Tony's tax work either. I don't know who was getting all the choice deductions for my expenses, but I know I wasn't. I eventually took my tax work to Jim Bruno, an honest, forthright Christian who knew the tax code. Finally I stopped overpaying the government and started collecting refunds.

Not that it mattered much. If there had been more coming in, there would have been more going out. Money and I have had many brief affairs, but never a long-term relationship. I've always satisfied an abiding love for expensive toys. And drugs.

I went to spring training in 1981 ready to pick up where I'd left off, but all the media wanted to talk about was the sophomore jinx. Was I worried about it? It had gotten Rick Sutcliffe the year before, hadn't it? Could I hold off the National League for another year with only two pitches? I had to answer the same questions every day, and it got tedious.

The truth is that I spent many sleepless nights worrying about the sophomore jinx, even though I thought it was probably only a myth created by the media. I'm sure more great rookies have succeeded than failed in their sophomore seasons, but all I ever read and heard about were the ones who flopped.

I had succeeded in my rookie year not by baffling the hitters with my limited assortment of pitches or by overpowering them, but by putting the ball where they were least likely to hurt me. I knew I could continue to get hitters out that way no matter how many different pitches I was throwing, as long as I had command of all of them. As I told the media, what happened to Sutcliffe was of no significance. He was right-handed, a lot taller, and he had a much bigger head than I had.

I don't know whether the Dodgers were concerned about the sophomore jinx, but they seemed to think I needed another pitch. Or at least Al Campanis thought so. He figured that if I had an off-speed pitch to mix with my hard stuff, the hitters wouldn't be able to time me. He wanted me to concentrate on the off-speed curve, so Perranoski and I went to work on it. I didn't want to mess with a successful formula, but, being a good organization man, I went along without making waves.

It wasn't easy for a stiff-wrist pitcher like me to learn a pitch that required a different wrist position and release. I even altered my delivery to accommodate the curve. The results were disastrous at first.

I don't remember a lot of the details because I was wasted most of the spring, but I know that maintenance men all over Florida were busy repairing fences damaged by bombs hit off my hanging curve. In 16 innings, I gave up 27 hits and had an ERA of 6.19.

Despite my poor performance, my position in the Dodger bullpen was solidified when Joe Beckwith suffered a serious eye injury late in the spring, leaving us a reliever short. Trying to duck quickly out of the way of a line drive hit up the middle, Joe detached some muscles, causing both of his eyes to turn out to the sides. It was scary. He needed surgery to repair the damage and was on the disabled list for all of 1981.

I suppose that when I saw the freak injury that Joe had sustained, I should have recognized my own fragility and appreciated the importance of taking good care of myself. But being in denial of my chemical dependency, I was deluded in my thinking. I hadn't had a serious sports-related injury up to that time, but who was I to think I wouldn't ever have one? I thought I was indestructible, and my view didn't change until I injured my elbow in 1984.

The Dodgers added to my feeling of relative security by refusing another trade offer for me. The Cubs wanted to send us Bill Buckner, who had hit a league-leading .324 in 1980, but insisted that the Dodgers include me in any deal. The Dodgers said they wouldn't trade me. That made me feel so good that I almost forgot I'd been a member of the Red Sox for four hours only three months before.

I got another ego boost late in the spring of 1981 when *Playgirl* magazine named me one of baseball's sexiest men. The caption beneath my (fully clothed) picture read, "Just out of college, this southpaw was named the Rookie of the Year in 1980. His boyish charm and devilish pranks are rapidly earning him a reputation on and off the diamond." Two things bothered me about that caption:

What were the "devilish pranks" it referred to, and how did *Playgirl* know about them? If the people at *Playgirl* could find out about my behavior, I was going to have to get better at hiding my drug use.

It wasn't long before Cindy latched onto a copy of the magazine. She wanted to know pronto what "off the diamond" antics *Playgirl* was talking about. "How would I know?" I answered. "Who knows where they get that stuff?"

In the spring of 1981, my cocaine intake escalated to the point of total preoccupation. Since the fall, except for the Fred Lynn trade, almost everything that happened had told me how great I was. My poor spring pitching didn't bring me down to earth because I knew it didn't reflect what I could and would do when things got serious.

I was a hotshot, infallible, the man of the hour. The Dodgers couldn't cut me; I was the reigning Rookie of the Year and the heart of their bullpen. I'd attained my place in baseball and in society, and I was going to stay there forever. Cindy was taking courses at UCLA and spent only ten days in Florida with me that spring, so there was no one around who could try to tell me what to do. Besides, spring training was just for fun. I was going to party.

I didn't see how increasing the frequency and quantity of my drug use could cause any harm. I was young and strong. Addiction was not a word in my vocabulary.

During spring training, another player and I were visited in our villa by a guy I'll call Jose, a coke dealer I'd met in L.A. through one of my teammates during the winter of 1980–81. The three of us were getting high one evening when Lasorda walked in. "Who in the hell's that?" Tommy asked.

"It's my cousin," the other player replied.

"Well, get your cousin's butt out of here," Tommy said. Jose left and came back later, but Tommy caught him in the villa and evicted him again.

About every other night in Florida, several guys on the team would get together and snort an entire eight-ball. That's three and a half grams worth $250 to $350, depending on the quality of the stuff. It was like potluck stew. Whoever wanted to participate brought some stuff, and we mixed it all together and had a feast.

How we managed to play ball on the following days is a mystery to me. Of course, some of us didn't play so well. There's no question that my lame pitching that spring wasn't caused entirely by the difficult process of learning a new pitch. Place much of the blame on my hyperactive beak.

On the other hand, I snorted significant quantities throughout the second half of the 1981 season and, miraculously, pitched pretty well. Maybe that's because by then I had devised a system for inhaling my fill at night, getting plenty of sleep and coming to the ballpark the following day with a somewhat clear head. It's also true that, even during the height of my addiction, my competitive instincts and my sturdy physical constitution took over when it was time to do my job.

When the 1981 regular season began, I tried to control my use. It was time to be serious again. I had told everyone within earshot that there would be no sophomore jinx for this boy. Now I had to prove it.

From opening day until the strike in June, I was on relatively good behavior, meaning that most of the time my use was beyond the social level but not outrageous. I was snorting two to three grams per week. Nevertheless, I spent approximately $3,000 on cocaine between the beginning of spring training and the first day of the strike, a period of less than four months. By cocaine standards, that's not a lot of money. But when you're making $65,000 in gross annual salary and you're taking on additional financial responsibilities every day, it's a lot.

Cindy had stopped snorting. She'd done it only a couple of times in Michigan, and only a few times since, so it was no big deal that she quit. She still smoked pot once or twice a year, an indulgence in which I refused to join. Cindy usually didn't know when I was high, but she objected when I was. My use in her presence was taboo, so I tried to hide it from her.

Small amounts of coke didn't dramatically alter my personality at that time. In fact, I had to do at least half a dozen lines before Cindy could tell I was high. After my use reached the addiction stage and the drug had control of my body, I had to suck up only a few grains of the stuff to cause personality changes that were obvious to anyone who knew me.

We opened the season at home with a three-game sweep of our 1980 tormentors, the Astros. The third game gave both Rick Sutcliffe and me a chance to redeem ourselves. Sutcliffe was trying to come back from a poor 1980, and I wanted to forget all about spring training. Sutcliffe, getting a start after spending most of the previous year in the bullpen, pitched strongly into the eighth, handing the game to me with a 3–1 lead, one out and runners at second and third.

As usual, I was facing a win-or-die situation. I had decided that I wasn't going to let the curve ruin my season. I could imagine the "Sophomore Jinx" headlines that would appear if I had a couple of bad outings.

So I junked the curve, at least in tight situations, until I could master it. I went back to my old delivery and my fastball/slider repertoire. If I had to pitch a long stretch, say four or five innings, I might pull the curve out of the closet. Even if I didn't get it over, the speed change could throw hitters off and keep them from sitting on the hard stuff. But in a short-stretch, pressure situation, I would rely on my command pitches.

The first Astro hitter I faced was Jeff Leonard, who flied to right to sacrifice in Houston's second run. Then I struck out Gary Woods to end the inning. In the ninth I retired Cesar Cedeno on an infield out and struck out Jose Cruz and Danny Heep. Spring training was ancient history.

My left knee, the one that had been injured in the auto accident in Alaska, acted up in spring training, and I continued to experience pain and unsteadiness after the season started. When I pushed off the rubber with my left leg, the knee would collapse inward. In order to keep my velocity, I began using more arm and shoulder motion to compensate for my inability to push off. If I had kept doing that, I would have hurt my arm and shoulder. So every day I had the trainer tape me from my ankle to the bottom of my butt, just to hold the knee and ankle in place so I could push off. Surgery was recommended, but I declined because I had a strange feeling that our team was going to do great things, and I wanted to be part of it.

I've always played hurt, but I've also stayed off the mound when I felt that an injury was sufficiently severe that I might hurt the team if I pitched. I told Lasorda when my knee was hurting too much for me to be effective. On one occasion, I took myself out of a game because I didn't want to blow a lead.

Still, I was pitching well. By early May I hadn't allowed an earned run. So when I had an indifferent outing against the Mets and Tommy publicly questioned my pitching and my injury, I didn't appreciate it.

It happened on May 9 in New York. With the score tied at 4, Castillo gave up a walk and a single, and I came in with men at first and third and no one out. Alex Trevino looped a single to center to score a run, and another scored when Ron Cey threw Doug Flynn's bunt away. We walked pinch hitter Lee Mazzilli intentionally, and I struck out Mookie Wilson, but Frank Taveras lined to center to score a third run before I got out of it. We lost 7–4.

Tommy told the writers, "To me, I don't think Howe is throwing the ball real hard, like he's capable of throwing. I don't know whether his knee is bothering him or not. They only tell you what they want you to know. You ask them and it's, 'Oh, I'm OK.' "

Tommy made it sound like I wasn't telling the team what, if anything, was wrong with me. I could understand Tommy's frustration at losing to a ragtag outfit like the Mets, but he was way off base. The next day I took a cue from Tommy and used the press to take a shot at him.

Hubie Brooks had made three errors in a row in the fourth inning to help us score four runs, and Welch took a 5–2 lead into the bottom of the eighth. When Joel Youngblood led off with a double, Welchie left and I came in. Youngblood scored on a single and a force, but then I closed the Mets down for the rest of the afternoon to pick up my third save. When the press asked what kind of pop I'd had on my fastball that day, I said, "Worse than yesterday." Which was true.

It made me uncomfortable to say that, though, because I'm not one to publicly confront management. I did it in the gentlest way I knew. I wanted to make a point to Tommy because it wasn't the only time he'd slighted me by public innuendo.

Throwing the ball hard isn't what really counts anyway, and Tommy, a former pitcher, knew that. Movement and location are far more important. Sometimes when I'm tired, my fastball may be several miles per hour slower, but it may be sinking and therefore more effective. That's why I've often done my best pitching when I've been out there a lot, like seven or eight games out of ten. Then I'm still strong enough to throw with better than average pace and my usual control, plus movement.

I'd been right about the Dodgers' prospects. By May 23 we were 28–11 and had a five and a half game lead over the Reds. I was 4–1 with four saves, and I had allowed only one earned run in more than 22 innings, an ERA of 0.40.

On the field and at the plate, we were essentially the same team that had fallen just short in 1980. Baker, Cey, Garvey, Rick Monday and the rapidly developing Pedro Guerrero supplied the power. Davey Lopes and the newly acquired Ken Landreaux had speed. What was different was the pitching. Fernando Valenzuela had replaced Sutton in the rotation, and Dave Stewart and Tom Niedenfuer had been added to back me up in the bullpen. We had more depth than we'd had a year before.

I'm a streaky pitcher, and my inevitable streak of several poor outings began May 27 in Atlanta, when I gave up a game-losing homer to the legendary Terry Harper.

I hate giving up home runs, not only because they represent total victory for the hitter, but because of the embarrassment that the umpires heap on the pitcher. When a homer is hit off me, I know it right away, so I don't have to stand and watch it leave the park. Before it has landed in a faraway place, I ask the umpire for a new ball. But umps won't give you one until the hitter has crossed the plate. I don't understand the reason for this, but it means the pitcher has to stand out on the mound with nothing to do but look disgusted while the batter circles the bases and the crowd either cheers or boos. It's the ultimate insult.

I've always taken pride in my ability to avoid giving up home runs. Until Harper cranked his shot leading off the bottom of the ninth to beat us 3–2, I'd only given up one in 107 major league innings. I had no excuses. I just fed Harper a straight fastball down the middle. If he couldn't hit that one, he should be playing sandlot ball. It was only his second big league homer.

I've given up more embarrassing homers than that. On July 9, 1982, that noted powerhouse Bob Dernier hit one into the third deck in Philadelphia. It was his third major league homer. Amid the applause, I'm sure I heard some fans laughing.

The Reds started closing in on us, and we had a mini pennant race on our hands. Both teams were anticipating the reality of a strike and a split 1981 season, which meant that the team that was ahead at strike time was guaranteed a playoff spot.

I wasn't at my best, and I was afraid I might mess up our chances to win the first half. On June 2 against Atlanta, Tommy called on me in the tenth with one out, a runner at second and the game still tied. I gave up consecutive doubles to Bill Nahorodny and Jerry Royster and we lost 3–1. Four days later in Chicago, I gave up three runs in the eighth to convert an 8–5 deficit into an 11–5 rout.

But when the strike came, we were still a half game ahead of the Reds, who had played one less game. The Reds went on to lose the second half to Houston by only a game and a half. The Reds whined and moaned all winter that they had been shafted because they'd had the best record in baseball but hadn't made the playoffs. Too bad. They had voted to go with the split season concept, just like everyone else. I had trouble mustering any sympathy for them.

The strike lasted more than seven weeks. For me it was a time of physical healing, financial difficulties and heavy drug use. I worked out a total of four times, twice the first week. The other two workouts consisted of playing catch on the road near my house.

The strike was good for my knee because it had time to heal without the stress of baseball. On the orders of Dr. Frank Jobe, our team orthopedist, I went to the stadium a few times to strengthen my hamstrings with a Cybex exercise machine. That tightened the left knee joint and reduced my discomfort. When I came back after the strike, I was able to throw more naturally.

The timing of the strike couldn't have been worse financially. Three days before the strike began, I closed on the purchase of a beautiful 2,600-square-foot house in Agoura for $189,000. We put all our cash into it and had to borrow from Cindy's parents to complete the deal. Meanwhile, I was on strike and no longer earning my usual salary. When I needed money for just about anything—including drugs—for two months, I had to borrow it. Fortunately, my credit was still good.

I had endless time to kill and no responsibility, so each day brought a new party. Sometimes it brought a continuation of the previous day's party. I didn't use every day, but there weren't too many days during the strike that I wasn't high. And when I partied, I snorted between one and two grams a day.

Suddenly I lost the ability to use the drug socially. I couldn't snort a little without snorting a lot. I don't know how it happened, but the drug grabbed me and wouldn't let go. I couldn't just be high for a while, come down and go home. I had to keep using to sustain the high. The fun of being high was lost in the obsession. I didn't know it then, but I was addicted to cocaine.

During the strike, I spent more and more time with Jose, the pusher who had come to Florida during spring training. Jose had sucked me in the way lots of pushers and other leeches prey upon athletes and entertainers. In the beginning he was my friend, laying the drug out for me whenever I wanted it and asking nothing in return. Then he started charging me for the coke and letting me run a tab. I ran up debts of hundreds and then thousands of dollars, and from time to time I had to make good on my debts.

As partying became a daily practice, I began to stay out all night about once a week. I'd come home sometime during the next morning or afternoon, depending upon how much coke we'd had to snort and how far we'd been able to stretch what we had.

I was saved from Jose and oblivion, at least temporarily, by my L.A. father, Mike Hernandez, Sr. Early in the 1980 season, when I was looking for a way to supplement my minimum major league wage, Dodger coach Manny Mota introduced me to Mike, the president of Camino Real Chevrolet in Monterey Park, a section of East L.A.

Mike is a self-made man, a son of the ghetto in East L.A., who has built and maintained an enormously successful auto dealership in his old neighborhood. He is shrewd, insightful and admirable. It was only natural that I, an automotive hound and the son of a General Motors family, went to work for Mike.

He gave me a job in sales. All I really had to do was show up, but I enjoyed working with GM products and I was a natural salesman, so I was able to move a few units.

The thing of greatest value that I received from Camino Real was a second family. The entire Hernandez family, especially Mike and his sons, Mike Jr. and Tom, have treated me like a son and brother since we first met. They are always looking out for me. They've never given up on me, although they have had good reason to do so. I've been fortunate to have them in my corner.

At one point during the strike, my debt to Jose reached $1,000 and he demanded payment. I had leased a 1980 Corvette from Camino Real, and I was thinking about selling it or turning it back to the dealership. Instead, I seized upon the idea of turning the lease over to Jose to extinguish my debt. The idea sounded great to Jose. That was the only way he could have obtained an expensive car like that. He had no credit rating and lived day-to-day off the proceeds of his drug sales.

I took Jose into Mike Sr.'s office and tried to pass Jose off as an upstanding businessman who could assume my obligations under the lease agreement. I thought I'd fooled Cindy into believing the story, but Mike could see through anyone I hung around with. Right away he pegged Jose as a slimeball.

"He's not getting anywhere near your car," Mike Sr. told me. "You drive it, it's yours. I'm gonna have this sonofabitch run out of town."

What Mike didn't know then, but soon discovered, was that his son Tom had also been buying coke from Jose. I've felt guilty for years now because I introduced Tom to Jose, and Tom got pretty screwed up.

A short time later, I took off on a binge with Jose and Tom, and, when I didn't turn up after a couple of days, Cindy told Mike Jr. that I was missing in action. When we sent Tom to McDonald's for grub, Mike spotted him. Mike followed Tom back to Jose's place in east L.A., and then he busted us and got Tom and me out of there.

Then Mike Sr. literally ran Jose out of town. Mike knows a lot of people in high places in the community, and he used his influence to make Jose disappear. I never saw him again.

My main source of whiff was gone, but in L.A. there was no shortage of sources. I could find another, and there was no question that I would, because the drug was now in control.

The second half of the season started shortly after the Jose bust, and I tried to change my pattern of coke use. I began to realize that heavy drug use would impair my pitching ability, regardless of how much sleep I got before I went to the ballpark. I didn't want to stop and couldn't, but I didn't want to use too much. I decided that the best way to keep myself from reaching out for the drug on a daily basis was to binge about once every two weeks, get the party-ing out of my system, then lay off between binges.

Of course, it didn't work that way. I made sure the binges hap-pened on schedule, but I couldn't stay away from coke in between. I was "chipping," snorting small amounts that added up to about a gram or two a week. I was still using almost daily.

The strike was settled August 9, and our first game of the second half of the season was scheduled for August 10 against the Reds at Dodger Stadium.

The front office began letting us use the stadium for workouts in early August. I guess the people in management were still mad at the players for being so brazenly disloyal to Dodger blue, because they wouldn't turn the stadium lights on when we worked out in the evenings. Shame on us for placing the quality of our families' lives ahead of the financial well-being of the organization!

My workout on August 2 or 3 was only the fifth time I'd thrown a ball since the stike began. I was throwing batting practice without a screen because I hated using one. It was about 6:00 p.m., and the fading daylight was casting shadows between the mound and home plate. I lobbed a couple of warm-ups, and Steve Yeager stepped in to hit. I threw a pitch and Yeager said, "I didn't even see that one."

"Neither did I," I said. "Go tell them to turn the lights on."

One of the coaches was standing nearby and he said, "Just throw the ball."

Yeager blasted the next one right at me, and I never saw it. The ball came in just under the bill of my cap and cracked me in the center of the forehead. I staggered, stuck my foot in the ball bucket, tripped and fell. As I was falling, I remember saying to myself, "I told you to turn the damn lights on."

I was conscious when I landed, and I heard voices all around me, but I couldn't see. It really scared me. A car was brought onto the field to take me to the hospital, and I was told later me that a clowning Terry Forster sprawled in front of the car so it couldn't be moved.

I spent the night in California Hospital. For the first three or four hours, I couldn't see. I fell asleep for a while, and when I woke up at 9:00 p.m., I threw up and then I was OK. Nobody could find Cindy until a couple of hours after it happened.

The next morning I checked out of the hospital. The doctors couldn't find a reason to keep me there. I wasn't allowed to work out for three days because things looked a little fuzzy. But by our first game of the second half on August 10, I was ready to pitch and Lasorda obliged me.

Jerry Reuss worked six shutout innings and permitted Cincinnati only three hits and two walks. I gave up nothing in three innings and picked up my sixth save as we won 4–0.

Cindy had been teasing me because I'd hardly picked up a ball in more than seven weeks. "How are you going to pitch?" she asked. "Forget it," I replied. But I knew Cindy was right and that I really shouldn't have been able to pitch, since I had hardly worked out at all since the strike began. Once again, God took care of me and restored my pitching ability.

I don't want to suggest that the Dodgers put forth less than maximum effort in the second half of the season, but it's true that the players were not exactly despondent after a loss. We had clinched a spot in the playoffs by virtue of our first-half division win. We sort of coasted to a fourth-place finish in the second half. Houston won it by a game and a half over Cincinnati.

My season was no improvement on 1980. I finished 1981 with a 5–3 record, eight saves and an ERA of 2.50. I was slightly less effective in the second half. I had no streak of ineffectiveness, but I had unpredictable bad outings about once every three games. In other words, I was inconsistent. My drug use definitely had something to do with that.

On September 3 I threw my all-time worst clubhouse temper tantrum after a frustrating loss to St. Louis. We'd entered the top of the ninth with a 3–2 lead, and I was on the mound with a chance for a save. But Bill Russell, our shortstop, wasn't going to let it happen.

Keith Hernandez singled, and then George Hendrick bounced softly to short. Russell thought he could get a force at second, but he didn't, and both runners were safe.

After I forced Hernandez at third on a bunt, Darrell Porter hit what looked like a game-ending double-play ball to Steve Sax, who'd been called up to play second with Lopes hurt. Sax fielded the ball cleanly and flipped perfectly to Russell for the force. Russell then cannonballed his relay into the seats, allowing Hendrick to score the tying run and Porter to reach second.

Lasorda saw me glaring at Russell and came to get me. "Take him out," I told Lasorda, gesturing toward Russell. "He's the one making the errors, not me." Lasorda brought in Dave Stewart, a righty, to pitch to right-handed hitter Sixto Lezcano. Lezcano hit the first pitch out of the park.

It seemed as if Russell saved his errors for times when I was on the verge of a win or a save. Actually, Russell was infamous for such feats and spread the wealth around fairly evenly. But I was in no mood to be reasonable about it this time.

I got to the clubhouse first, took a bat to a set of lockers and sheared them nearly in half. Then I punched the glass out of a fire extinguisher case. Just as the rest of the guys were getting to the clubhouse door, I picked up a shopping cart and threw it against the top of the door.

Dusty Baker reached the door when the cart crashed into it, and he turned around and told everyone, "Don't go in there. That sonofabitch is mad. He's mad. Don't go in there."

Finally, after I'd picked up and thrown everything that wasn't bolted down, I calmed down. Everyone came in and tried to console me. Everyone, that is, except Russell, who wisely kept his distance. I went out that night and got blasted on a little bit of everything.

———————

The intradivisional playoff miniseries opened in the Astrodome. We had the home advantage, so Games Three, Four and Five would be played in L.A.

We dug ourselves a deep hole right away, losing the first two games by scores of 3–1 and 1–0. Denny Walling's single with two out in the bottom of the 11th beat us in the second game. I had pitched a shutout tenth in that game.

I still thought we could win the series because I didn't think Houston could beat us in L.A. On the trip back, I told Lasorda I was available to pitch as often as he wanted. I was tired, but I had all winter to rest. I was determined that our playoff chances weren't going to slip away this time.

In the third game, we led 3–1 after seven, and Tommy called on me to pitch the eighth behind Burt Hooton. I retired the Astros in order and struck out two of them. My adrenaline was pumping so furiously that I was throwing as hard or harder than I'd thrown all year. We won 6–1.

Lasorda didn't need me in either of the last two games, because Valenzuela and Reuss pitched beauties for us. In the fifth game, Reuss had a five-hit shutout going with two out in the ninth. In the bullpen, Coach Mark Cresse said, "Yeah, we're gonna win it," and began gathering the gear.

I'm superstitious about stuff like that. "Hey, man, don't take off yet," I said to him. "Don't leave, because something weird happens when you leave before the end in games like this."

"No way," Cresse said. "I'm going to get me some grub and a bottle of champagne." He began to walk out.

Reuss had two strikes on Dave Roberts. Jerry threw again and Roberts swung and missed. But Mike Scioscia missed the ball completely, and it went all the way to the backstop. Everyone froze for a moment. Then Scioscia started after the ball, and Roberts, realizing he wasn't out yet, sprinted for first. Scioscia got to the ball and threw Roberts out at first by half a step, ending the game. The final was 4–0.

Cresse said, "I'll never do it again."

Now it was party time. It was my first playoff victory celebration, and I was as excited as I'd ever been in my life. After some debate, we let the wives into the locker room for the party.

The women were anxious to get in, but once they did, I think some of them would rather have been elsewhere. Some of them dressed for the game as if it were a photo session for the cover of *Glamour* magazine. They didn't appreciate getting doused with beer and champagne and pelted with peanuts by ecstatic ballplayers.

I hugged another player's wife and she said, "You stink."

"What do you expect?" I replied. "I just got 14 bottles of champagne poured over me."

We sobered up in time to open the League Championship Series at home on October 13 against the Expos, who had eliminated the

Phillies. Happy Hooton pitched a super game for us, holding Montreal scoreless into the eighth, when Welch, pitching out of the bullpen in the playoffs, squelched a rally. Meanwhile, Cey and Russell drove in runs for us in the second, and Guerrero and Scioscia cranked homers off Jeff Reardon in the eighth to give us a 5–0 edge.

Gary Carter and Larry Parrish began the Expo ninth with doubles off Welchie, and I got the call. I'd had several days' rest, and I was strong and felt great. My ball had a lot of movement on it.

Warren Cromartie singled hard to center—I wasn't sorry to see him go to Japan after the '83 season—and they held Parrish at third. But Jerry White popped to second, and I got Chris Speier to hit into a game-ending double play, our fourth DP of the game. We were one up, but not for long.

Ray Burris threw a five-hitter at us in the second game in L.A. Then Steve Rogers tossed a seven-hitter, and White belted a three-run homer as they beat us 4–1 in the first game in Montreal. Once again, we had our backs to the wall, one game from elimination. This time we faced the formidable task of beating Montreal two straight in their own frozen stadium.

Formidable, but not insurmountable, not for this team. We'd gotten into the good habit of picking each other up when things looked bad. So many players were contributing, and someone was always there to deliver the big hit or to choke off an enemy rally with clutch pitching or fielding. Our theme song was Carl Carlton's "She's a Bad MamaJama." Don't mess with us, 'cause we're bad. Don't count us out, 'cause we're coming back to kick hell out of you.

We broke open a close game with six runs in the last two innings for a 7–1 win in the fourth game. Garvey and Baker drove in five runs between them. Hooton gave up only an unearned run. I got to close it out, picking up a couple of strikeouts in the ninth.

The deciding game was a dogfight, played in miserable weather. Rain delayed the start of the game for 26 minutes, and temperatures hovered near the freezing mark. That kind of weather doesn't bother me, though, probably because I played in it every spring in high school and college.

Valenzuela and Burris dueled to a 1–1 standoff after eight innings. In the ninth, the Expos brought in Steve Rogers, who had stuck our bats up our butts in the third game. He was back with two days' rest to hold us off for an inning or two. For one of the teams, this would be the last game, and the Expos were pulling out all stops to get to the World Series.

Rick Monday was our third scheduled hitter in the ninth. As he was getting ready to leave the on-deck circle for the plate with two outs and no one on, I trotted down from the far end of the bench, where the relievers sat in Montreal then, and called to Monday: "Hey, Mo, he's gonna try to sneak a fastball by you and get ahead of you. Just crunch it; look in and crunch it." Then I turned to the Dodger bench and said, "I'm calling it right now: dinger."

The first or second pitch Monday got was a fastball, belt-high, a mistake, and he ripped it over the fence in right center. As he trotted around third, Monday pointed at me and hollered, "You called it!" It was an eerie feeling to have called one of the most dramatic homers in postseason history.

Welchie came on to get the last out behind Fernando in the Expo ninth, and we had pulled off our back-from-the-dead act again. Before we left the field, we mocked the Expo fans by singing "Valdaree, Valdarah," the chorus with which they'd saluted us after the third game. Then we had our second date in a week with a few dozen magnums of champagne. We were getting to be connoisseurs.

It was the Dodgers and the Yankees in the World Series, a media natural. The pressure that the descending hordes of reporters placed on us was enormous. Never before had I experienced such tension and pressure to win. It drove a lot of people berserk in both organizations. In fact, it was in this series that Yankees owner George Steinbrenner got into his legendary elevator brawl with a Dodger fan.

The players did whatever they could to blow off steam. For instance, before the player introductions prior to the third game of the series in L.A., Jerry Reuss decided that the importance of pitchers was being downgraded because they were the last players introduced and they had to stand a long distance from the manager. Jerry and I planned to correct that problem. When he and I were introduced, we went over and stood right next to Lasorda. Then we concentrated on blowing the biggest bubbles we could with our gum. We were just a couple of excitable boys having a good time.

The series opened in Yankee Stadium, traditionally a Dodger graveyard. We didn't do anything in the first two games to dispel the notion that we couldn't win in that park. Reuss didn't pitch well in the opener. He was gone by the third and we lost 5–3. In the second game, Tommy John shut us out on four hits, 3–0.

I got my first World Series experience in the eighth inning of the second game. It was the first time I pitched in the House that Ruth Built. There were 60,000 animals screaming their frustrated urban lungs out and millions of fans watching on worldwide TV. The noise and pressure were awesome. I tried to concentrate.

I retired Dave Winfield on a fly to center, but Lou Piniella and Greg Nettles singled, and Lasorda lifted me. Bob Watson singled off Stewart to drive in a run, and Stewart then fired a wild pickoff throw into center, allowing Nettles to go to third. From there, Nettles scored on a sacrifice fly.

Once again, things looked grim for Dodger blue. Las Vegas was offering something like 22–1 odds against the Dodgers winning four straight after falling behind 2–0, even though we were virtually unbeatable at Dodger Stadium in the playoffs (4–1 up to then). I hope a lot of Dodger fans took that action and wiped out a few bookies. We knew we had the Yanks right where we wanted them.

Fernando staggered the route for us in the third game, giving up four early runs but hanging on for a 5–4 win. Cey hit a three-run homer for us.

In the fourth game, Welch didn't have anything, and we fell behind 4–0 by the third. It was the first game of the series for Reggie Jackson, and he allowed a fly ball to bounce off his chest in the sixth, helping us score three runs to tie it at 6.

I entered the game to pitch the seventh, which passed without incident. In the bottom half of that inning, we scored the lead run, and I came to the plate with runners at first and second and one out. I didn't expect to hit, but Lasorda was nearly out of pinch hitters and I was his remaining bullpen, so he let me bunt. I told Lasorda that I'd either get the bunt down or Tommy John was going to hit me, because I was willing to take one for the team.

Actually, it wasn't a gamble for Lasorda to let me hit. Whenever we were home, all of the pitchers practiced bunting, and we were all pretty good. Tommy John was not a tough pitcher to bunt against, because he threw either a sinker or a fastball that wasn't hard enough to chip your teeth.

He threw me a fastball waist high, and I put it neatly down the third-base line for a sacrifice. Lopes then drove in my insurance run with a high chopper in front of the plate.

I needed the extra run. With no one on in the eighth, Reggie Jackson hit a whistling homer that would have knocked down the fence if it hadn't cleared it. After the game, my dad asked me what kind of pitch I'd thrown Reggie. "A change-the-score pitch," I told him.

I got in trouble in the ninth on a single by Rick Cerone and an error that was charged to me. Bobby Murcer hit a bouncer to Garvey, who fumbled it about three times before he could shovel it to me. I had arrived at first after a world-class sprint and waited while Garvey groped for the ball. The American League umpire ruled that I missed the base—which was garbage—and I was assigned an error.

With two outs and two on, Willie Randolph hit a long fly ball to deep center. There was no doubt that the ball would stay in, but the media still made a big deal about our close escape. I had myself a World Series win, even though I didn't have real good stuff that day, and the series was all even.

When Randolph's ball was caught, Lasorda came out to hug me. I was so tired that when he squeezed me, I spit tobacco juice down the back of his jersey. Perranoski saw it all and started laughing. "What's so funny?" Tommy asked. "He just busted his ass."

"Oh, nothing. My mistake," Perranoski chuckled.

Game Five was a classic Dodger win: great pitching and just enough offense. Reuss threw a five-hitter. Guerrero and Yeager hit back-to-back homers in the seventh off Ron Guidry to give us a 2–1 win. In the eighth inning of that game, Goose Gossage nearly decapitated Ron Cey with a 94-mile-per-hour fastball. The Penguin not only lived, but was back for the next game.

Now the Yankees had their backs to the wall, and our juggernaut was rolling. It didn't matter that we were back in New York.

Our first try at Game Six was rained out, so Cindy and I spent most of the evening in our hotel room. We got into an argument, and Cindy went to bed. I poured myself a little pile of coke and got in beside her. As she slept, I snorted my pile and got a good buzz going. I didn't sleep most of that night.

When I got to the stadium the next day, a little green pill was waiting on the shelf of my locker. I don't know how it got there, but I seemed to find the pills before important Dodger games. I noticed that other players had received the same gift. I took my medicine. Apparently, other players did too, because everyone seemed unusually fired up and tensions ran high. There were a few near fights around the batting cage.

Game Six was a competitive pitching duel between Tommy John and Burt Hooton for four innings. Then Bob Lemon, the Yankees' manager, yanked John for a pinch hitter in the bottom of the fourth. We lit up George Frazier, Ron Davis and Rick Reuschel for seven runs in the fifth and sixth innings, and the rest was easy.

Lemon has been widely criticized by the media for pulling John, who may have been his most reliable starter, so early in the game. But as usual, the media were wrong. John was not sharp. With each succeeding inning, balls were being hit harder and harder off him. He had given up six hits in four innings when he left. We'd have gotten him soon. Lemon's mistake was summoning George Frazier to replace John. Frazier had nothing going for him all series. He lost three series games, including the sixth, to set a record.

Despite all that was written about the Yankees' bullpen, ours was consistently better. Ron Davis and George Frazier were generally ineffective as middle relievers and setup men. When a Yankee starter couldn't take them to the eighth or ninth, when the Goose could rescue them, the Yanks were in serious jeopardy.

Hooton tired in the sixth, and I came in with the bases loaded and one out. I surrendered a run-scoring single to Lou Piniella and that was it. The Yankees got only one more hit and a walk off me the rest of the way. I also had three strikeouts.

I had no interest in messing around with any breaking stuff that night, especially with a six-run lead. When I came in, I met Yeager on the mound and told him, "Just put one down and move it around. We're going after them."

Reggie Jackson and I had a little feud going, and he'd won round one with his homer in the fourth game. After that shot, Reggie answered critics by saying, "Ask Steve Howe if I can still hit a fastball."

My answer probably would have been, "Beats me." Reggie didn't realize that his homer had come off a hanging slider that didn't break and looked like a slower fastball. He might have been able to hit a fastball if he knew what one looked like.

When I saw Reggie in the seventh inning of Game Six, I decided to reacquaint him with the fastball. I blew three heaters right past him. As he was walking back to the dugout, I yelled to him, "That's a fastball. That was three fastballs."

The three and two-thirds innings I pitched in Game Six were the longest innings of my life. They seemed to go on for an eternity. They lasted so long that I even got to hit twice. (It would be more accurate to say that I stood at the plate twice. I struck out both times and didn't get a whiff of the ball.) I couldn't wait to finish it, and I kept trying to calculate who the last hitter would be. Some guys on the bench figured it would be Bob Watson, and they were right.

Watson got to hit in the ninth only because Dave Lopes bobbled a grounder by Jackson with two out. I decided to let Watson clobber a high-and-away fastball, figuring he could hit it into the vast wasteland of center field in Yankee Stadium and no harm could come of it. Sure enough, he lifted a high fly to center.

As the ball left Watson's bat, I threw my hands up in the air and Yeager started for the mound. As the ball was caught, I leaped into Yeager's arms with my hands high. I came down and jumped again, and this time I clobbered Garvey, who had just arrived at the party, with an elbow to the chin. I nearly knocked him out.

Moments later I was in the dugout, preparing to enter the tunnel to the clubhouse with Danny Ozark, a Dodger coach and a wonderful man who had endured countless frustrations as the successful but unappreciated manager of the Phillies in the 1970s. Some obnoxious Yankee fans—is there something redundant about that phrase?—were hanging over the dugout roof, trying to grab our hats and equipment.

Danny looked at me and said, "I always wanted to get to this point, just once in my life, so I could do this."

I said, "Go for it." Danny reached up and drilled one of the fans right between the eyes. Then he said, "Awright, let's go party."

In addition to the usual champagne spraying, pouring and drinking ceremonies, we got a good food fight going in the clubhouse. The wives were there waiting for us, and I took them several bottles of champagne. Reggie and Lou Piniella came over, congratulated us and told us we were the better ballclub that year, which was very gracious of them.

We were a good team that had become great with the emergence of Fernando Valenzuela. We had a workable blend of veterans and good young players, and we had no real weaknesses. We had guts and determination. We were lucky to have had no major injuries to key players. Those factors separated the 1981 Dodgers from the 1980 edition, which was good but not quite good enough.

As the insanity ran its course, what had happened began to hit me, although I didn't completely sort it out until a couple of days later. In only my second year in the big leagues, I had reached the pinnacle. Any kid who ever wanted to be a professional athlete has dreamed of winning a world championship, regardless of his sport.

Yet for all the time I spent hoping to reach that point and thinking about how it would feel, I just couldn't articulate how I felt about what I had experienced. The value of winning isn't in money or trophies or rings, although I didn't turn down any of that stuff. What counted for me was that my team had run the course and proved itself the best, and I had helped make it that way. At the age of 23, I was at the top.

Our flight from New York back to L.A., on the Dodgers' team plane, was nothing less than an airborne, world-class party. Just about everyone was ingesting some form of mind-altering chemical. I kept going to the john so I could snort my way to greater appreciation of our championship. Cindy thought the champagne was making me pee an awful lot. The plane was flying at 38,000 feet, but I was at about 43,000 most of the way.

Steve Garvey has said that a couple of hours out of New York on the flight home, he stood at the back of the plane, looking out over his slumbering teammates and reflecting on the magnitude of our accomplishment. That's not quite accurate.

Garv wasn't the only guy on that plane who couldn't sleep. True, most of the wives passed out early, but at least half the team was well on its way to getting so wired that the party didn't stop for about four days.

There were 10,000 people waiting to pounce on us at the airport in L.A. at about nine that morning. I had a plan of escape, but the whole experience, enhanced by all the drugs I'd inhaled, made me as paranoid as I've ever been in my life, and that covers a lot of ground.

I made a beeline through the terminal, but our path through the crowd was narrow, and people kept pounding me on the back and yelling at me. Cindy was right behind me, and a lot of the blows landed on her head. I was so anxious that the hair on the back of my neck was standing straight up, and my heart was pounding so hard I thought it would blow up and I'd collapse. By the time we cleared the crowd, we were in the middle of the airport parking lot.

The motorcade through downtown L.A. the next day was calmer, even though a couple hundred thousand people showed up. The only scary part was when some of the cops on horseback were shoved against our floats.

If L.A. loves anything more than its Dodgers, it's a good party. Its players, including one 23-year-old nurturing a growing addiction, felt the same way.

8

Obsession

It took awhile before I realized it. Anytime I thought about it or talked to him about it, he denied it. He would swear to God he wasn't doing anything wrong, and I kept talking to him and I said, "Steve, remember one thing. You've got a great future. You've got a wonderful family. Don't do anything to destroy them. Remember, when you sleep with dogs, you wind up with fleas. You be careful who you travel around with, who you hang around with."

He swore up and down that there wasn't anything wrong. Then when we found out that he began to lie and miss planes and stuff like that, that's when we knew what the problem was.

—Tommy Lasorda
Manager, Los Angeles Dodgers
October 1986

Following the series and a short Hawaiian vacation, I settled into a comfortable world champion's off-season routine, which consisted of party, party and party again. As if I had needed one, I now had a reason to celebrate, a reason I could trade on at least until I had to report to Florida in February for spring training.

Wherever I went, great mounds of white powder followed me around, formed broad rails and sailed up my waiting nostrils. I wasn't spending much of my postseason earnings on the stuff either. Everyone wanted to give me a congratulatory slap on the back and a few dozen snorts.

If Cindy thought I had a problem, she didn't say so. Not that I gave her a chance. I saw nothing wrong or threatening about what I was doing. Certainly I didn't look at myself as an addict or even a heavy user.

In November 1981 I took off on a lengthy binge that marked my first sustained loss of control over the drug. It began when I met some guys in a bar in Marina del Rey. They invited me to join them for some blow. I had never seen these guys before, but it sounded like a good idea. My impulsive side, which gets me in trouble more often than not, took over.

I was gone for five days. To maintain the high, we snorted a couple of lines every half hour. I ate once. If I slept at all during the entire binge, it wasn't for more than a few hours. I had no contact with Cindy. I was too messed up to speak coherently to her on the telephone. Not surprisingly, she worried that I was dead.

I wondered, as I snorted my brains out, what Cindy might be thinking. I felt bad that I didn't call her, but I didn't dwell on it. When those feelings began to crowd my euphoria, I knew how to handle them: "Hey, pal, I need another blast." I was partying and I wasn't supposed to feel guilt.

When I finally turned up at home, I gave Cindy one of my patented garbage excuses. I thought I didn't owe her more than that. I blamed all our marital disharmony on her.

I couldn't put my finger on what was wrong with our relationship. I only knew that I hated being controlled, and Cindy tried to control me by laying down rules and directing my conduct. In my denial of my addiction, I had to blame somebody to alleviate my guilt, so I told her that she was suffocating me and that she had to give me more time to be with my friends. I watched her eyes cloud with hurt, and she couldn't respond. She accepted the notion that I didn't want to be home because something was wrong with her.

That was my power play, and it worked. It diverted attention from where I had been and what I was doing, and it established a basis for future escapes to the refuge of cocaine. The sickest part of all is that once I realized that my tactic had succeeded, I felt no remorse. Instead, I felt relief because I knew I'd be able to get away with periodic disappearances. It was not until years later that Cindy's pain got through to me and became mine.

Cocaine was the source of my personality distortions and deliberate insensitivity, and also a major cause of the marital problems I couldn't pinpoint, but I didn't understand that. I recognized intellectually that there was something wrong with blaming a cocaine binge on my wife, but Cindy's pain wasn't reaching me emotionally because the drug was destroying my ability to feel. I thought coke had nothing to do with what was wrong between us. If I had admitted that the drug was at fault, I might have thought I should stop using it. But I didn't want and wouldn't allow my reasoning to move in that direction.

The great Marina del Rey binge of 1981 was not without immediate consequences for me, however. Cindy didn't just sit around for five days waiting for me to turn up at home or in a morgue. She alerted both the Dodgers and a private investigator that I was missing. I was well hidden, so the private eye couldn't find me. But now the Dodgers knew there was a problem.

During my absence, Cindy and the Dodgers decided I was an alcoholic. I thought that was bizarre because I was so heavily into cocaine that I was hardly drinking, and then only to help me down from a binge. Ever since Bob Welch's treatment for alcoholism after the 1979 season, the Dodgers had been looking for signs of alcohol abuse among players. As late as the end of 1981, they never suspected that drug abuse could be a source of trouble.

The week after I returned, the Dodgers and the players' union arranged for me to talk with John Newton, a Union 76 officer who counseled employees of that company on alcoholism. Newton is a rehabilitated alcoholic. Rumor has it that while driving drunk on the freeway in L.A. one night, he decided to pull over to the side of the road for a nap. Unfortunately, he pulled over to the left, turned off his car engine and lights and nodded off in the high-speed lane. He was lucky he wound up in jail instead of the morgue.

Newton gave me a 20-question test that's supposed to determine whether someone is an alcoholic. I answered the questions honestly and I flunked. Newton told me I should watch my drinking. Hey, no problem.

Cindy and I went to Alaska for Christmas, and I was full of holiday spirit. 'Tis the season to be wasted, fa-la-la-la-la. I was counting on a blizzard, and I knew some friends in Fairbanks were always well supplied. Just to make sure, I took along a half ounce of coke.

I was high every day on that trip. Several of us did everything under the influence. We snowmobiled on coke; we played cards while we snorted.

Cindy was not participating, and I lied to her about my use, but she knew what I was doing. She was beginning to get worried. Both her sister and her best friend told her to loosen up and have a good time, and even suggested to her that her marriage might work better if she would join in. Eventually Cindy did try that, but in Alaska she initiated search-and-destroy missions for stashes of coke. I'd hidden the stuff in a pull-down fan in a bathroom, and she never found it.

As often happens during group binges, things got crazy. One night two of us went out, befriended a derelict and brought him home to party with us. We'd never seen the guy before. He could have been a cop or a mass murderer for all we knew or cared. At home, where Cindy and her sister and two little kids were sleeping, we passed him off as a long-lost buddy. Cindy and her sister didn't believe us, and they made us take the guy home.

I was straighter during the New Year's Eve party than at any other time while I was in Alaska. Some strange people showed up, and I found myself protecting Cindy and playing the role of enforcer. Somebody had to do it. Everyone else was too far gone.

One obnoxious guy, who had known Cindy a few years before, decided he liked her in mature form and began following her around. Another guy started spilling drinks and then spit on the carpet, right in the middle of my brother-in-law's beautiful house. I threw both of those clowns out the door.

This confused Cindy, who'd been ready to declare me a hopeless addict. Suddenly I was being mature and responsible. For one night, anyway, I conned her into believing that my problem wasn't serious.

Cindy still believed a lot of my stories, or so I thought. A good example was an outrageous lie I told her that winter. Cindy was taking a photography class for her interior design program at UCLA. She built models for her portfolio and stored them in the attic space above the guest bedroom of our house in Agoura.

When I came home from a binge or finished off a gram, I'd chuck the empty vials up into the same attic space. One day Cindy went to pull down a model, and about 25 vials fell on her head. She wanted to know where they'd come from and I said, "I don't know. They're somebody else's." Cindy said there was no way that could be true, because the house was brand new. I wouldn't budge on my story, so Cindy finally gave up and acted as if she believed it. Maybe she just wanted to believe things weren't as bad as they appeared.

———————

During more than seven years of cocaine use, I learned quite a bit about the drug and my response to it. The negative effects of cocaine are devastating, and every cocaine abuser I've known has readily admitted it. But coke is such an overwhelming force that most abusers will ignore its drawbacks until they've lost almost everything in pursuit of it.

What did I like about cocaine? Its virtues make a brief but powerfully seductive list of attractions.

First, cocaine is a "miracle" drug. If you've gone without sleep for two days and you're thoroughly exhausted, only two lines of cocaine will revive you and make you feel as you would several hours after awakening from a full night's sleep. It's a feeling of normalcy without the jagged edge you'd experience if you tried the same trick with coffee. In my experience, no other substance, not even speed, can revive the body that way without producing an accompanying discomfort that reminds you that your glow is artificial.

Then there's the euphoria, which arrives several minutes after you snort the first line or two. You feel wonderful, pleased with everything going on around you. You sense that you can accomplish anything you want, that nothing is impossible.

You spend hours trying to recapture the euphoria. Experiencing it once is not enough. But the euphoria is elusive. That's why cocaine is so deceiving and addicting. It disguises itself as something wonderful, and once you are hooked, it's hideous.

Cocaine's darker side creates unpleasant changes in your personality and approach to life and causes havoc within your body. Once you've become obsessed, chances are you'll never be free without help.

Persistent use of the drug diminishes your sense of responsibility until it's nonexistent. When things have to be done, you'll avoid doing them or be unable to do them because you're in pursuit of coke, or high and unable to function, or coming off a high and trying not to get caught.

I missed several team flights because of cocaine. I left my wife and daughter so I could get high without worrying about the responsibility of taking care of them. Like my father had done when he was drinking, I missed ballgames, banquets and other events that people were counting on me to attend. I knew I was supposed to be there, but the great deity cocaine spoke from within me and said, "The hell with it. I am more important."

Cocaine blocks responses of guilt and compassion that you're supposed to feel when you fail people who are depending on you. As long as you're high, you don't feel the pain, but when you're coming down, the guilt is twice as devastating.

Your reaction is to tell yourself you don't want to feel guilt or compassion. Because coke suppresses those emotions, you snort some more. So you develop a cyclical pattern of behavior that feeds both your abuse of the drug and your evasion of responsibility and guilt.

The problem is that continued use never eliminates guilt and anxiety. Snorting to escape the pain just doesn't work. At best, it offers relief so temporary it can be measured in minutes. You can deflect guilt by distraction—playing cards or games like backgammon—when you're high, but when you crash, the guilt will creep back in and take hold, more intensely than ever.

When you come down off your cloud and go home, the guilt goes with you. I became addicted when I had shouldered a lot of responsibility: I was married and had a sizable mortgage, and I was an important player on a major league baseball team. By mid-1983 I also had a daughter. As my responsibilities grew, so did my sense of guilt when I returned from a binge.

In the early stages of addiction, the guilt is almost constructive. When I'd get home, I'd do all the household chores I'd neglected, treat Cindy like a queen and behave like a model citizen around the ballpark. That would last for a few days, until I got loaded again.

Later, when addiction became firmly rooted, my response to guilt changed. I'd say to myself, I make the money. I pay the bills. If Cindy doesn't like what I'm doing, she can hit the door. I'd lost all sensitivity to the interests of others, even my wife. Cocaine had made it impossible for me to function as a normal human being.

Cocaine caused major damage to my marriage. Cindy didn't think I should be using the drug, so my lying and sneaking around created conflict. Cindy was spending so much time trying to baby-sit me and control my use that she had no time for herself, and she became resentful.

My relationships with others were also damaged. Ron Perranoski had been like another father until my addiction took over. I became sassy and arrogant, and Ron and I stopped riding to the ballpark together. I didn't want him to know I was letting him down, so I created conflict to establish distance between us.

I lost all concern for the consequences of my drug use. I didn't care who was hurt, even though the list of those who suffered included me. I lost my job, and I almost lost my wife lots of times. Amazingly, it didn't get through to me for a long time that cocaine was the villain. I couldn't see it. That's what's so baffling and dangerous about the drug.

I lost a lot of self-esteem off the baseball field. Fortunately, I retained it on the field, the only area of my life in which I thought I had control. I knew I could retire the guy with the bat in three strikes or less. I was lucky to have baseball, because it was my only source of self-worth when my addiction raged out of control.

It was when I stepped off the mound, took off my uniform, threw my glove in my locker and reentered the real world that I got into trouble. My power in fantasyland didn't help me deal with the crises of real life.

Coke magnified feelings of inadequacy that I'd battled since adolescence and reaffirmed to me that I couldn't be counted on to fix things, or even to handle simple chores. I figured I had nothing to lose by getting high, because I was nearly worthless when I was straight.

When you're high and the initial euphoria has worn off, strange things happen in your head. Sometimes I recalled deep, dark secrets, things for which I was sorry and didn't want anyone else to know about, like when I'd been delinquent as a teenager or deceived Cindy. On other occasions, I painted mental pictures of childhood events, but the pictures often portrayed the opposite of how I really felt about those events. Cocaine enabled me to mask my feelings of pain, fear, discomfort and inadequacy. Not until I stopped abusing substances could I tell people how I really felt.

A cokehead's thought and behavior patterns are never consistent. After I'd abused for an extended period of time, I was subject to bizarre mood swings even when I wasn't snorting. I was alternately irritable and passive, sometimes within the same five-minute stretch. The explosiveness of my temper, a problem throughout my life, was magnified. I'm still moody, but my mood swings are less frequent and less severe than when I was snorting.

Paranoia is a by-product of cocaine abuse. Mine surfaced when I got off the plane in L.A. after the trip back from the World Series in 1981. It grew in direct proportion to my celebrity and reached all-time highs after my addiction became public knowledge in late 1982.

I was sure that everyone, especially in L.A., knew who I was and knew I was an addict, and if they saw me they'd all be looking for signs that I was screwed up. So I became a closet addict. I hid in padlocked houses and apartments when I got high, and I spent a lot of time peering out from behind blinds and curtains and through the peepholes in hotel room doors, expecting the cops or the mind police to arrive any minute to take me away. I never went out on the street when I was high.

I acted this way regardless of whether I was getting high in a secluded hideaway, miles from civilization, or in a room at the top of a high-rise metropolitan hotel with tinted windows. I've even seen people on coke throw things through third-story windows because they were sure someone was looking in. One night in Chicago, during a blowout while I was a Dodger, I taped the curtains to the window frames in my hotel room so no one could see in. I was staying on the 18th floor.

I didn't want Cindy to know I was getting high, so my paranoia extended to her. For about two years, when she came to hug me, I turned my head away because I was sure she was looking up my nose for traces of white powder. She's since admitted to me that half of the time she really was checking out my beak.

It's probably a good thing I didn't go out when I was seriously partying, because I would have embarrassed myself. I've seen guys walk into bars, playing Mr. Savoir-Faire, wearing their Bill Blass perfume and flirting with the ladies, never realizing they were also carrying two big eau de cocaine rings around their nostrils after a snorting session. That could have been me too.

Physically, cocaine races, drains and fries your system, steadily robbing it of nutrients and energy. A two-day binge is probably as debilitating as running a marathon. Your nose runs and sometimes bleeds; your nerves are shot; your eyes itch. When it's over, it's awfully tough to go out and fire a baseball 90 miles per hour with control.

Somehow, I performed. I didn't have a heart attack, and I didn't lose my hand-eye coordination. God was looking out for me. Cindy and many others were constantly lifting me up in prayer. Of course, it's possible that the full effects of my abuse won't appear until later. My career, and even my life, may be shortened by all the coke I snorted.

The most frightening and effective thing I could do to discourage others from turning to cocaine would be to include in this book before and after photos of Howe on a binge. I wish I had pictures like that. The after shots wouldn't be pretty.

Cocaine suppresses your appetite, so on a binge you might go several days without eating anything solid. If you have any taste for alcohol, you'll drink double or triple the amount you'd normally have at a party, partly because alcohol is a depressant and counteracts and moderates the effects of coke.

The combination of cocaine and booze dehydrates you, and the effect of dehydration and lack of food is to make you look like a skeleton, a concentration camp prisoner. When I got high, I sweated profusely, my eyes sank back in my head and glazed over, and I slouched around, partly because I didn't have the energy to hold myself upright. When I looked in the mirror, though, I said to myself, "I don't look too bad. I just need a little sleep. Or another blast."

Oddly enough, although cocaine is a stimulant, it didn't make me hyper, probably because I normally go through life at 100 miles per hour. In fact, coke pacified me and mellowed me to the point that I couldn't perform tasks that required minimal concentration, such as driving. For most people, coke offers more of a body high that makes them want to go out and raise hell. Different strokes for different folks, I guess.

If you snort enough in a short period, your nervous system can go haywire. On the way down from one of my worst binges, when

I consumed about 15 grams in three days, my nervous system decided it was going to play hopscotch all over my body. I developed a bad case of twitches that I couldn't stop. It was horrifying.

You'll pay little attention to sex when you're high. Contrary to one popular legend, cocaine is not an aphrodisiac. In fact, it has the opposite effect, cutting your sex drive. When obsession sets in, the pursuit of cocaine is enough to make you forget about sex.

Hygiene is something you just don't care about during concentrated snorting. I rarely bathed during a binge, and I usually slept, if at all, on a couch or the floor.

Doctors estimate that if you consume a gram of coke in a short period, it takes your body three days to recover. Imagine the recovery period required after a three-day, two-gram-a-day binge. It would take close to two weeks to crawl back, and the recovery would be that rapid only if you didn't snort while recovering. That means that from the latter part of 1981 through late 1985, my body was suffering almost constantly from the effects of cocaine abuse.

Because I was snorting so much and still pitching well, I thought I was physically invincible. True, I had knee problems in 1981 and a sore shoulder that required cortisone shots in 1982, but I pitched through both ailments.

I never had to spend months in the weight room to get in shape. My body always bounced back, despite the abuse I heaped on it. If I needed training, I could accomplish in a couple of weeks what it took other players several months to do.

At Michigan, trainer Gus Crouch discovered that I have an exceptional wingspan because the bones running from my shoulders to my elbows are extremely long. He also found that I'm one of the few players with perfect balance between front and rear shoulder muscles, and that I have natural hyperextension of my elbows. Guys who blow out their shoulders, like Mark Fidrych, the former Tiger pitcher, usually don't have that shoulder balance. I have a body that was designed to throw things. That's why I never had a serious arm or shoulder injury until I pinched my ulnar nerve in late 1984.

When I got to the Dodgers, I became a leader in designing weight training programs for pitchers. Because of my training in exercise physiology, I understood what had to be done to build and maintain strength in a pitcher's arm, and I often did arm, shoulder, wrist and hand exercises after games on nights when I hadn't pitched.

I told myself that cocaine couldn't hurt my body. It certainly wouldn't kill me. I thought the only ways I could die were by auto accident, getting shot during a fight or having a heart attack while making love when I was 80.

Now I know better.

Compared to the party-hearty environment of L.A., Vero Beach seemed tame during spring training in 1982. Cindy kept an eye on me, and baseball drew my attention away from chemicals.

There were a couple of natural party situations in which I shared blasts with friends. Once we had visitors from Canada, and that prompted the destruction of an eight-ball in three days.

I pitched better that spring than I had the previous year. If I was not quite the ruthless terminator I had been in Florida in 1980, I was still calmer and more efficient than the celebrity-conscious, carefree Howe of 1981. I can't remember specific pitching performances that spring—too many poisoned brain cells since then—but I remember pitching well.

When the season began and I got back to L.A., I was sucked back into my 1981 crowd. When I was with them, I snorted up a snowstorm. Even when I wasn't with them, I got into a pattern of continuous, daily use away from the ballpark.

Cindy came to most of the Dodgers' home games. When she was there, we'd go home together. When she wasn't, I went out to party and often didn't come home at all. I'd get high, crash with my friends and go to the ballpark at the usual midafternoon time the next day.

After a few all-nighters, I'd put in an appearance at home before heading for the stadium. Cindy stayed up much of each night I was gone, frantic with worry, suspecting there might be another woman in my life, and not knowing whether I was alive or dead until she checked the box score the next morning.

When she confronted me, I'd say, "I can't talk; I'm in a hurry. I'll talk to you about it later." I was buying time to come up with a credible excuse. It was obvious that I was using, and Cindy knew it, but I didn't want her or anyone else to know how much.

When we came home together after a game, I had a plan to get high that worked every time. I asked a guy I'll call Alex, a friend and coke dealer, to leave a packet at a designated location among some trees in front of the garage at my house.

I didn't want Cindy to see Alex. She disliked him and suspected he was a dealer, even though I tried to assure her otherwise. Alex was also an addict. A couple of years later, he got busted and went to jail.

As soon as we walked into the house, Cindy would begin preparing dinner. I took the dog out for a walk, and that's when I picked up the stash Alex had left.

After dinner, Cindy went to bed. When I was sure she was asleep, I went into the den and snorted while I watched TV. I got blasted until five or six in the morning, then slept until two the next afternoon, when it was time to go play ball. Cindy got up in the morning and went about her business, never knowing what I'd been doing all night. I guess she thought I was too keyed up to sleep after the games.

Through nearly the entire 1982 baseball season, I snorted two grams or more per day. In little more than a year, my habit had grown from a cozy campfire into a full-blown, life-threatening, home-wrecking California brush fire.

Never during my addiction did an extended period of time pass without something bizarre happening. As you might expect, some of the wildest incidents happened in New York.

I think it was in 1982 that I got high under rather unusual circumstances. I went with several Mets and someone who said he was a business associate of Dan Ackroyd and John Belushi to a place in New Jersey called the Blues Brothers Club. It was a huge warehouse that was nearly empty. There was a bar, and a woman was standing behind it, but when I asked for a drink, she said, "We ain't got no booze here."

There was one light bulb in a corner, so we sat in that corner and got wasted. One of the guys went into a bathroom to wash up, but there were no lights and he cut his hand on a broken mirror. The whole experience was spooky.

On another New York trip, probably that same season, some of the Mets took me to Studio 54, which was still a pretty hot disco. We got down to some serious snorting with a well-known comic entertainer and some NBC and CBS executives. At one point, on my way to the john, I was so blasted that I almost fell off the second deck of the disco.

Cindy began to tune in to the severity of my problem again toward the end of the season. She hadn't been able to slow me down by going to home games, so she joined me on a late-August road trip to Chicago, Pittsburgh and St. Louis and snorted limited amounts of coke with me. She was trying to regain control.

The script didn't play quite the way Cindy had written it. I gave her the coke to hold in her purse and told her to use it whenever she wanted. Of course, I also used it whenever I wanted, which was usually when she wasn't looking. Cindy periodically checked her purse to make sure the stash was secure. As often as not, it was missing.

Cindy's experiment had its comical moments. She didn't know how to snort, and she blew out as much as she took in. Cindy decided after three weeks that getting high with me was neither helping our marriage nor limiting my use. I was still going out and using when I wasn't getting high with her. Again she became the narc, and I started sneaking around and lying to get blasted.

It was in Pittsburgh that Cindy realized how out of control I was. We were riding in the back of the team bus, and I was snorting and laughing because I was getting away with it. Cindy said, "Those guys are going to see you. What are you doing?" I just looked at her and laughed. She told me later that she realized at that moment that my cocaine abuse had advanced from a game to a sickness.

Cindy became pregnant with Chelsi on that road trip and learned of it a few weeks later. The new restrictions on Cindy's activities affected my addiction. She couldn't follow me around or go to many ballgames, and I was free again. I was already snorting as much as I could without dipping a straw into a baggie in the bullpen, but now it was easier to get away with it. The only restrictive influences in my life were baseball and guilt.

I didn't enjoy the 1982 baseball season much, partly because my life consisted entirely of playing ball and sitting in curtained rooms snorting little packets of white powder. I didn't pitch as well as I thought I should.

I finished with numbers that would have made most relievers deliriously happy. I was 7–5 with a 2.08 ERA and 13 saves. I had allowed only six unintentional walks in nearly 100 innings, and at one point I had permitted only one earned run through 39 appearances. But I was inconsistent, and I never felt I was throwing the ball well. To make matters worse, we blew a lead down the stretch and lost the division title to Atlanta on the last day of the regular season.

I don't know how we managed to stay in contention all year, because we always seemed to be struggling. Guys were griping about playing time and how they were being used. The bullpen was in turmoil. Tom Niedenfuer, who had pitched well for us in 1981, was cut at the end of spring training in 1982, although he returned before the season was a month old.

I began the season with several strong performances. Then on April 18 in San Diego, I inherited a 3–2 lead and a couple of baserunners in the eighth. I got ripped, allowing both runners to score and giving up five more runs without getting anyone out.

By June 14 I had five wins and only two saves. I accumulated so many wins because I wasn't protecting leads in save situations, and I was leading the bullpen in pissing off the starters. Fortunately, my teammates were scratching out some runs to bail me out.

Not all of my failures were my fault. In Philadelphia on May 10, I relieved Niedenfuer in the bottom of the tenth with the score tied, runners at first and third, one out and Pete Rose at the plate. I'm sure I fanned Rose with a 2-and-2 slider, but Dutch Rennert saw it inside. After I threw a classic Howe fit on the mound, Rose got a hit and we lost.

Beginning in mid-June, I had my only real hot streak of the year. I made seven strong appearances in a row and earned saves in four of them. I guess Tommy Lasorda thought I was pitching well. A few days before the July 13 All-Star Game in Montreal, he told me he was taking me along to be one of his eight pitchers on the National League staff. I was thrilled.

Typically, the press reported that the only reason I made the team was because Bruce Sutter was hurt. Tommy stuck up for me, telling the press that Tom Hume had filled Sutter's spot and that I would have made the team on merit anyway.

No question, the All-Star Game was the highlight of my season. It was an honor to be there among the best players in the game. The media hype was unbelievable, rivaling the World Series. There was a nice banquet at which we were given commemorative rings. Everywhere we went we were showered with gifts and publicity.

Before the game, National League President Chub Feeney came into our clubhouse and gave us a pep talk. The National League had won ten in a row, but Chub wanted more blood. "You better win this one," he said. "We need to keep the streak going."

And so we did. With one out and one on in the ninth and the National League holding a 4–1 lead, Tommy brought me in to face Kent Hrbek, Minnesota's big, left-handed rookie phenom. I threw one pitch, a slider, and Hrbek popped up feebly to short center.

The little fat guy waddled out to the mound again, intent on letting everybody play. "Great job," Tommy said. "I'm going to bring in Hume."

"OK, fine," I said, "but you aren't getting the ball."

"What do you mean?"

"This is my ball. I got him out, and I might not ever make it here again. I'm taking it with me." I walked off the mound with the ball, and I still have it. Hume retired Buddy Bell and the game was over.

After my one-pitch outing, a reporter actually asked whether I'd had good stuff. "How would I know?" I said.

The only other bright spot in my season was when my teammates flattered me by making me their alternate representative to the Players Association. I held the position for three weeks, then quit. I didn't want to go to meetings, I didn't want to assume responsibility if I could avoid it, and I didn't want to do anything outside of playing ball that would cut into my high time.

After the All-Star Game, I didn't pitch well until late in the season. My knee was bothering me again, and I developed tendonitis in my pitching shoulder. It got so bad during the second half of the season that I couldn't brush my hair or my teeth with my left hand, and I couldn't lift my elbow anywhere near the level of my shoulder.

Our trainer, Bill Buhler, known to the players as the Federal Buhler of Investigation or the Federal Bureau of Buhler because he was always nosing around, apparently didn't believe that the tendonitis was a problem. "You just can't play hurt," he told me.

I got angry because I'd proved him wrong, but I also wasn't going to pitch with a sore arm anymore. So in mid-August, after we returned from a road trip, I took a cortisone shot from Dr. Frank Jobe, our orthopedist. The man with the needles. Whenever we saw him, we asked whether he had his needle kit. He always did.

I'm scared of needles. It didn't help when, just as the doc was about to stick me, Ron Roenicke walked right in front of me, saw the needle and said, "Oh, my God!"

Then Dr. Jobe stuck me, and the pain was incredible. Cortisone works by attacking inflammation, and for the first several minutes after an injection, there's an intense burning sensation. At least the shot brought me temporary relief from the tendonitis.

Cindy heard that I'd gotten a shot, and she stood in the corridor outside the clubhouse crying. I had to go out and calm her down before I could deal with my pain.

Throughout the season, I was unhappy with the way Tommy was using me. I seemed to be getting more long relief assignments than usual, coming into games in the seventh inning or even earlier. Maybe it was because Niedenfuer was smoking when he got back from Albuquerque, picking up five saves in little more than three weeks.

Like almost any manager, Tommy will ride a good horse until it dies, and that's how he handled Niedenfuer, who flamed out quickly. After picking up his fifth save on May 22, Buffalohead didn't get another for nearly three months. Still, for a while, I thought I'd lost my job.

Given my immaturity and a coke-addled mind subject to severe mood swings, it was not unusual for me to respond irrationally to almost anything that happened in my life. I got mad when the sun came up; I got mad when the sun went down. I was pissed off when Tommy pitched me too much, and I ranted and raved when I didn't pitch enough or at the right times.

In the second half of the season, I was only 2–4, but I had six saves in seven tries. I had several good outings in mid-September, but then I failed to protect a tie in San Diego on the 22nd and gave up a run in the eighth inning to lose a game to the Giants on the 24th. Even though I had two more decent games after that, Tommy might have been nervous about using me with the season on the line in the final series at San Francisco.

We needed a win on the final day, October 3, to finish in a tie with the Braves. With the score tied at 2, Niedenfuer took the mound for us in the bottom of the seventh and got into immediate trouble. Bob Brenly singled and went to third on Champ Summers's double. Niedenfuer struck out pitcher Greg Minton, but the top of the order, lefties Max Venable and Joe Morgan, was coming up.

I was ready in the bullpen. It was the kind of situation in which Tommy had been using me ever since I'd been a rookie. I wanted in, but Tommy called for Terry Forster, the other lefty in our bullpen. I was crushed and humiliated.

Terry struck out Jim Wohlford, a right-handed hitter who was batting for Venable. Morgan had given me trouble in '80 and '81, but he was hitless against me in '82. In fact, eight days earlier, I'd popped him up with a man on. Tommy stuck with Forster, and Morgan hit a hanging slider for a three-run homer. We couldn't come back, and the pennant was lost.

When it was over, I cried in front of the TV camera, but Jim Hill, the reporter and a former football player, had the grace not to use the footage. Jim interviewed Forster too, and Terry, great competitor that he was, could have killed himself.

This is no reflection on Terry Forster, who was a fine pitcher, but I know that if Lasorda had put me in to face Morgan, we would have won. I had outstanding stuff in the bullpen, but I never got a chance to use it. Tommy told me he wanted to save me in case I was needed in later innings. I didn't believe that, because he'd had me warming up since the fourth. I now know why Lasorda may not have used me when the chips were down in San Francisco, and why he used me with decreasing frequency during the stretch run: The Dodgers were aware that I had a problem with cocaine abuse.

Probably around midseason, without my knowledge, Mike Hernandez, Sr. warned Manny Mota that he suspected I was heavily into drugs. I don't know whether Manny told the front office, but I believe he did. Neither Manny nor anyone else in the Dodger organization said a word to me about it for the rest of the season.

The Dodgers may have been taking a see-no-evil, speak-no-evil approach to protect the image of the organization. They did the same thing in late June after Don Newcombe was quoted in a Santa Monica newspaper as saying that the Dodgers had a "very serious problem" with drug and alcohol abuse among the players.

Newc, a former pitcher and alcoholic, was the Dodgers' director of community relations and had helped the club set up a program to monitor drug and alcohol use. Believe me, he was in a position to know what he was talking about. The Dodgers denied that there was a problem, and Newc backed off. The Dodgers were not yet ready to deal publicly with the issue. To this day, most baseball organizations would rather sweep such stories under the rug than respond constructively to the problem.

Tommy Lasorda may have been thinking about my cocaine problem when he had to choose a left-handed reliever in the seventh inning at San Francisco on October 3. The pain of disappointment and defeat that I suffered on that day lived with me throughout the troubled winter that followed.

One factor that may have hurt our team in 1982 was the distraction of nonstop media attention focused on Steve Garvey's season-long contract negotiations with the Dodgers. Garv was Mr. Dodger, and a lot of people were worried that he might leave. But I don't think any of his Dodger teammates were too distressed when his talks with the Dodgers failed and he signed with San Diego.

Garv didn't spend much time with the rest of us. He rarely went out with us to drink a few beers and share a few chuckles. Because he went his own way, some players got the impression that Garv thought he was better than the rest of us.

If Garv was misunderstood, it was because he never let anyone know what he was all about. All we saw was the public person, the super-intense ballplayer, the smiling mannequin on the TV promos. I'm not condemning Garv for being a private person. But maybe his desire to excel was so strong, and his personality so serious, that his relations with his teammates were hampered.

As a player, Garv worked his butt off, and he contributed with an excellent bat and above-average fielding. On the other hand, Garv couldn't throw or run, and guys hitting ahead of him in the lineup became annoyed because he wouldn't take a pitch so they could steal. Garv never took many walks. It seemed that he cared more about personal goals than team objectives. For example, his consecutive-game streak became an obsession. He even began his book by talking about it.

Garv wound up signing with the Padres for little more in annual salary than the Dodgers had offered. The Dodgers wouldn't budge from their policy of offering only performance contracts. The Padres, on the other hand, were willing to write a pile of incentive clauses into his contract.

———

My first major coke blowout of the 1982–83 off-season happened in October. My sister, Kathi, was visiting, and I knew Cindy wouldn't want me going on any road trips, so I set one up by picking a fight with her. I left in a huff without telling her where I was going.

One of my friends was a pilot. Three of us jumped into his plane and flew to Lake Powell, on the Arizona-Utah border. We were going to meet four more guys there, and we were loaded down with a week's provisions: ten cases of whiskey, almost five and a half ounces of cocaine and ten steaks. We didn't figure to be doing too much eating once we started snorting.

For three solid days, all I did was snort, drink and break fishing poles. I'd tie the poles to the side of the boat and forget they were tied up when I went to see what was nibbling. After I snapped a couple of poles in half, they made me stop fishing.

We were gone five days and couldn't finish all the liquor and drugs. By the time we left the lake, no one wanted to see the stuff anymore.

It was either during that binge or one that occurred within the next two weeks that Cindy went to talk to my agent, Tony Attanasio, about my problem. Tony told her the Dodgers already knew about it and wanted to give me a urine test because it was time to negotiate a new contract.

When I resurfaced, Cindy told me Tony wanted to talk, so I called him. "The Dodgers want to test you," Tony said. "Could you pass it if they gave it to you tomorrow?"

"No."

"Do you need help? Would you like us to help you?"

I thought about it. Cocaine wasn't as much fun as it used to be. I was causing my wife untold pain and anxiety. I was not happy with the way my life had been going for nearly a year. The weight of the obsession, and the financial burden of satisfying it, were becoming intolerable. But I liked the drug. I didn't want to stop using it.

More important to me at that moment, though, the Dodgers had me cornered. They knew I had a problem. Perhaps if I took the initiative and asked for help, they wouldn't penalize me. I could put them off by going in for treatment, and when everything had quieted down and blown over, I could start getting high again as long as I was cool about it.

I said yes.

Cindy, who had initiated the quest for assistance, didn't realize that "help" meant a visit to a distant rehabilitation center for more than a month. She was upset when she found out.

But by then I was signed, sealed and delivered. With my authorization, Tony requested that the Dodgers arrange treatment for me. I was assigned to The Meadows in Wickenburg, Arizona, where Bobby Welch had been treated for alcoholism three years before.

9

Project Rehab

The biggest shock I had with him was when he came back that first spring and he and Cindy were staying in a motel. After all the problems, he was going to come back. I was in my uniform, and he was late again. I asked Tommy if it was all right if I went over to the motel, and he said, "Yeah, you're the closest to him."

I went over to Vero Beach and sat down and talked to him. That was my first experience with him after he was down at The Meadows. I don't think he was clean. He was very nervous and hyper. I thought it was because he was coming back and going to meet the press.

It was like I was his father. I said, "You know, I just don't understand why you're putting your career, your family and everything else on the line with that stuff. What are you doing?"

He said, "Everything's fine; everything's going to be OK." Just gave me all that baloney.

He finally made it the next day, and he just freaked out on the mound. He was in a little area where we throw on the sidelines, and he just couldn't take the pressure. I've never seen anybody like that. They had to take him into the infirmary and calm him down. He just went berserk on that mound.

—Ron Perranoski
October 1986

130

It was a few days before Thanksgiving when Tony Attanasio requested that the Dodgers provide treatment for my chemical dependency. I was sure I'd have a couple of weeks, or at least until after the holiday, to give myself a major-league send-off. I was stunned when they told me I'd have to begin treatment the next day.

I went right to my source and bought two grams. I snorted it all on the flight to Phoenix and got fractured. The flight takes only about 40 minutes, and I must have visited the bathroom 40 times. Each time I emerged, no doubt, I looked a little more damaged. I'm sure my fellow first-class passengers thought either I had a serious bladder problem or I was a terrorist setting up a hijacking.

When I got off the plane, there was a guy waiting in a station wagon to take me to The Meadows. It's 48 miles from Phoenix to Wickenburg, but I needed a longer ride than that to return from the cosmic journey on which I'd just airmailed myself. A drive from Phoenix to New York might have done it. When I got to The Meadows, I was still in la-la land. Boy, was I in for a shock.

I wasn't at The Meadows because I was convinced that I needed help. I knew I was snorting too much, but I didn't yet see that it was affecting my family life and my career. I would have preferred to handle it on my own, which means I probably would have tried to regulate my use by periodic binges, a technique that had already failed. Or I would have done nothing at all.

I wanted to display a constructive attitude so my position in contract talks wouldn't be jeopardized. The way I plotted it, I'd emerge from The Meadows with a clean slate. Everybody, including the Dodgers, would assume I was drug-free forevermore, and the cloud of suspicion would be removed. I could still get high, as long as the Dodgers didn't find out.

My agreement to go to The Meadows was not well thought out. I didn't realize I'd never be above suspicion. I never considered that the baseball establishment wouldn't understand that drug dependency is a sickness, and that baseball eventually would punish me as a repeat offender. Had those possibilities occurred to me, I might not have agreed to enter The Meadows.

What could I have done instead? Maybe I could have gotten Attanasio to stall the Dodgers for 48 hours, tell them I was on a fishing trip or something. Assuming I could have stayed clean that long, I would have tested negative if the Dodgers still wanted to test me. Then I could have sought rehabilitation privately.

I thought that if I went to The Meadows, manageability would be restored in my life, enabling me to continue to use drugs. But I didn't want to be at The Meadows, so I rebelled against everything associated with the place. It's located in the most desolate desert I had ever seen, surrounded by cacti, tumbleweed and small, bare hills. It's probably the perfect place for a rehab center, miles from civilization and the nearest bar or drug dealer. I hated it.

The photographs in the brochure make The Meadows look like a country club. Not quite. There was no water in the swimming pool, and the volleyball net had a hole in it. There wasn't much to do for recreation except take walks.

I've always loved water, and there was no water around The Meadows for miles. When the staff went to town for supplies, I asked them to bring me some land-shark repellent.

My first activity was detoxification. I suppose I needed it. They took me into a room, gave me a pair of pajamas and took away my clothes. They know you won't try to escape by walking or hitching a ride to town in pajamas.

They went through my belongings, searching for drugs. They took my shaving lotion because they thought I might drink it to get high. They lifted my razor blades so I wouldn't slash my wrists. Then a doctor searched for contraband in every orifice of my body. I felt like a criminal.

I was put in a detox room by myself for three days with a book on alcoholism that had been published by Alcoholics Anonymous. I didn't read it, even though the only other thing I could do in there was talk to myself.

In the middle of my first night, tossing from the discomfort of my narrow institutional bed and the down side of a blowout, I fell out of bed and woke up when I hit the floor. I couldn't believe where I was and what had happened. I wanted to escape, but I didn't know where they'd hidden my clothes.

After detox, I was allowed to come out of my cage, put on clothes and mingle with other human beings. My treatment began. The first stage of treatment at The Meadows is completed when a chemically dependent person admits he or she is powerless against drugs and alcohol. Normally, the first step is completed in a week or two. So strong was my rebellion against The Meadows' program that I didn't get there until my fifth week.

I didn't think I was an alcoholic. I hadn't drunk much in the past year. I drank a lot only when I was trying to counteract the effects of coke. I was supposed to be so tough and strong that substances couldn't control me, and it was embarrassing enough to admit I was a cokehead. I was also haunted by the thought that if I confessed to alcohol abuse, I'd be following too closely in Dad's footsteps. I believed Dad's problem and mine were different.

The program at The Meadows was a dinosaur, directed almost exclusively toward alcoholism. I didn't think I had a tendency to abuse substances in general. I'd chosen coke after experimenting with other drugs, so there must have been a reason why I was dependent only on cocaine. I thought The Meadows should have treated me for that problem instead of trying to invent others.

My counselors and therapists persisted on the alcohol issue. When I finally made the required admission, I did it to get them off my back and to get me out of there, which couldn't happen until I'd completed four steps. I still couldn't believe that someone else might know more than I did about something.

I wasn't allowed to telephone Cindy for a week. Then the counselors let me talk to her twice a week, and calls were limited to five minutes. They were trying to cut me off completely from my normal environment so they could treat me in a sterilized setting, but that made me feel like a convict with no rights.

For the first several days of treatment, I wasn't allowed to talk. Counselors and other members of my therapy group sat around and told me what a worthless, evil person I was. I couldn't respond. I had to sit there and take it.

They tried to tell me what my feelings were. "Aren't you hurt, Steve?" they asked. "Don't you feel angry? Admit that you feel a lot of anger." I never admitted anger, but in fact I eventually got angry—at The Meadows. One day they gave me a bataca, a sort of tennis racquet with a leather cover, and told me to work out my anger by banging on a Styrofoam cube. I caused so much damage that they took away the bataca and never let me use it again.

The Meadows was trying to break me, reduce me to an emotional basket case so that I would always associate certain negative thoughts and feelings with drug use. Then they'd build me back up by proving I could get through life without the assistance of chemicals. If I had not been so closed-minded and had accepted what

The Meadows was trying to show me, the program might have worked.

The Meadows' treatment didn't work because I was unwilling to look honestly at what chemicals had done to my life. In addition, I'd been taught that emotions interfere with an athlete's performance. I was the iceman of the Dodgers, the guy who pitches only when a game is at stake. My job was to ignore 50,000 screaming fans, knock the hitter on his butt, get him out with a series of perfectly placed pitches and walk off the mound as though nothing important had happened. Off the mound, my state of mind was much the same because drugs suppressed my ability to feel. It was just about impossible for me to admit to strangers at The Meadows that I was inadequate, angry, hurt or out of control. The Meadows couldn't break me down because I wouldn't allow it.

Another reason The Meadows couldn't help me is that I hadn't reached bottom by losing everything. Drug use had not cost me my family or my job. I could count on making a good living in the future, even though my finances were in sorry shape by the end of 1982. I insisted that I could handle the cocaine problem my way, when in fact I wasn't ready to stop getting high.

One thing I believe today is that I couldn't pick up the pieces of my shattered past and go forward without the help of Jesus Christ. Today I am sober only with his and others' help.

The only person at The Meadows who came close to reaching me was Mavis, my counselor. Mavis was sharp and knew how to get under my skin, to get a rise out of me. But she couldn't break me. I'm sure Mavis knew I wasn't ready to graduate to clean living when my five weeks at The Meadows were up.

After three weeks of "treatment," it was time for family weekend. The addict's therapy is designed to include his family because addiction affects—and infects—the whole clan. I was hurt and disappointed when no one from my family came down from Michigan. I felt deserted. Cindy's parents stopped by for a short time. Basically, my family weekend was Cindy, and that was traumatic enough.

There was a lot of crying and hugging at the Phoenix airport when Cindy arrived. I was scared and a little shell-shocked by what had happened to me at The Meadows, and Cindy was scared because she realized that my addiction had grown to be more than just a Howe family problem.

The rules prohibited physical contact, let alone intimacy, between family members during the weekend. Cindy and I ignored that rule from the first night to the last that she was there. We had an emotional and physical need that was more compelling than any rule.

Family therapy began the day after Cindy's arrival. The program called for all family members, one by one, to openly discuss the cruel, irresponsible and bizarre things their favorite addicts had done.

Cindy was so nervous before the session that she was practically hysterical. They wanted her to show me how much my conduct had hurt her and our marriage. Cindy was inclined to protect me, and she thought the therapy would hurt and anger me. Naturally, the counselors picked Cindy to speak first. They didn't push her hard because she was pregnant, but the experience was very painful for both of us.

They sat Cindy directly in front of me, facing me. Through a series of questions, the counselors explored Cindy's emotions, getting her to admit that my conduct as an addict had hurt, angered and victimized her. Cindy made a most convincing victim: petite, blond, pregnant and innocent. The counselors sounded like prosecutors cross-examining an accused murderer. I wanted to stand up and say, "Hey, leave her alone. I'm the one on trial here."

They asked Cindy whether her estimate of her self-worth was low. "I don't know what you're talking about," she said. Today she agrees that their question hit close to the mark, but she didn't realize it then.

When Cindy began to get into the details of what had happened between us, I did what I could to cut her off. I had a lot of emotional power over her, and I knew how to use it. By grinning in a certain way and using my eyes, or by pretending I was about to cry, I got through to her mothering instincts and made her break off her monologue. The counselors noticed what I was doing and jumped all over me, which made me angry but didn't stop me from sending messages to Cindy.

Still, Cindy exposed enough raw nerves to further damage our relationship. If I had let The Meadows' program help me, it would have helped my marriage as well, despite all the harsh words that were said. Instead, I came away from family weekend believing that Cindy had hurt and exposed me unnecessarily.

It seemed as if The Meadows wasn't helping any of the other drug addicts I met there either. One of them, a football player from Oklahoma State, went berserk almost every day. From down the hall I could hear him yelling profanities and then, crash! He probably broke more things than anyone else who was ever confined at The Meadows. He didn't get to use the bataca for long either.

I left The Meadows a few days after Christmas with a hostile attitude. I hated everybody and everything. I hated Cindy for telling Tony Attanasio about my problem, and I hated Tony for telling the Dodgers. I hated the Dodgers for sending me to a place that told me I was an alcoholic. I hated The Meadows for the way they handled me and for failing to explore the problems created by my family background. I hated my family for not being there when I needed their support.

I was such a walking time bomb that I was afraid I was going to kill someone or hurt myself if I didn't medicate. So I took the easy way out—I got high. There was a hiding place in my house where I'd left a small stash, not more than a few lines, really. The day after I left The Meadows, I raided it. Happy New Year.

I'd agreed to go to The Meadows only after Tony had gotten the Dodgers to promise that they wouldn't use my addiction and treatment as evidence against me at my salary arbitration hearing in January. I had voluntarily (well, almost) brought my problem to the Dodgers and handled it their way. It would have been a low blow for the team to use it against me under those circumstances. My case was supposed to be a Dodger family secret.

Within a week after I returned to L.A., and only a few weeks before the hearing, news of my treatment hit the papers. I certainly wasn't the source of the leak. I'm sure it came from the Dodgers' front office. Someone was more concerned about the size of my salary than about my recovery. They threw me to the wolves just to save a few bucks.

Because I hadn't reached an internal reckoning with my addiction, I was far from prepared for public disclosure. Suddenly the world knew that Steve Howe, the professional iceman, was a dope fiend. It blew me away.

The arbitration hearing further wounded my shaky state of equilibrium. I'd asked for $450,000 for 1983, and the Dodgers countered with an offer of $325,000. Given what I'd accomplished and what other quality relief pitchers were earning, my demand was fair. The Dodgers spent several days trying to prove otherwise.

I'd totally and proudly committed myself to the Dodgers for three years. Regardless of whether I was hurt, I'd always answered when Tommy Lasorda had called on me. I'd been an essential player on a championship team that remained a strong contender. It was devastating for me to sit at a table across from my employers, with Cindy at my side, as they picked apart my career and belittled my performance.

I'd doubted my value as a human being off the diamond, but I'd always believed in my invincibility on the field. Now the Dodgers were impersonally dismantling my only source of self-assurance at a time when I needed all the confidence I could muster.

Drugs hung over the hearing like a giant thunderhead, but the Dodgers never mentioned the subject. After letting the world in on our dirty little family secret, they didn't have to. I lost the arbitration and signed my 1983 contract for $325,000. The good news was that my salary had tripled, but the bad news was that now I had three times as much money to spend on getting blasted.

As soon as I arrived at Vero Beach for spring training, the pressure began to build. I was a rare specimen under the microscope of public attention, an addicted ballplayer who'd been through rehab. Maybe it was my imagination and latent paranoia at work, but people around the ballclub seemed to be looking at me differently.

I quickly found out who my real friends were on the team. Most of the guys treated me with the same fellowship and good humor as always, even making cracks about my habit and my nose. I was actually relieved by that kind of abuse. It was a sign that things were normal around the Dodger clubhouse. Of course, some of my old buddies were drug users themselves, and they realized that what had happened to me could just as easily have happened to them.

There was a small group of players who treated me as if I had AIDS. Their attitude was that my illness and the publicity it created were bad for the Dodgers and bad for baseball. They expected me to account to the team for everything I did that was out of the ordinary. I resented it, and I've never been shy about expressing my feelings about stuff like that. Inevitably, personality conflicts developed.

Rick Monday was one guy I clashed with from time to time. Rick was one of the game's senior citizens, and he was from the old school. I guess Monday decided that because I was an addict, I was a suspect. When I was late during spring training and during the season, he wanted to know why. When I showed up late for a game in July, he was quoted as saying, "There are 24 people who want to know what in hell is going on."

At the time, I didn't think I owed Monday or anyone else an explanation. When my screw-ups affected the team, I thought an apology was due, but never an explanation. I had personal problems just like anyone else. The reasons were my own business. Fortunately, most of my teammates understood that. But as I look back now, I believe that I did owe the team an explanation. My anger was a cover-up because I couldn't tell them I was getting high.

The news media were all over me like piranhas in a feeding frenzy when I got to Florida. They loved it when they had an excuse to intrude into a ballplayer's private life. My visit at The Meadows was the biggest Dodger scandal since the Garvey exposé in *Inside Sports*.

I tried to be as cooperative as possible with the media. I knew they had a job to do. Within limits, I tried to help them do it, figuring that it was in the best interest of the team to maintain positive relations with the media. Rarely did I refuse an interview, so I resented it when reporters manufactured quotes, published misguided opinions without the benefit of research or knowledge and dug into the players' backgrounds, all to build controversy and sell papers or attract viewers.

I was misquoted; so what else is new? No big deal, unless it hurt someone. But I didn't much like it when I was quoted and never interviewed. On one occasion, after a doubleheader in Pittsburgh in which we'd won the first game, I was quoted as saying I'd expected the Pirates to roll over in the second game. I couldn't believe it. I hadn't spoken with any reporters, and I never would have made a remark that would give another team ammunition for a vendetta.

Members of the Clarkston High School baseball team, with Steve second from the left, cheer their team on. (W. F. Datwyler)

Steve relaxing between innings during a Clarkston High School game. (W. F. Datwyler)

Coach Paul Tungate presenting an award to Steve on Steve Howe Night at Clarkston High School on December 19, 1980, as Cindy looks on. Steve had recently been named National League Rookie of the Year.

Left to Right: Dodgers Jerry Reuss, Rick Monday, Steve Yeager and Steve Howe prior to a game in 1983.

Steve showing his form while pitching for the Los Angeles Dodgers. (Los Angeles Dodgers)

Steve reflects his team's winning mood in the 1981 World Series. (Los Angeles Dodgers)

Steve and his daughter Chelsi at the snowmobile races in Kalispell, Montana, winter 1987.

Steve tests his Polaris Indy 650 racer on a field near Kalispell, Montana, in December 1987. (Diane Ensign)

Kalispell Assistant Chief of Police Don Hossack nabs Steve in the act of building the perfect snowball in December 1987. (Diane Ensign)

Cindy and Steve at the Professional Athletes Outreach Conference, November 1987.

Steve on the mound at Arlington Stadium. (Texas Rangers)

A family gathering in Wichita, Kansas, in August 1988. Left to right: Virgil Howe, Steve's father; Brian; Steve; Chelsi; Barbara Howe, Steve's mother; and Steve's grandmother.

Chelsi, Steve, Cindy and Brian Howe in January 1989.

In four and a half seasons with the Dodgers, I developed strong views on which reporters were honest and objective, and which were opinionated, consistently negative and ignorant.

Among the good guys, Jim Hill of Channel 2 was a former football player who understood athletes and treated us fairly. So did Tommy Hawkins, a radio sportscaster who had played with the Lakers in the NBA. Among the beat writers, Ken Gurnick of the *Herald-Examiner* and Gordon Verrell of the *Long Beach Press-Telegram* did an excellent, objective job. Jim Murray of the *Los Angeles Times* isn't considered the dean of sports columnists for nothing; he was fair and knowledgeable. The guys who wrote for *Dodger Blue*, the Dodgers' own publication, never offended me, but that's not surprising.

Most of the rest of the writers and reporters wrote garbage or were gutless back-stabbers who wouldn't face you after they ripped you in print. Some of them had the gall to trash the team, then show up in the clubhouse after a win and eat Tommy Lasorda's food and drink his beer.

Some of the fools never let me forget I had a cocaine problem. From the day they first heard about it, until I left L.A. in 1985, they hounded me and strained to find signs that I was back on the stuff. The pressure they created was unbearable. But I fell down often enough to give them reason to believe they were on the right track.

During spring training in 1983, they demanded details of my addiction and treatment. I avoided them for a couple of weeks, but I realized they wouldn't go away, so I called a press conference on March 4 to end the inquisition. No one from the Dodgers pushed me to do it. Kenny Landreaux, our center fielder, had also undergone drug rehabilitation that winter, and he refused to tell the press about it.

I sat at a card table in the press room, facing dozens of reporters. I rambled on for what seemed like hours about my addiction, family history and treatment, and I answered a lot of questions. I don't know if I made any sense. I was more nervous than I'd ever been before. Conflicting thoughts and emotions were fighting for control of my head. Throughout the session, I battled to maintain my composure. I had never before sat in front of a group of strangers and discussed the most intimate and embarrassing details of my life—not even in group sessions at The Meadows, where I'd never completely opened up. It was one of the hardest things I've ever done.

Although I didn't plan it that way, the press conference turned out to be another in a series of cons to divert attention from my drug problem. As I described my treatment at The Meadows and how it had helped me turn away from coke, I was thinking: I can't wait to get back to the condo and catch a blast. I hate to admit it, but it didn't bother me to deceive the fans and the press. I was just another addict hiding behind a carefully constructed wall of half-truths.

Maybe no one saw the lies because the truth, to the extent I revealed it, was so juicy. The press was particularly attentive when I told them how I'd gotten high within the hallowed walls of Dodger Stadium. No ballplayer had ever told stories like that.

I was especially paranoid about getting high in the stadium, with all the security cops and Dodger employees around, but the extra element of risk actually made it more exciting. If I'd been caught catching a blast in the stadium parking lot or on the team bus, two locations where I regularly lifted off, the consequences would have been equally severe. Still, I felt safer outside the stadium, where Dodger blue seemed to be less of a threat. In the back of the bus, I was surrounded by teammates who I knew wouldn't give me away, and in the parking lot I could see people coming. I had to be more careful in the stadium.

Doing it in the clubhouse was too much of a risk, even for me. But there are tunnels leading from the locker room to parking lots where I left my car, and sometimes I had a bump in a tunnel. I got caught a few times, but only by teammates. Some of them were in the tunnels on days they weren't playing, sneaking women down from the stands. When they nabbed me, I had to pay the penalty: "All right, Howzer, give me some of that stuff."

I didn't pitch when I was high because I feared the drug might disrupt my control, which was how I made my living. That doesn't mean I never pitched under the influence. Quite a few times I didn't give myself enough recovery time from an all-night binge, and I was still on my way down when I was called in to pitch. It was a bad feeling.

I was a quick worker in those games. I wanted to get it over and get out of there so I could go to sleep or, better yet, start the cycle over with another binge. Even though I had to ice my arm, exercise, shower and dress after I pitched, I was still one of the first guys out of the clubhouse when I was coming off a binge.

If pitching on the way down ever hurt my performance, I don't remember it. Somehow, I pitched through it. Even when my addiction was at its worst, I rarely got ripped.

When the commissioner's office heard what I'd told the press at Dodgertown, they sent their in-house investigator, Harry Gibbs, scurrying down to Florida to talk to me. Gibbs met the team in West Palm Beach, where we were playing an exhibition game.

Lasorda came into the clubhouse, took me aside and said, "Let me introduce you to somebody. This is Harry Gibbs. Harry'd just like to chat with you a little bit." Gibbs and I went into a nearby room and closed the door.

Gibbs's idea of a chat was more like a Nazi interrogation. "Who'd you get the stuff from?" he demanded. "Who'd you buy from? Who'd you do it with? Which other players use it?"

I said something like, "This is my problem, and I went in and took care of it on my own."

Gibbs replied, "If you won't tell me, we're going to make it very difficult for you. We're going to be watching you." They did, and they were. Our meeting was the beginning of my intimate relationship with the commissioner's office. Unfortunately, I would have the pleasure of dealing with Harry again.

I was so intimidated by Gibbs that I began snorting with renewed enthusiasm. By Cindy's estimate, I was loaded 90 percent of spring training that year, and I stayed out about six out of every seven nights. When I did get home, I was late.

I have to rely on Cindy's memory for a lot of details. Most of 1983 is kind of hazy to me. Her memory is probably reliable because I made that spring unforgettably miserable for her. Cindy was seven months pregnant, and I was staying out all night snorting coke. I was also telling her I didn't think I wanted to be married anymore.

My paranoia reached new dimensions during that period, mostly because my addiction and treatment were public and the press was on me. There was also a drug dealer in Florida to whom I owed money, and he hadn't forgotten about me. I spent most of the spring riding around with a gun, just in case.

That spring the Players Association gave us a dues refund. Mine totaled $2,500, but Cindy never knew refunds had been passed out until she heard about it from another player's wife. By then the money was gone, spent on coke. Cindy and I got into a nasty argument when she found out.

I didn't get to keep the fruits of my dues refund for long. We were out riding in the car one day when Cindy found a baggie full of coke under the seat. The baggie held half an ounce, about $850 worth, and it was the real good stuff. "Oh, gosh," Cindy said, "look at this!"

I was dying inside. I was afraid to admit that the stuff was mine. Cindy had turned me in once to Tony Attanasio and the Dodgers, and I thought she might do it again. "I don't know where that came from," I said. "It must belong to the guy I let in my car last night."

Cindy called my bluff. "Well, pull into this gas station up here, and I'll go dump it in the toilet," she said. I was sick about it for a week.

10

Grasping at Straws

We thought he was in good hands. I took it that when he got through with the camp over in Arizona, the rehabilitation center, he would be cured, because we had such good fortune with Bob Welch. Bob Welch went over there, and boom, he was rehabilitated and everything was fine.

Then I learned that the biggest thing is after they get through the rehabilitation center. If there's anything that I consider important looking back, it's why we were not advised that they have relapses. I thought these fellows graduated like they do in colleges, and I was under the assumption that everything was all right. But apparently everything wasn't all right. They do have relapses. And I know that there are people who probably hound them and try to sell them the stuff that they used to get free.

> —Al Campanis
> Former Vice President and
>   Director of Player Personnel
> Los Angeles Dodgers
> October 1986

As the 1983 baseball season loomed, my addiction began reaching out with increasing frequency to claim its second victim: Cindy.

She was closest to me, the only person who saw me with any regularity when I was away from the relatively stable environment of the ballpark. It was never in doubt that the fallout would settle on her and our marriage would deteriorate.

Cindy was so much like Mom that it makes me believe that men tend to marry women like their mothers. Both are controllers who tried, at different times and with no success, to direct every facet of my life in order to make me the kind of person they thought I should be. Cindy admits it and now says that only people who don't believe in themselves try to control others. She didn't recognize that in 1983.

Our marriage hadn't been a model of mutual support and fulfillment. We didn't communicate and we led largely separate lives. She went to school and had her own set of friends. I played ball, hung around with my friends and spent a lot of time with my mistress, cocaine. Until I became obsessed with coke, I expressed some interest in what Cindy was up to and how her life was going, but by 1982 it never crossed my mind to ask.

Before she got pregnant, Cindy went to most Dodger home games. We spent time together in the car on the way to the ballpark and back. We ate dinner, and then we went separate ways. Cindy headed for bed; sometimes I followed, but usually I couldn't relax. I'd sit up much of the night watching TV, shooting pool and snorting coke. For most of my life, I've been in a big hurry to go nowhere.

Even when Cindy went on Dodger road trips, we scarcely saw each other. During the day, she wanted to shop and see the sights. I wanted to sleep so I'd have the energy to perform, and a tour bus trip around a city in the heat of midday wasn't my idea of a good time.

I could have postponed my gratification to do what Cindy wanted, but I was too immature to understand how much it would have helped my marriage. I was finding out that you have to work to make a marriage succeed. I already had a job, and I'd never liked working overtime. It was one of my many personality defects.

As my cocaine indulgence grew into addiction, Cindy began delivering a message that was familiar to me, attacking my self-worth, a very small target. "You're no good," she said. "You're hurting me and you're hurting our marriage. You're throwing it all away, everything we've got."

She threw in words like "never" and "always" to drive home her point, as in "You're never going to get it right," and "You're always late," and "You never say how good I look." "Never" and "always" don't recognize positive exceptions and don't hold much hope for improvement. I reacted with hostility.

I didn't want to deal with what Cindy was saying, even though every passing day was proving her right. Such heavy discussions interfered with getting high, so I avoided them until she cornered me. Then I admitted that I had a problem, but I told her it was her fault because she wouldn't leave me alone. It was like I was saying, "If you'll just leave me alone and let me kill myself, I'll be fine."

By the beginning of spring training, Cindy wasn't in a position to exercise much control. She was entering her seventh month of pregnancy, couldn't join me on road trips and couldn't party with me. Her attempts to control my coke use by snorting with me were ancient history. Now she took a strong antidrug stand, but she was powerless to stop me.

Cindy was so firm in her opposition that I couldn't tell her I was up to my old tricks. She was obviously frightened at the possibility that her husband, the father of her soon-to-be-born child, was out of control again. I did what I could to keep the truth from her, even though I was taking full advantage of her pregnancy. I wanted Cindy to think I wasn't the hopeless, coke-driven derelict that her instincts told her I was.

My main weapon of deception was the con, which I raised to the level of an art form during more than four years of trying to conceal constant cocaine abuse. A con is a kind of lie—it is sophisticated play-acting designed to make things appear to be what they aren't. Some of the cons were successful; others were so transparent that they failed miserably. All of the cons had a common theme—they were schemes I thought up so I could snort coke with as little interference as possible.

Here's an example of how I used a con on Cindy: Not long after I left The Meadows, my parents visited us in Florida. When I'd discussed my coke problem with Cindy, I'd often blamed my Dad, and I knew Cindy believed me because she had agreed that Dad must have set a terrible example. Blaming Dad was a con I had used to set up future cons.

Dad and I went to a bar for a few drinks. After a couple of hours, I left old Pudge at the bar, telling him I'd be back in a few minutes. I was gone for well over an hour, and when I came back I was blown away. Pudge was pretty hot about it.

When we got home much later than expected, Cindy was on my case right away. "Dad didn't want to leave the bar," I told her. "I tried to get him to leave, but he wouldn't."

Then I went over to a desk, pulled out some Alcoholics Anonymous materials I'd been given at The Meadows, and pretended to read them carefully. Cindy smiled with approval and sat with me, and we discussed some of the things in the pamphlets. I used the pamphlets and Dad's old drinking habits to deflect Cindy's attention from where I'd been and what I'd been doing. The con worked.

It may be hard to believe that Cindy didn't know I was snorting my brains out almost every night. I'm not sure I believe it myself. But Cindy says she was told that sometimes an addict's behavior doesn't change right away when he sobers up, so she thought I might be staying out nights because I wasn't coping well with sobriety. We were also going through a period when, according to Cindy, she couldn't always tell I was high. But when the cons worked in early 1983, it was mostly because she wanted them to.

My cocaine abuse eventually became so obvious that the cons lost effectiveness as a cover. Throughout the first half of 1983, I resorted to power plays to keep Cindy from exposing my relapse to the Dodgers. During spring training and through the first month of the regular season, when I sensed that Cindy's gullibility and tolerance were exhausted, I'd tell her, "I don't know if I want to be married anymore."

"This is a nice time to be telling me, when I'm seven months pregnant," Cindy would answer, and floods of tears and harsh words followed. When it was over, she backed off for as long as a couple of weeks. By making her feel she was losing me, I revived her protective impulses and shut her up.

I took that whole riff a big step further in late April, a few days before Cindy's friends threw a baby shower for her. I was doing some deep thinking as we rode home in near silence from a home game. The pressure Cindy had been applying was making it impossible for me to use coke without guilt, and difficult for me to use at all. If I was going to keep getting high, I couldn't do it around Cindy.

I also wondered whether my relationship with Cindy might in some way be contributing to my addiction. Had she set off a sickness inside me that drove me to snort? Perhaps I was using the drug to escape from the world she was trying so hard to mold for me. The only way I could find out for sure was by taking her out of my life for a while. My thinking was irrational. Not much that I did in 1983 off the mound was rational or logical.

Without warning, as we stepped out of the car at home, I told her, "I have to go."

"What?" asked Cindy. "Where are you going?"

"I'm leaving. I just can't handle this anymore. I have to go." I went to our bedroom, threw a few clothes into a bag and walked out the door, leaving Cindy crying hysterically in the living room.

I reached bottom at that moment. When you leave your wife, who's in her ninth month of pregnancy, so you can pursue a more important interest in getting high without hassles, you've got nowhere to go but up.

But right then I had nowhere to go at all, so I drove around and finally booked in at the Westlake Inn for the night. The next day I found a friend who let me crash at his place.

Then I went to see Cindy. I told her I didn't want a divorce, I still wanted to see her, and I wanted to support the baby completely. But I also said I didn't want to have to be where she wanted me, when she wanted me there, because I couldn't meet those expectations.

Neither of us told any of our friends about the separation. I was too ashamed to tell anyone. Publicly, we played the roles of happy, expectant spouses. On the day of the baby shower, I entertained the guys at our house while the women gathered at a neighbor's home across the street. At the end of the shower, I walked over and gave Cindy a big kiss and flowers.

While my personal life was at its most chaotic, my pitching was at its best. The only explanation I can offer for that phenomenon is that baseball was my island of refuge. On the mound I was able to shut everything else out and perform like a machine. I forgot about drugs, rehab programs, jeering fans and prying reporters. I saw only a catcher, a hitter and a plate.

With the exception of Steve Sax and his bizarre inability to make 65-foot throws from second to first, our whole team, especially our bullpen, was hot at the beginning of the year. I had two saves and a win in my first three appearances, all against Houston, by April 12. Through April, I pitched 11 and two-thirds innings, allowed one unearned run, permitted only one inherited baserunner to score and had four saves.

May was more of the same. On May 17 I lost to Montreal, but it was on an unearned run that Niedenfuer walked in after I'd left in the 15th inning. By the end of the month, I'd pitched 22 and a third innings without allowing an earned run. I had seven saves and had walked only five, a couple of those intentionally. Control, which was so noticeably absent from the rest of my life, remained one of my greatest attributes as a pitcher.

Still, the Dodgers were watching me closely. They had good reason to, but they took the evil-eye routine to extremes, feeding my paranoia.

Trainer Bill Buhler, the Federal Buhler of Investigation himself, was so offended by my addiction that he wouldn't talk to me, but he studied me so closely when he looked at me that I was sure that he, like Cindy, was checking my nostrils for signs of abuse. I don't know what he expected to find up there. Close examination wouldn't have revealed more than a few boulders of compacted powder in my nostrils and sinuses.

When Buhler spoke to me at all, it was to get on my case about smoking cigarettes. I know smoking is a disgusting habit, and I've tried to quit lots of times. I'm smoking a pack or less a day now, and that may be the best I can do. Athletes don't want it known, but a lot of them smoke. Buhler was down on all the Dodger smokers.

Al Campanis, then the Dodgers' director of player development and in effect the general manager, also reminded me now and then that I would always be a suspect in his eyes. Al would point a finger at me and say, "I'm gonna be watching you."

I thought Al was out to get me. He's a former teacher with old-school values and a spare-the-rod-and-spoil-the-child attitude, so I didn't expect him to respond to my problem with compassion and understanding. Instead, he got his message across with threats of surveillance and punishment.

His threats weren't idle. During the 1983 season, I noticed I was being followed. Sometimes the surveillance was conducted by police who used Catalinas and other inconspicuous American cars. Private investigators also tailed me in a variety of vehicles. If they were trying to conceal their activities, they did a poor job of it.

One night, on Sunset Boulevard, I got out of my car and threw a brick through the windshield of a car that had been on my butt for several miles. I defied the driver to report me to the police, but he ignored me and drove off.

At other times—especially when I was on my way to score some coke from my dealer friend, Alex—I avoided confronting the investigators. I had my Porsche then and outran the turkeys.

Later, after Alex got busted, I found out that the Malibu Sheriff's Department had been following me at the request of the Dodgers. One of their reports said, "We undertook surveillance of Mr. Steve Howe, but he lost us at speeds in excess of 100 miles per hour."

All the unwanted attention finally got to me. Within a couple of weeks after I left Cindy, I really began to worry that coke was going to get me in serious trouble with the Dodgers. I cut way back on my use, almost to the point of not using at all. This would have been a great victory, except that I temporarily replaced cocaine with alcohol.

I had become a basket case, a bundle of nerves that was primed to explode at any time. I needed something mood-altering that would make me feel better and wouldn't cause me trouble with the authorities. Alcohol was legal, and the Dodgers might even be relieved if they caught me drinking. I drank enough to approximate the calming effect coke had on me.

The temptation of cocaine was always there. It ambushed me in mid-May, after Cindy and I had gotten back together, as her due date approached. My brother Chris was visiting us in L.A. Family visits were always a convenient excuse for a party.

We were playing a series in San Diego. The team let me commute from my house to Jack Murphy Stadium in San Diego—a drive of about two hours—because of Cindy's condition. I had been snorting the night before and the morning of one of the games. Chris and I took off for the ballpark, and I took some more blasts as I drove. The Dodgers had to play that day without me. I couldn't show up wasted, so Chris and I pulled off the interstate north of San Diego and spent the night in a motel.

Someone from the Dodgers called Cindy and wanted to know where I was. Cindy was through telling lies for me. She said, "I thought he was in San Diego with you." Uh oh.

The next day I had to face the music. Perranoski and Campanis were waiting for me, and Al was livid. "You think this ballclub revolves around you?" Al steamed. "Well it doesn't. I'll trade your ass! If you screw up again, I'll trade your ass!"

The hot seat I'd been sitting on since January was turned up to about 12,000 degrees. It was hot enough to keep my addiction in check for about a week.

After the San Diego series, the Dodgers left on a road trip to Montreal, New York and Philadelphia. Cindy was about ready to deliver, and I'd promised her I'd be there. After we got to Montreal, she called and said she was beginning labor. I headed home and called her from Las Vegas on the way. Sorry, false alarm. I rejoined the team immediately in New York.

I wasn't there long. Early on the morning of May 22, the call came again. I woke Tommy and got his approval to leave, then went straight to the airport. I got to the hospital in L.A. by late morning. Cindy was still working on it. I cheered her on until late that night, when Chelsi was born.

I went home mentally and physically exhausted, and more than a little mixed up. I was overjoyed that I had a daughter, but I felt distressed and guilty about my marriage. I had a lot of phone calls to make, so I decided it wouldn't hurt to snort a few lines to keep me awake for a while. A few lines turned into many lines, and a while became all night.

By 3:00 a.m. I was fried, and it seemed like a great idea to call Peter O'Malley with the news. He must have been annoyed, but, as always, Peter was a gentleman. When I told him, all he said was, "That's great, Steve. Glad you called. Is Cindy OK?"

Maybe I should have called Peter three hours earlier, before I got started with the coke, to tell him how bad I felt and what I wanted to do about it. He might have talked me out of it or sent someone over to settle me down. But I never phoned the bullpen, so no one came in for the save.

I was scheduled to see Cindy and Chelsi at the hospital on the morning of the 23rd. Then I would jump into a waiting limo bound for the airport and fly to Philly in time for that night's game. Cindy had set the whole thing up from her hospital bed and had even bought my plane tickets. I wasn't very cooperative, though. I fell asleep only a couple of hours before I was supposed to see Cindy at the hospital.

When I didn't appear on time, Cindy called one of our neighbors, who came over to check on me. She found me passed out in the bedroom. When she woke me, I made her take me to the airport right away. But as soon as we got off the freeway, I freaked. I was afraid that if I got on that flight, I'd still look wired six hours later when I rejoined the team. I made her take me home again.

Meanwhile, Campanis was calling all over L.A., trying to find out when he could have me in uniform again. He even called Cindy at the hospital before finally reaching me, minutes after I got back from the airport. With Al's pointed words of encouragement, I hustled back to the airport and flew to Philly, getting there in time to warm up at the end of the game.

The sportswriters were surprised to see me in the locker room. "What are you doing here?" asked one. "You look like dogmeat."

"Campanis told me to be here," I said.

When the writer asked Al about it, Al said, "I told him to stay home." For once, the reporters were nice to me. They toned down my unprintable, insulting reply after I'd heard what Al said, but Al got the message. I was back in the doghouse. I was about to get in a lot farther.

We returned to L.A. on Thursday, May 26, to kick off a home stand with a series against the Giants. I brought Cindy and Chelsi home from the hospital that day, then left and stayed out until 3:00 a.m. Friday. I missed my appointment Friday morning with Dr. Robert Woods, the team physician, for a glucose tolerance test, a diabetes screen I'd requested because Dad had tested positive. I didn't pitch on Friday night, and on the way home I stopped at the Westlake Inn for a beer.

I had never met the guy sitting next to me at the bar, but he recognized me and started telling me how great a pitcher he thought I was. It made me feel better than I'd felt all week. A celebration was in order. "I can do a little bit of the good stuff," I told myself. "I'll even give him some."

I had a baggie in the car and we took it over to his house. We sat up all night. I ignored the warning signals that were flashing in my head. The messages said: Day game tomorrow! No recovery time!

When it was time to leave for the stadium on Saturday morning, I hadn't slept at all, and I looked and felt like a derelict. No way could I walk into the clubhouse and nonchalantly suit up when I was still ripped. As I neared the stadium, I began driving around in circles, cruising through neighborhoods I'd never been in, just to kill time. After a couple of hours of aimless touring, the car overheated and broke down, right in the middle of the barrio.

It was more than an hour after I should have arrived at the clubhouse. It was so hot I couldn't sit in the car. Although I couldn't have been far from the ballpark, the neighborhood was unfamiliar and threatening. I wondered whether I'd have to fight my way out of there, and whether my car would be trashed if I tried to reach the stadium on foot. I found a phone booth and called Lasorda. "Tommy, I'm on my way, but I'm going to be a little late," I told him.

"Where are you, Howzer?"

"Don't worry. I'm on my way."

I called Cindy. Lasorda had already called her to see if she knew where I was. "Why don't you call him and tell him where you are?" Cindy suggested. "He'll send someone to pick you up."

I called Tommy and told him what street I was on, and he said he'd send Bob Smith, the team's director of security, to get me. Bob never found me, because in my condition I really didn't want to be found.

After another hour or so, I called Cindy again and asked her to come get me. She was still weak from childbirth and shouldn't have been driving, and the only car available to her was my high-performance Porsche, but as usual Cindy was there when I needed her.

This time, though, Cindy wasn't buying my standard denials and excuses. "The man I married wouldn't have stayed out the second night after his baby was brought home from the hospital," she said. "I don't know who you are right now, but it isn't you."

"Well, I'm using, just a little," I half admitted.

Cindy told me she'd learned from Tony Attanasio that the Dodgers suspected I was getting high and were ready to release me. "You're out of control," she said, "and if you don't go back into treatment, you're canned, you've had it."

When we got home, I called Tony, who'd already spoken to the Dodgers about possible treatment for me. "I blew it, man," I said. "I need to go back in."

"I know, kid," Tony said softly. "We'll get you some help."

The Meadows obviously wasn't the answer. The next day, Ron Perranoski drove me down to CareUnit, a rehabilitation facility in nearby Orange County.

I learned a lot about myself and my disease at CareUnit, where the program was less oppressive and more cocaine-oriented than the boot camp for lushes at The Meadows. One thing I didn't learn at CareUnit was how to get off coke and stay off.

At CareUnit I was allowed to wear regular clothes and to talk to people right away. The Dodgers sent a scout to catch me, so I worked out almost daily and kept my arm in shape. Cindy and Chelsi spent a lot of time camped out at the home of Burt and Ginger Hooton, who lived nearby, so Ginger could watch Chelsi while Cindy came to visit me. The therapy sessions were more open and useful, probably because I was becoming less afraid of understanding and expressing my emotions.

I hadn't been very concerned about getting in touch with my emotions while I was growing up in Clarkston. The inhabitants of blue-collar, suburban Detroit were tough and stoical, and only women and nerds spent a lot of time worrying and talking about "feelings." It was acceptable to actively express anger, but it showed weakness to display hurt and fear, so I learned to suppress rather than deal with those emotions.

The CareUnit therapy sessions, administered by Dr. Michael Stone, took me back to high school, when I'd first used booze and drugs to suppress the hurt caused by my girlfriend's infidelity. The counselors got me to admit the sadness and hurt I'd experienced on that and other occasions, and to describe how I'd felt when I'd used chemicals to relieve my emotional discomfort. I began to see that chemicals don't eliminate negative emotions, but offer only temporary relief. When you come down, the pain is still there.

Using substances to suppress emotions stunts the addict's development as a person. I was extremely immature at that stage because I'd never learned to handle problems. It was so much easier to get blasted and wipe the rest of the world out of my picture. When an addict kicks his habit and reenters the real world, his emotional development resumes.

I also learned that, regardless of why I'd used coke, I had to reorder my priorities if I was going to leave my habit behind. For nearly two years, the order of my priorities had been coke, career and family. That's no way to live, and it only spreads the suffering. In addition to accepting his helplessness against drugs and alcohol, an addict has to believe that he can handle life without drugs, and he must choose sobriety as his top priority.

Although I was more receptive and cooperative this time around, there remained one aspect of my treatment that I couldn't handle at all. That was family week, when most of my family flew in from Detroit to join in therapy sessions. At The Meadows I was hurt because the family didn't seem to care enough to help. Now that they'd come to the rescue, I couldn't face them.

I was still carrying around a lot of excess psychological baggage relating to my parents—some lingering resentment over the consequences of Dad's drinking and issues I'd never resolved with my mother. My counselors at CareUnit told me that I had to deal with those family matters if I wanted to clear my head and get on with a more constructive life. I agreed, but I just couldn't sit there and confront Mom and Dad. I knew they'd think I was placing all the blame on them (and I was). I couldn't hurt them that much. I told the counselors I wouldn't do it.

The counselors and Dr. Stone asked Cindy to carry the ball. She was the only one, other than me, who could tell my family what I was thinking. She wanted so much to help me that she agreed to do it, even though she must have known it would permanently damage her relationship with the family.

The confrontation was even uglier than I'd anticipated, and it was my fault. While I'd been telling Cindy how badly my parents had screwed me up as a kid, I'd also been telling Mom and Dad that Cindy was a controlling bitch who was making my life miserable. It's a classic symptom of addiction: An addict pins his problem on everyone but himself.

During family week at CareUnit, Cindy and my family blamed each other for my sickness. They battled during counseling with Dr. Joseph Pursch, the director of CareUnit, and again at a group therapy session at which other substance abusers and their families were present. Accusations and harsh words flew from both sides, while I sat and said little. More harm was done than good. When things got hot in the group session, my brother Jeff stood up slowly, glared down at little Cindy and said, "I've had about enough. I'm not going to sit here anymore and listen to you run my family down." Then he stomped out.

Cindy's parents were also there, but they wisely stayed out of the crossfire. At the suggestion of the counselors, Cindy and I went out to dinner with my parents. We didn't have a good time. The tension was so overwhelming that I could barely eat, and, when it was over, I threw up in the parking lot.

At first I thought Dr. Pursch was a major part of the problem, but then I thought everybody was a part of my problem. The man made a great first impression because he was charismatic and knowledgeable. He also said many negative things about The Meadows.

But by the time I left CareUnit, I was sure that Dr. Pursch wanted to establish his reputation as well as help me recover. I was outside his office one day, waiting for my session with him. I heard him talking to someone on the phone, discussing the possibility of becoming Major League Baseball's substance abuse guru if he could keep me in line. From that point on, in my anger and denial, I was subconsciously going to show Dr. Pursch how far he was going to get with me and Major League Baseball.

Everyone involved wanted me to get out of rehab and back to the mound as soon as possible. The Dodgers were in a pennant race and needed me. I wanted to pitch, not sit for hours before groups of fellow addicts and discuss my innermost feelings. I didn't want to face my disease, so naturally I didn't want to talk about it with other addicts. I wanted to do what I did best: play baseball.

Pursch also worked overtime to turn me against Cindy. When he first interviewed me, I made the mistake of repeating some of the negative things I'd said to my parents about Cindy. Pursch grabbed ahold of that theme and wouldn't let it die. He told me that Cindy and I were two sick people who fed off each other and would be better off apart. "I think you and Cindy should separate," he said to me more than once.

Cindy says Pursch gave her the same advice and told her I'd never be able to take care of her. Cindy says she thinks Pursch wanted her out of the way so he could control me and work for my recovery without interference.

Again, God asserted his control of my life. I was sick and I blamed Cindy for many of my problems, but I knew in my heart that I wanted to spend the rest of my life with her, however long that was to be.

We put together a little motorcade to the stadium for my triumphant return and press conference on June 24. Tony Attanasio and Pursch led the way in their matching Mercedes, and Cindy, Chelsi and I followed with Larry, my aftercare sponsor, a recovering addict I'd met at CareUnit.

Larry was a great guy and a baseball fan, and he was excited about being part of my recovery. He caused a sensation around the clubhouse because he didn't quite fit the Dodgers' clean, conservative, button-down image. He was six-foot-three, about 270 pounds, bearded, with one earring and otherwise short hair that ended in a tail.

I was much more relaxed for this press conference than I'd been for the March interrogation in Florida. I was becoming accustomed to my role as the addict returning from his latest rehab. Thanks to Pursch's coaching, I had all the right answers. Unfortunately, I still wasn't willing to live by them.

I was anxious about how Dodger fans would react to my second fall from grace, but I shouldn't have worried. Dodger fans have high expectations, and the players are under a lot of pressure. But when it comes to sickness and personal adversity, the fans are loyal, understanding, remarkably generous and thoughtful. After Chelsi was born, fans sent us all kinds of presents for her, everything from handmade blankets and clothes to dolls and toys.

I've always understood that I wouldn't have had a career without the fans, and I've tried to treat them as I hoped they'd treat me. Every kid who comes to the ballpark with his glove hopes to catch a ball or get an autograph. When I was about ten, I was crushed when Mickey Lolich, one of my heroes, brushed me off when I asked for an autograph at Tiger Stadium. When I made it to the majors, I always took time to sign autographs, and I've never refused one to a kid.

The fans welcomed me heartily when I came back in late June. I felt relatively clearheaded, physically strong and ready to pitch. But I was still on the disabled list, and I had a new problem: The Dodgers and the commissioner's office were thinking of punishing me for my relapse.

Their investigation began with the second visit in less than four months from Harry Gibbs, the henchman for Commissioner Bowie Kuhn. Harry's writers hadn't come up with any new material. It was another round of, "Where'd you get the stuff? Who'd you buy it from? Who'd you do it with? Why'd you do it?"

Tony Attanasio and Roy Bell, my attorney at the time, represented me at the commissioner's "hearing." Bob Walker, the Dodgers' attorney, and a representative from the Players Association also participated. It was a hang-'em-high court, and not even Clint Eastwood could have saved me.

The commissioner's office had made up its mind to nail me for being a repeat offender. Tony and Roy argued that because they'd instituted drug policies and procedures after my first rehab, I couldn't qualify as a repeat offender under those policies. Most of the time I just sat there and doodled, like a little kid bored with the conversation at a party for adults.

We tried to negotiate a settlement with the Dodgers, but they wanted me to accept punishment and forget about filing a grievance under the terms of the collective bargaining agreement between the players and the owners. I wouldn't give up my right to a grievance, so there was no settlement.

On June 28 Commissioner Kuhn and the Dodgers decided to fine me $53,867, my pay for the month I'd been unavailable to the team. It was the largest player fine in baseball history. I was placed on three years' probation, and I had to submit to periodic medical examinations, including blood tests and urinalysis. Testing had been suggested by Dr. Pursch, who told the press that testing was a routine part of CareUnit's aftercare procedure. I was also supposed to attend Narcotics Anonymous meetings.

Reaction from the media was mixed, but I got a lot of support from *Sports Illustrated* and from Jim Murray of the *Los Angeles Times*.

Both said, in columns that appeared shortly after the fine was announced, that organized baseball should worry about rehabilitating players with drug problems and leave punishment to the legal authorities. Amen.

Sports Illustrated also spotted an inconsistency in the position of the baseball establishment. When I first admitted my coke problem and entered The Meadows in November 1982, the Dodgers and the commissioner's office treated my addiction as an illness or disability. The second time it happened, it was suddenly a career-threatening criminal offense, although there had been no change in the drug or the problem.

I was never warned that if I came forward again and asked for help, I'd be penalized. If I had known the new rules, I would have hidden my relapse as best I could. Since then, I'm sure other players, knowing what happened to me, have chosen to live with their habits rather than seek treatment. The price of recovery has become almost as great as the price of dependency.

If the pressure on me was great when the season started, it was enormous when I returned to the Dodgers' roster in late June. I knew that if I was ever late for a game or team function, I'd better be in the hospital or dead, because otherwise the Dodgers would assume I was snorting again. It was not the most favorable atmosphere in which to resume my career.

On June 29, in my first appearance in 43 days, I gave up a meaningless eighth-inning run to San Diego in a 13–2 loss. The run was scored as unearned at the time, but the next day the official scorer changed an error to a hit, so it turned out to be the first earned run I'd given up all season.

I gave up my second earned run the next night, and this time it cost us a game. Luis Salazar doubled with two out in the ninth to give San Diego a 7–6 win. I felt out of sync.

Tommy Lasorda wasn't shy about giving me chances to get my act together. On July 1 I pitched the bottom of the tenth in Houston to pick up a save. It wasn't pretty—the Astros got two hits. But at least I'd made a contribution. Three days later, Jose Cruz crushed a high fastball out of the Astrodome in the bottom of the eighth with no one on, and I had my third loss.

Back at Dodger Stadium, the support of the home crowd settled me down. In my first three home appearances since CareUnit, I gave up one hit and no runs in five innings and picked up two saves. On July 13, though, I lost to the Cardinals, setting up David Green's game-winning single with a wild pitch. My inconsistency was driving me crazy, and I was afraid Tommy would give my job as closer to someone who was more reliable. I was a disaster waiting to happen.

I didn't pitch the following night, and Dusty Baker and I went to TGI Friday's for a bite after the game. Dusty was one of my closest buddies on the team, and he was spending a lot of time with me then, probably to make sure I stayed out of trouble.

Everything was fine until Dusty left Friday's. Then I hit the bar for a quick beer, and I started talking to a former semipro hockey player who told me he owned a Toyota dealership. "Hey, man," he said after a while, "I got some really good stuff here." I was in one of those impulsive moods that used to hit me about every 45 seconds or so. He didn't have to ask twice.

Off we went to his house. The stuff was not only good, it was plentiful. We snorted all night, and it was late morning before I fell asleep on his floor.

When I woke up, the first clock I saw said 5:00 p.m. I should have been at the ballpark for our Friday night game by 4:15. My first thought was, Uh oh, I'm in deep stuff now. I started to drive to the stadium, but realized I was still too screwed up to meet Bill Buhler's prosecutorial stare, let alone pitch. I turned around and went home.

It was 6:30 when I got there, and Cindy was waiting, suspecting the worst and finding confirmation in the condition of my eyes. I couldn't tell her I'd been getting high. I was sure she'd turn me in again, and my career would be history. I was hoping she'd go along with a believable story, like a broken-down car, that I could tell the Dodgers to get off the hook. But before Cindy even asked for an explanation, she told me that Dodger Vice President Fred Claire had called looking for me, and she'd told him I hadn't been home the night before.

I had to make up a story on the spot, so I did the best I could under the circumstances. I told Cindy I'd been having an affair.

Cindy began asking a lot of questions. My answers weren't convincing. The woman's name, I told her, was Debbie Mansfield. The name rolled easily off my tongue because I knew a guy named Darrell Mansfield, a Christian rock singer. I said I didn't want to continue the affair, and I'd broken it off the night before, but I'd sat on the beach all night and most of Friday because I didn't know what to do with myself. Then I told her that Debbie and I had never slept together.

Hey, I never said the story was foolproof. But for a head full of cocaine, with no time to think, it wasn't bad.

"You're lying," was Cindy's analysis.

I called Fred Claire and told him I was on my way to the ballpark. Fred told me to come straight to his office. Cindy went with me, and we arrived at 8:00 p.m., about 20 minutes after the game had started. Cindy told me on the way down that she didn't want to hear the Debbie Mansfield story again. She left Fred's office before I could begin telling Fred and Al Campanis about my night on the beach.

Fred and Al didn't say much, but Al's face said, "You're full of it, kid." I felt trapped. The story was getting weaker by the minute. I thought the Dodgers would lock me up in a padded room if I stayed with it. On the other hand, if I admitted I was back on coke, the Dodgers might suspend or even release me. I hung tough with Debbie.

Tony Attanasio arrived, and he went in to meet with Fred and Al while I sat in another room with Cindy and my aftercare sponsor, Larry, who'd dropped by for the show. Finally, I confessed to Cindy and Larry. When Tony joined us, I told him too.

"They want you to take a urine test," Tony said. Fortunately, I was caught in the middle of a developing dispute between the Players Association and Major League Baseball. Partly because of the wonderful example I'd set, the commissioner's office was pushing for random urinalysis for all players. The Players Association was vigorously opposed.

On the advice of Tony and the union, I refused the test. The Players Association had already filed a grievance (which was later dropped) against the testing requirement of my probation conditions, so I didn't want to consent to a test.

Early Saturday morning, without the Dodgers' knowledge, I drove to CareUnit and for the first time peed into a plastic container, a procedure at which I would become an expert. The Dodgers had threatened to suspend me for refusing a test. But I had nothing to lose by taking a private test. Traces of cocaine will show up in your urine 48 hours after your last snort, and I'd had a taste about 24 hours before I provided a sample, so I figured a positive test was guaranteed. I told myself that my predicament was nobody's fault but mine, and I'd have to accept the consequences of a dirty test if the Dodgers found out. On the other hand, if the test came back negative, I'd run to the Dodgers with the results.

After another meeting Saturday morning, the Dodgers suspended me indefinitely. Twelve hours later, the test came back negative. I later learned that the lab technician hadn't tested the sample for cocaine. I wondered whether Dr. Pursch fixed the test to protect his interest in my recovery.

When the Dodgers saw the test result on Sunday, they reinstated me. My suspension lasted one day and cost me $1,889, not much more than I'd pay for an ounce of coke.

When I was at CareUnit for my test, Dr. Pursch wanted to know what had happened to me, so I dusted off Debbie Mansfield and tried again. Finally, I'd found someone who embraced the story with enthusiasm. Pursch had every reason to want to believe it. It fit his theory that Cindy and I were bad for each other and should split up, and it saved him from an embarrassing public admission that his CareUnit program had failed to cure my chemical dependency.

When the team left on a road trip after Sunday's game, Pursch called Cindy and invited her to visit CareUnit for counseling. Cindy was badly shaken, hurt and vulnerable. She kept telling me she thought she'd failed somehow. She agreed to go to CareUnit, but she was in for a surprise. Instead of therapy, Pursch repeated some old advice: "End your marriage."

Did I learn anything from my narrow escape from severe career damage? Sure. I learned that testing is unreliable, and that sometimes when you screw up you can get away with it. It was a dangerous lesson. Nothing had happened to change my priorities. I knew I'd get high again before long.

Tommy Lasorda didn't put me on ice for a few days to make sure I wasn't wacko. He threw me right back into the wars on our eastern swing, and I was ready. I got a win on July 19 in an 11-

inning game in Pittsburgh, and I followed that with another score-less outing. In my third appearance of the Pittsburgh series, I took the loss on two runs in the ninth.

The way we lost that one reflected a trend. The team had been in first place in the division on the first of July, but by the end of the month, we were five and a half games behind Atlanta. We were playing poor fundamental baseball.

It was on that road trip—through Pittsburgh, St. Louis, Chicago and on into San Francisco—that fans started to taunt me about my drug problem. I heard the insults when I was in the dugout, when I was warming up in the bullpen, even on the street. I didn't hear them when I was on the mound; my wall of concentration held firm. It was ironic that the abuse began in earnest on that trip, because I was behaving for a change.

Opposing players and coaches, many of whom understood my struggle from personal experience, rarely made cracks, even in jest. The exception was Frank Robinson, once a great player and more recently a manager, who proved in San Francisco on July 31 that class and decency had nothing to do with his approach to managing.

During my four seasons, Candlestick Park had never been a friendly place for the Dodgers. We won more than our share of games there, but the intensity of the rivalry brought out the ani-mals in the stands. With the possible exception of New Yorkers, the Candlestick fans are the most radical I've ever encountered.

A true Giant fan will use almost any object as a missile. In 1982 some loony tune made the near-fatal mistake of hitting Reggie Smith in the chest with a batting helmet on Helmet Day. We went into the stands after the guy. I got a grip on his shirt and tried to pull him back onto the field, where he'd have been fair game for a pounding, but the guy had a death grip on the railing. I think he lost two or three fingers and sued the Dodgers and the city of San Francisco.

In the Candlestick bullpen, we were pelted with fruit, beer bot-tles, smoke bombs and M-80s, before they installed a roof to give us a little protection. Manny Mota, one of our coaches, liked to stand around with us in the pen, but he stopped doing that in San Francisco after he got hit in the head with an orange. One night a guy dropped an M-80 over the railing into my lap and took off running into the stands. I winged it back at him, and it exploded just as it hit him in the back of the neck. What goes around, comes around—and fast.

Even the stadium ushers were targets of the fans. If the ushers got someone mad, you saw a flock of orange jackets hauling butt down the aisles toward the field, trying to avoid a barrage of bottles.

That was the friendly atmosphere in which we played a doubleheader on July 31, 1983. In the first game, Lasorda brought me in to pitch the ninth and protect a 2–1 lead. After my first pitch to Jeff Leonard, Robinson strolled out of the dugout and asked the home plate umpire, Lee Weyer, to check me for foreign substances that I might be using to doctor the ball. That's the first and last time I've ever been accused of loading up a baseball. Everyone in the league knew which guys did it, and I wasn't one of them. Frank was just trying to shake me up.

"Shit, Frank," I yelled at him, "I'm 25 years old. I don't need to cheat. Especially to beat your team."

"F— you," said Frank. As he walked back to the dugout, he turned to face me and put his fingers to his nose. In response, I stepped off the mound and licked my fingers with an exaggerated motion.

Robinson wasn't finished. When he got to the dugout, he yelled, "Hey, Howe!" When he was sure he had my attention, he snorted dramatically several times.

At that point, I was ready to take a piece out of Robinson. I began calling him every name I knew to get him out on the field, but he wouldn't leave the safety of the dugout.

To show Frank how much he'd shaken me, I struck out Leonard and jammed Darrell Evans so badly that all he could manage was a little grounder. I thought I heard Evans say something smartass as he trotted by. "You pizza-face sonofabitch!" I hollered. "If you got something to say, come back here." Darrell, who's really a pretty good guy, just kept going.

After I retired Joel Youngblood to end a perfect inning and record my 11th save, more words were exchanged and a brawl almost erupted on the field. Dusty Baker and Ron Perranoski were ready to kill and had to be restrained. I offered to fix Giants' first-base coach Don Buford's knees for him. The fans got into the act, and one marksman skulled Dave Anderson, our backup shortstop, with a grapefruit, dropping him to his knees. After some milling around, everyone retired to the clubhouses. We were so fired up that we lost the second game of the doubleheader.

———————

After a short home stand against Cincinnati and Atlanta, we returned the visits on a road trip that ended in mid-August. Larry went along, and my parents met us for a harmonious few days in Cincinnati. I'd been clean for nearly a month, but I was churning inside from the effects of fan abuse, Frank Robinson and my own urges. I didn't want to take the risk of getting high again, but I felt that if I didn't make a significant change in my life soon, I'd go nuts. As usual, I thought the solution was to tinker with my marriage.

About the time the team returned to L.A., I met a guy named Ricky through some friends. Ricky was single and didn't snort coke, but he was a serious drinker. We stayed out for a night getting drunk together, and a friendship was born. Ricky offered me a place to crash if I needed it. I took him up on it right away and walked out on Cindy again.

Cindy freaked, and who could blame her? I'd twisted her head in so many directions that it's a wonder she didn't snap. When I moved out, she called that well-known marriage counselor, Joe Pursch, for advice and encouragement. "Maybe that's Steve's way of telling you the marriage is over," Pursch told her. I drank heavily during the five weeks I stayed with Ricky. I knew the Dodgers wouldn't ask me to take a urine test for alcohol. I was drinking Bailey's Irish Cream, a gentleman's drink but not exactly a light snack. When I woke up the morning after a Bailey's session, I felt worse than I felt after a two-day coke binge.

My body seemed to be ignoring the abuse, because I began to pitch well. After giving up a two-run, ninth-inning homer to Bob Watson to cost us a game in Atlanta on August 13, I pitched well in seven of my next eight appearances through September 9 and earned five saves, for a season total of 18. By September 19, after two more good outings, my ERA, which never climbed as high as 2.00 all year, was back down to 1.44. The team was smoking too. We'd fallen six and a half games out in mid-August, but by September 9 we were back in front by three. We got there by beating the hell out of Atlanta in head-to-head competition.

We were in the middle of a pennant drive, an experience every ballplayer yearns for, but my thoughts were on everything but baseball. My urge to get high was growing stronger, and so was my guilt. I couldn't believe I'd left my wife and three-month-old daughter so that I could feed my disease. I was every bit as irresponsible and worthless as my mother had forecast.

I started snorting coke again in mid-September. Full obsession returned after only a taste. Within days I was back to a couple of grams a day. There was no one to stop me, and there was no one around to hide it from, except the Dodgers.

I got ripped the night of September 21 and went to bed in plenty of time to recover before our off-day flight to Atlanta for a crucial showdown series. But the freeways were jammed with rush-hour traffic. As I sat on the freeway in gridlock, I realized I was in serious trouble again. Our charter flight left without me, and I couldn't catch a commercial flight until 3:30 that afternoon.

It was late that night, eastern time, when the plane arrived. At the end of the jetway stood Bill Buhler and Billy DeLury, the Dodgers' traveling secretary and one of my best friends in the organization. Buhler was carrying a container for a urine sample. He wanted me to oblige him immediately.

We must have spent a couple of hours in the airport concourse, talking about options. I couldn't submit to a test; I knew the result would be positive. I called Roy Bell, my lawyer, and Peter Ciccarelli, Tony Attanasio's assistant, for advice. I finally refused the test and we went to the hotel. Buhler said we could discuss the test again in the morning.

As soon as I woke up, I got Roy Bell on the phone again and told him I wanted to come home. "I can't handle this pressure anymore," I said. "They're driving me crazy." True, I was a basket case, a set of loose wires, but most of all I wanted to avoid the test. Roy advised me to come home for treatment. Before Buhler came looking for me, I checked out of the hotel and flew back to L.A.

When Cindy and Chelsi met me at the airport, they saw someone they probably didn't recognize, someone who wasn't making sense. By late afternoon Friday, I was back at CareUnit. They took a urine sample, about 40 hours since I'd snorted, and it came back negative. I doubt that the test result convinced anyone that I was clean.

The Dodgers suspended me indefinitely, this time for leaving the team without permission in Atlanta. After a couple of days, the team began to make noises about wanting me back. They were wrapping up the division title and hoping I could pitch in the playoffs. I liked that idea, but Roy Bell and Dr. Michael Stone told me to forget it. I wasn't pitching again in 1983.

Before the Dodgers-Phillies playoff series began, Mike Schmidt of the Phils said he didn't think the Dodgers could win without me. Unfortunately, Schmidt was right, and the Dodgers were eliminated in four games. Even if my absence wasn't the cause of our defeat—and we'll never know—I'd let my teammates down again, this time when the stakes were highest.

11

Lost and Found

I couldn't walk away from the relationship. I wanted to. Believe me, I wanted to get involved with somebody else. I wanted some excuse to get me out of the emotional hell I was in. It was just pure hell for me. But I couldn't; I couldn't leave him. Don't ask me why, whether it was love or what, I don't know. But I couldn't leave him, so we decided to keep trying. One more time.

—Cindy Howe
September 1986

The doctors and counselors at CareUnit tried to figure out why their message wasn't getting through. After they'd interviewed me for hours and given me psychological tests, Pursch told Cindy I was suffering from a "narcissistic personality disorder." In other words, I was obsessed with serving my urges, often at the expense of everything else. Pursch told Cindy that if I was ever going to kick coke, I'd have to work very hard to change my approach to life, and Pursch didn't think I was capable of making that change yet. Cindy says she thought they were trying to tell her I wasn't going to recover.

Drs. Pursch and Stone recommended that when I finished treatment, I go into a halfway house rather than go home immediately. I wouldn't do it. I didn't want to be away from Cindy and Chelsi, and I suspected that the halfway house proposal was another one of Pursch's schemes to break up my marriage. And what if the press found out? The embarrassment would kill me. My image of a halfway house was a place for total degenerates who were unable to function in the real world, not for an accomplished professional.

I didn't care that a halfway house can provide a system of mutual support to help addicts stay clean. With my attitude, a halfway house probably wouldn't have worked. I still thought I knew better than anyone what was best for me. I thought all I needed was a magical prescription for abstinence.

I was at CareUnit for 28 days. At home, I found things hadn't been going well for Cindy. Aside from her predictable anxiety over the drug-clouded future of her own family, she'd had to fend off attacks from my family. Mom and Kathi had called and accused Cindy of hoarding my money, something Cindy says she didn't do until later. If she was stashing cash, she was doing a lousy job of it, because we were broke within three months after I left CareUnit.

Pursch recommended a counselor to Cindy, and Cindy convinced me we should go to counseling if we wanted to revive our marriage. We went to several sessions, but there were wounds that weren't going to heal easily. In a strange way, though, Cindy got us back on track.

Just before I walked out on Cindy in late April 1983, we hired a guy I'll call Tom to lay tiles in our kitchen. We often invited people who had done work for us to be our guest at a Dodgers game, so Cindy invited Tom.

Tom picked Cindy up and took her to the ballpark. On the way to the game, Tom told Cindy that he and his wife had divorced because of his wife's infidelity. Cindy told Tom that I'd left her.

Cindy was impressed that Tom was considerate enough to ask her out to dinner during my next road trip. It helped Cindy's self-esteem, which was low because I had been totally neglecting her. Cindy was only a few weeks from delivery and very round from her pregnancy.

According to Cindy, after Chelsi was born she didn't even talk to Tom until the Debbie Mansfield incident in July. Although Cindy didn't believe my story, she behaved as though it were true. When

I was on another road trip, she called Tom for advice on how to deal with a cheating spouse. They began to talk on the phone from time to time.

After I went into CareUnit in September, Cindy called me one Friday night and told me she was on her way to a meeting of a local chapter of an anonymous fellowship organization for families of chemically dependent people. Cindy's behavior patterns have always been predictable. When we hung up, I thought: Bullshit! Cindy's chapter doesn't meet Friday night.

When she visited me at CareUnit the next day, I asked her, "Where were you last night?"

"I went over to see Tom."

"What were you doing over there?"

"I wanted to see if I wanted him more than I wanted you."

I couldn't believe I was being compared to Tom, who, as far as I could tell, had nothing going for him. Still, I was amazed to find that I felt threatened and angry. In my twisted view, it was fine for me to walk out on Cindy, but I was taking care of her needs and paying her bills, so it was against the rules for her to go out with another man, especially one I'd hired to lay tiles in my kitchen.

I asked Cindy, "What'd you do when you went over there?"

"Oh, nothing, we just sat there with Chelsi and watched TV. Oh, and we smoked a joint."

Here's little holier-than-thou, Miss Antidrug Cindy, sneaking off to get stoned with the tile man after preaching to me about drugs. I was offended. Cindy really hadn't done anything terrible, although she wasn't setting a good example for me. She had smoked grass before on occasion, but I didn't want her getting high with another man.

If Cindy told me about her evening with Tom to make me jealous and improve our marriage, she succeeded. I found I didn't want to lose Cindy. We talked it out and decided to try to make things work. I moved back home after I was released from treatment.

———————

Unlike The Meadows, CareUnit prescribed an aftercare program that was supposed to reinforce the treatment I'd received. After both my visits to CareUnit, my aftercare program included regular attendance at meetings of Narcotics Anonymous or another mutual support group for addicts. When I left CareUnit the second time, I was ordered to attend 90 meetings in 90 days.

As usual, I didn't follow orders. I went to a few meetings, then stopped. I had better things to do. Another reason I quit was that I began using coke again soon after the end of treatment. I couldn't face my fellow addicts at meetings and lie to them about how well I was doing.

My new sponsor after CareUnit II was Clancy, also known as "The General." A recovering alcoholic, Clancy was one of the most successful people in L.A. in the field of outpatient care for the chemically dependent. He ran the Midnight Mission for skid-row types, was involved in numerous anonymous support groups and sponsored dozens of recovering addicts. His speeches on his own alcoholism, and on the disease in general, are both scary and inspiring.

Clancy ran tightly structured programs and expected total compliance with his orders. Every Saturday Clancy held a mandatory softball game for those in his care. Clancy let me know at our first meeting that the new guys shoveled the dogshit off the field before the softball game. It was beneath my dignity to shovel dogshit, so I never went to a game. I should have shown up and shoveled, to humble myself. It might have provided the attitude adjustment I needed.

Clancy learned my game quickly, and he knew how to deal with me. He'd seen so many addicts that he was familiar with all personality types and tricks of the trade. But just when Clancy began to get through to me, I shut him out. I still wasn't ready.

Ten days after I left CareUnit, there was a birthday party for Clancy. I was advised to be there. I strolled into my house a couple of hours before the party, still on the way down from a classic all-night blowout. Cindy worked frantically to get me dressed and ready.

Although the evening represented another failure for me, there was one thing I did right. For the first time in my life, at the age of 25, I tied my own necktie! You'd be surprised at the number of athletes who can't knot a tie. Only a couple of the Dodgers could do it, so everyone's ties were knotted before we left on a road trip, when ties and jackets were required. Those ties stayed knotted for the whole trip. When we wanted to take our ties off, we loosened the knots and slipped the ties over our heads.

As Cindy and I drove to Clancy's party, I knew it was no use trying to fool him. Clancy would take one look at me and know where my nose had been. At the restaurant, I went right up to him and told him what had happened.

Clancy understood and forgave me. Before his recovery began—he'd been sober for 20 years when I met him—he'd suffered from an alcohol dependency so great that it had driven him into the nuthouse more than once. Clancy had fallen down lots of times before he finally stood up and stayed up. "Sometimes you don't get it right at the beginning," he said to me.

A couple of weeks later, trouble found me again. After Care-Unit, the Dodgers ordered me to take periodic urine tests, administered by Dr. Forest Tennant, and I passed several. Late in November I met a guy named Steve, whom I'd heard of through my first major coke supplier in L.A. Steve had his own coke problem and always had some around. I began chipping with him, and in a matter of days the chipping turned into a string of full-fledged snortathons. I quit all my aftercare activities.

I was in control most of Thanksgiving week, and I had a clean, happy Thanksgiving with my family. I was surprised when I tested positive on the Friday after Thanksgiving. I guess my most recent blast-off hadn't passed out of my system.

I called Pursch, the source of helpful negative test results in the past, and told him, "There's no way that test should be positive."

"Well, why don't you come on down here and give me a test?" Pursch said. I did, early the following week, too soon after another party, and Pursch also came up with a positive. Both Tennant and Pursch tested me again a few days later—both positive.

The commissioner's office was paying close attention. Tennant sent his test results to Bowie Kuhn, who was pondering whether to punish me again for my September relapse. I'm sure the latest evidence of my continuing drug abuse made Kuhn's decision easy.

On Thursday morning, December 15, Fred Claire invited Cindy and me to his office. Fred said the Dodgers would do whatever had to be done to help me get off drugs. He suggested that I accept treatment from Tennant, and I agreed. Fred also told me that Commissioner Kuhn had suspended me for the entire 1984 season for the "integrity of the game" and for violating the terms of my probation.

Tony Attanasio and Roy Bell had warned me to expect some kind of disciplinary action, probably a suspension, but a year seemed like forever. At first I was stunned and sad. I hadn't been able to fool all the people all the time. My world of cons, lies, broken promises and emotional instability had finally collapsed, and I was going to pay for it. The more I thought about the suspension, though, the more my sadness turned to anger. Although the fault was mostly mine, I didn't think the penalty was fair.

On the day he announced my suspension, Kuhn also suspended three members of the 1983 Kansas City Royals—Willie Wilson, Jerry Martin and Willie Aikens. All three had been convicted of attempting to distribute cocaine and sentenced to three-month terms in a federal penitentiary. Kuhn suspended them for one year each, but their suspensions were reviewable in May of 1984. As it turned out, all three of the K.C. players were reinstated before the midway point of the 1984 season. Wilson is the only one still playing in the majors.

How could the commissioner justify penalizing me more severely than the K.C. guys? He couldn't. They were criminally convicted drug traffickers. I was an addict who had neither dealt drugs nor embarrassed my team and the game by being arrested, dragged before a court of law and sent to jail. If the commissioner was really concerned about the "integrity of the game," as he said so often, shouldn't he have come down harder on criminal traffickers than on a user? He seemed to be saying that the Kansas City guys had learned their lesson, but I needed to be taught one. He was going to teach me how to stay straight by taking away my living for a year.

I wanted to file a grievance contesting my suspension, but at about that time Tony Attanasio washed his hands of all my problems. That's when I met Jim Hawkins.

Jim is primarily a bankruptcy lawyer, and he'd helped a friend I'd met in my aftercare program. It was mid-December when I visited Jim's office. I liked him right away. He was a recovering alcoholic with long-term sobriety and he understood my problem. Jim said the chemically dependent should not be treated as criminals. He was on my side.

Once I was satisfied that Jim was the right lawyer to represent me, I fell asleep on the floor of his office while he was talking to me. I was so mentally and physically exhausted that I just checked out, something I've been able to do anywhere, anytime, in any position. I guess that gave Jim a pretty good idea how serious my problem was.

Within a couple of weeks, Jim filed for bankruptcy on behalf of Cindy and me. I'd spent tens of thousands of dollars on drugs, but that wasn't going to bankrupt me on a salary of $325,000 a year. What sent me over the financial edge was my taste for high living and expensive toys, especially high-performance cars like Porsches and Corvettes. Having an expensive sports car and snorting coke were part of the L.A. scene that I had joined. I lived to the limit my salary would allow, and then some. I had no sense of how to handle money, and I wouldn't listen to direction from my agents. I'd taken several loans from banks to finance my lifestyle. My suspension told the banks that I no longer had a guaranteed income, so they demanded payment on the notes they held. There was no way I could pay them.

Hawkins and the Players Association filed a grievance over my suspension. A hearing was set for late January, but it never took place. Neither the Dodgers nor the commissioner's office wanted a confrontation with the union over drug testing. Finally in May, the Dodgers called a meeting the night before another scheduled hearing. Fred Claire and Bob Walker, the Dodgers' attorney, were there with Jim Hawkins and me.

At the meeting, Claire and Walker told us that if I dropped my grievance and agreed to spend all of 1984 in rehabilitation without playing, the Dodgers would pay all my expenses—an action the commissioner had approved—and would petition the commissioner to officially reinstate me. Once the commissioner canceled my suspension, the Dodgers would begin to pay me full salary. Not a bad deal.

We didn't have many cards to play. Hawkins had told me that because I was in bankruptcy, any contract to which I was a party could be voided. I could have claimed that my contract with the Dodgers was no longer effective, making me a free agent. But we never seriously considered free agency. I didn't want to leave the Dodgers. I accepted the deal, and I was reinstated by midseason.

For several years after the Dodgers drafted me, I worshiped the organization. But beginning with the team's disclosure of my addiction and rehabilitation before my arbitration hearing in January 1983, a series of events proved to me that the Dodger image was not what I had thought it was.

Although the Dodgers carefully created the appearance that they were treating their people well, the organization never really appreciated what the players did for them. The case of Dusty Baker is a great example.

In February 1984 Dusty was in the early stages of a lucrative long-term contract with the Dodgers. He'd spent eight productive seasons in Dodger blue and was only 34 years old. The team tried to waive him, and he became a free agent. Dusty's crime? He had "too much influence" on younger players.

Dusty was smart and he was a natural leader. Most teams place a lot of value on veterans who take younger players under their wing and help them adjust to the majors. Dusty did that for me in 1980 and became one of my best friends on the team. Dusty was also an independent thinker who didn't automatically swallow every propaganda pill the Dodgers fed him. Dusty's independence was probably his downfall. He told young players the facts of life in the majors, things that management probably didn't want them to hear. He told players about contracts and bargaining, and directed them to his brother, an investment counselor, for financial guidance. The Dodgers seemed uncomfortable about that.

Perhaps coincidentally, but probably not, Baker was one of three exiled Dodgers who were my closest friends on the team. The Dodgers traded Bobby Castillo to Minnesota in January 1982, although Castillo returned to the team in 1985. In August 1983 they traded Dave Stewart to Texas for Rick Honeycutt. In 1987 Stewart blossomed as one of the best starters in the American League.

Maybe the Dodgers thought that by getting rid of Stewart and Baker, they could solve my drug problem. After all, those were the guys I was hanging around with, and I was doing drugs, so they must have been influencing me, right? Wrong. Nobody on the Dodgers pressured me to do drugs. The decision and responsibility were mine. If the Dodgers thought the causes of my problem were external, they found out otherwise. Even with Stewart, Baker and Castillo gone, I was still snorting.

Another noncoincidence: Stewart and Baker are black, Castillo is Hispanic, and Al Campanis was making the Dodgers' personnel decisions at the time. I discovered after my first rehab, but before Stewart and Baker were shipped out, that Al was not exactly a liberal on racial matters. Al would call me into his office and ask me which black and Hispanic guys on the club were snorting coke. He probably assumed that drug abuse wasn't a white problem and I was a victim of bad influences.

Then Al would say, "Why do you hang around the blacks and Hispanics so much? Why don't you hang around with Rick Monday or Ron Cey, guys like that?" Monday and Cey are white. Now you know why I wasn't surprised when Al told the world on national TV that blacks lack the "necessities" to manage in the majors.

Strangely enough, Al's racial stereotypes were later reflected in public comments made by Don Newcombe, the director of the Dodgers' Employee Assistance Program and a former pitcher for the team. Newcombe, who is black, suggested that it was the black players on the team who needed drug counseling. A lot of the black guys were mad about that.

Once the Dodgers knew about my problem, Al began to pump me for information about any player who wasn't performing well. When Steve Sax couldn't make the throw from second to first, Al asked me whether Sax was into coke. Al asked the same question when Pete Guerrero hit a bad stretch. I refused to be Al's source. I always reported his inquiries back to the players in question, so they were under no illusions about the way the front office operated. By the time I left the team in 1985, I'd lost a lot of respect for Campanis and the organization. It was hard to believe that kind of stuff was going on.

Because I'd lost control for a few weeks and gotten caught, I was about to miss an entire season of baseball. I had to be careful about getting high. I had a good idea when I'd be tested, so I knew when I could get blasted and give myself enough recovery time to provide a clean urine sample. After my suspension, I fell into a pattern of one serious binge every month, with a little chipping in between when I knew I was safe. Cindy says she and Jim Hawkins joked throughout 1984 that my binges were more regular and predictable than a woman's menstrual cycle.

During the most difficult stages of my addiction, Christmas was an uncomfortable season for me. I enjoyed giving gifts to others and making them happy, but I'd screwed up so many times that I didn't feel I deserved to receive gifts.

Christmas was especially troubling in 1983. Cindy's parents and my brother Chris were staying with us. Chris made me nervous. I thought he was telling Mom everything that was said and done in my house. I also resented Chris for taking advantage of me. He came and stayed whenever and for as long as he wanted, had the run of the house and drove my cars, but he wasn't exactly grateful. He was using me. Maybe it bothered me because Chris reminded me of myself.

Part of me wanted to be there for Christmas, but I didn't want to ruin everyone else's fun, so I stayed away. By doing so, I ruined everything anyway. I went out on Christmas Eve and got thoroughly hammered at a friend's apartment. I was still wasted when I got home at 7:00 a.m. Cindy had saved some presents, and I opened them, and then I crashed until dinner.

We managed to get through Christmas dinner before everyone's emotions blew sky-high. Cindy and I went at it and I almost walked out. Then Chris started on me. "How can you live with yourself?" he wanted to know. "You treat everybody like dogshit." I didn't want to hear it. I destroyed a calculator that I had bought Cindy for Christmas by heaving it against the wall of the garage, and then I took off in my truck. I drove around the block and quietly came back because I wanted to spend some time with little Chelsi. I watched TV for a while, then fell asleep.

I had been a Christian since 1980, but increasingly over the last four years, Cindy had been asking me to take my faith more seriously. In 1984 I was willing to give it a try. Early in the year, we began counseling at the Church on the Way, a charismatic church whose members believe in speaking in tongues as a form of spiritual language. We went as a family, and in late February or early March I was baptized and began speaking in tongues right away. Later in March, Chelsi was dedicated at the church.

As Cindy had hoped, these religious experiences provided a sense of purpose and direction in my life. They made me feel like I was in control of my family's destiny. But the sudden change in lifestyle scared me. Was I ready to make a complete change and place my family's interests first? As Joe Pursch had told Cindy a few months before, I wasn't ready. The night after my baptism, I went looking for a party and had no trouble finding one.

When I disappeared for a couple of days, Cindy turned to her church friends for help. Too many people knew about my latest fall off the wagon, and I was catching flak from all sides. In late March I retreated to Michigan to relieve the pressure. I think Cindy feared I might not be back, but I knew I couldn't just say good-bye to my adorable blond, blue-eyed daughter. I needed a change of scene.

Something fundamental had changed in my relationship with my family. I'd embarrassed them a few times too many, and they weren't sure how to deal with me anymore. Kathi and I had been especially close in high school. We'd confided in each other about everything, and Kathi had even picked out my clothes in the morning because I was so bad at matching them. Now there was distance between us, and it wouldn't be long before we hardly spoke. Generally, the reception I got from my family was a little chilly. Maybe I should have gone to Florida instead.

When I got back to L.A. in April, I flunked one of Dr. Tennant's urine tests. That was no big deal in 1984. The Dodgers weren't horrified, because Tennant had told them I might have problems for a while.

By early May, Cindy was working on an interior design project for Charlene Tilton, who had become Cindy's friend through the church. Chelsi spent a lot of time with a babysitter because I was too busy getting high to take care of my responsibilities.

One day Cindy called me from our babysitter's house and said, "Steve, I can't take this anymore. I've just had enough. I'm staying here tonight, and I want you to be gone when I come home tomorrow."

I was a little stunned, but I figured Cindy would calm down in a few days and I'd prove to her I could be a responsible, considerate person. I miscalculated the depth of her distress, however. Instead of inviting me home after a few days, she filed papers in court for legal separation.

When the papers were served on me, it was as though someone had dropped a live grenade in my hands. Suddenly little Cindy was serious and assertive again, no longer the rug under my feet. I saw how roughly I'd treated her, how much my family meant to me and how coke was ruining everything. I was so remorseful that, for one of the few times in my life, I was panic-stricken. I went over to the house and broke into tears as I actually begged Cindy for forgiveness. "I swear I'll stay clean," I said.

Cindy coldly turned me away. "I don't believe you," she said. "You're not willing to do what it takes. I don't want to hear any of your bullshit. You had your chances, lots of them. Now all I want is for you to leave me alone." Nothing I could say that night would change her mind.

To make matters worse, Cindy started seeing Tom the tile man again. Tom lived north of L.A., but by coincidence he was handling a tile job in the L.A. area, and he called Cindy at about the time she filed for separation.

When Cindy admitted she'd been talking to Tom, I became even more frightened that I'd lose her. To keep tabs on her, I began doing things I never imagined I'd do, like calling up her classes at UCLA to find out if she was really there. I'd always thought guys who did stuff like that were lovesick wimps.

One time when I called, I found out that Cindy had left class early. I was at the house with Chelsi, and when Cindy got home, she answered my prying questions by telling the truth, as usual. When I asked where she'd gone, she admitted that she and Tom had met for a drink after her class. I urged her to forget Tom and give our marriage another try. I'd gone back to work full-time for Mike Hernandez at Camino Real Chevrolet, and I presented that to Cindy as evidence of my new sense of responsibility. Cindy knew me well enough to be skeptical. She wanted more time to make sure I wasn't trying to con her again. We talked late into the night, and I stayed over.

When the phone rang the next morning and I answered, the person at the other end hung up. I was sure it was Tom, and it pissed me off. "He's chickenshit," I told Cindy. A few minutes later, a woman called and asked for Cindy. The woman was Tom's ex-wife, and Tom had persuaded her to call Cindy with a message from Tom. Now I was mad, but Cindy sternly advised me that our relationship would be dead if I went tile-man hunting.

Cindy says her relationship with Tom never went beyond friendship. I have no reason not to believe her. I found out years later that Cindy had told Tom that no matter what happened, she loved me and was going to be faithful to me.

I knew I wouldn't be allowed back into my marriage unless I behaved. I slipped up once, on Memorial Day weekend, when I disappeared for a few days. "I've been trying to get you for two days," Cindy said when I surfaced. "Where were you?"

"I went to the beach with some of the guys from the program," I said, referring to the rehab program. "Sorry, I should've called and told you." I had to lie because Cindy was softening and I didn't want to blow my chance.

In early June Cindy let me come home with the understanding that she'd boot me again if I screwed up. She assured me that Tom was completely out of the picture. We began attending counseling sessions at the church.

Everything went well until July 4, when I disappeared again and missed a big holiday picnic for the guys in the rehab program. Cindy walked out on me for a few days, but she came back just as I was concluding that I'd finally ruined my marriage for good. I believe that God helped us stay together over the years, and I'm sure that Cindy and I would not be together today without his help.

I didn't get high again until just before the motor home trip that took me to Whitefish for the first time. The trip was a perfect family experience. We drove north through California and Oregon to Washington, then east for stops in Whitefish, northern Minnesota and Detroit. For three weeks we saw the country, visited friends, fished, swam and camped. Thoughts of coke flashed through my head from time to time, but I was surprised at how relaxed I was away from the pressures and temptations of southern California.

I'd been doing charity work since early in my major league career, especially for kids. In 1981 I made so many appearances at Children's Hospital in Northridge that the hospital put me on the cover of its magazine. When I saw those poor kids—some of them terminally ill—fighting for their lives and never giving up, it made me wonder why I seemed to place so little value on my own health.

I worked a lot with kids in 1984. I visited hospitals, counseled troubled kids and got involved with the Boy Scouts in East L.A. Mike Hernandez wanted to revive the Scouts in his old neighborhood, and at Mike's request I agreed to be chairman of a dinner sponsored by Mike and the Dodgers. The Boy Scouts would get a chance to meet ballplayers, and revenues from the sale of tickets would support the Scouts. It was a great idea and it was rewarding work for me. The first dinner was scheduled for June of 1985.

I was a member of the Union 76 Speakers Bureau for three years, and I participated in Ron Perranoski's golf tournament for charity, which the players called the "Polish Open." Ron used to give out sets of three forest-green golf balls, which were always a big hit. I worked on the Special Olympics and programs for muscular dystrophy.

Whenever I was asked to help, I said yes. Charity work was the only activity that gave me a sense of self-worth away from the ballpark. Kids really listened to me when I was counseling, probably because I was a living example of why they should stay away from alcohol and drugs. It was easier for me to admit to kids that I'd screwed up than it was for me to confide in doctors, therapists and baseball executives. Maybe I trusted the kids because I knew they wouldn't use my problems against me.

There were plenty of people I learned not to trust while I was in exile. They were high-profile business types who exploited my name when I was hot, but wanted nothing to do with me when I was out of baseball. Ever since I'd come to L.A., they'd invited me to come to their sporting goods stores, restaurants, nightclubs and workout facilities. Everything was free for me as long as they could trade on my name and picture. But all the snakes crawled back in their holes when Bowie Kuhn dropped the hammer on me. I could still visit their establishments, but nothing was free, regardless of how much I'd helped them.

Believe it or not, the Hollywood people were more genuine and far more trustworthy, especially when I was out of baseball. I met lots of them and occasionally even partied with them. They remained friendly and helpful when I needed them. My fellow pro athletes, guys I knew from the Rams and Lakers, understood my situation better than anyone else. They told me to hang in there and things would work out.

I met John DeLorean at about the time of his trial for coke dealing. His story showed me I wasn't the only guy in the world who had been targeted as an example by the authorities. I believe the jury's verdict of acquittal in DeLorean's case was the right one, because I'm convinced he was set up.

The people whose warmth made the most lasting impression on me were friends we made through our church. Cindy's involvement brought her lots of new friends, and our house was often full of Christians engaged in biblical discussions or prayer. Unfortunately, I was often the object of the prayers.

These Christians' selfless expressions of love amazed me, but at times I couldn't stand to be around them. When I was getting wasted and my self-esteem was at its lowest, I didn't believe scum like me was worthy of their prayer, so I stayed away. Why, I wondered, would these people have anything to do with me? But when I allowed them to get close to me, they made me feel a lot better about myself.

Our closest friends from church were Pam and Tony Hart. Just being around Tony had a calming influence. One night during 1984, they were at our house for dinner. I was out doing some chipping, not a major blowout, but enough to get me buzzed. I came home and stumbled into the middle of dinner. Everyone knew I was high, and I was embarrassed and wanted to get away.

Tony wouldn't let me leave. He made me sit on a chair in the living room, and he proceeded to take off my shoes and wash my feet, as Jesus had washed the feet of his disciples to show he was their servant. I was too shocked to stop him, and after a few minutes I understood the significance of what Tony was doing. He made me feel important and worthy, and no drug I've ever taken could duplicate that feeling.

One guy who has stuck with me through all my screw-ups is Dale McReynolds. When Mac signs a player for the Dodgers, the player becomes a member of Mac's extended family. Like a doting father whose sons have left the nest, Mac keeps tabs on his boys. When I've deserved a kick in the ass, Mac has delivered it. More importantly and far more frequently, he's offered support and encouragement in countless letters and phone calls.

When I was suspended, Mac called immediately. "I'm not giving up on you," he said. "You're part of my life. I signed you and you did well for both of us. Besides that, I think you're a great kid. Don't quit on me. You can beat this thing." Whatever happened, I had one true friend in a small Wisconsin town.

I didn't always appreciate Mac's help. Sometimes I argued with him, telling him I knew what I was doing and could handle my own problems. A couple of years ago, when I couldn't find my ass with both hands, I threw out a lot of his letters in a fit of rage. But Mac's advice and support have meant a lot to me. When I messed up, I knew I was letting Mac down, and that made me feel like a cockroach.

By September it seemed like a lifetime since I'd played ball. The Dodgers were as anxious as I was for me to start preparing for 1985, and they arranged for me to pitch in both the Arizona Instructional League and the Dominican Winter League.

The Dodgers would be snooping around, armed with urine sample beakers, so I couldn't take the risk of getting high once I got to Arizona. I got ripped right before I left, but I stayed clean while I was there.

It was a strange experience to be back in the Instructional League, surrounded by rookies and minor league players who were working on technique and trying to impress the Dodgers' staff. My perspective had changed since I'd last been there, five years before. Now I was an established veteran whose talent and potential contribution to the big club were beyond doubt. But in a way I was no different from the other players in Arizona. I had something to prove.

Although it felt great to take the mound and throw in the warm Arizona sunshine, I began to feel the pressure almost immediately. The younger players looked at me curiously. I wondered what they were thinking and saying behind my back. I renewed my unpleasant acquaintance with the media, who seemed to have forgotten me for most of the year and were no longer crawling over my back fence and peering in my windows in Agoura. Out of sight, out of mind, I guess. The press got wind of my presence in Arizona, showed up and began asking the predictable, obnoxious questions. "What did you do all year? Have you finally got it beat? Have you lost anything on your fastball?" And of course, "Can you handle the pressure once the season starts?" I wanted to hide behind a big cactus.

Instead, after a couple of weeks in Arizona, I plotted an escape for a risk-free blowout. I asked for and was granted a Thursday and Friday off so I could go to L.A. and tend to "business matters." If I could stay out of sight until Friday, I wasn't likely to stumble into a drug test until at least Monday, when my urine would be free of evidence. Cindy had been going home every week anyway to attend classes at UCLA on those days, so she thought it was a great idea. Cindy, Chelsi and I left our rented Arizona condo and babysitter on Wednesday afternoon and flew to Burbank, where I rented a car for the weekend.

I dropped Cindy and Chelsi off at home and told Cindy I had to go pick something up and I'd be back soon. "Soon" was a day and a half later.

Cindy was on the warpath. I'd taken the baby's car seat with me, and Cindy had been trying to wrap a seatbelt around little Chelsi while driving her around. "I'm not going back to Arizona with you," she said. "It's stupid if you're just going to get loaded. I can stay here and relax."

I went back to Arizona during the weekend, told the Dodgers I thought I'd trained enough, packed up all the stuff in the condo and drove back to L.A. with the babysitter. Cindy was noticeably relieved when I left for winter ball a couple of weeks later. She needed an extended vacation from me, but she'd get only about three weeks.

Licey, a team that plays out of Santo Domingo, is the Dodgers' connection in the Dominican Republic. Lots of guys from the organization play for Licey, either to impress management or just to stay in shape between seasons. In the Dominican you don't take the risk of using contraband. If they catch you, you're liable to rot in a gritty jail for years.

I was pitching well and was in my second week with the team, in mid-November, when it happened. I threw a fastball and felt a twinge, as if someone had stabbed me in the back of the elbow. Later, much later, the Dodger orthopedists discovered that a calcium deposit had pinched down and blown the ulnar nerve right out of its joint.

My elbow felt terrible. It hurt, and I couldn't throw or even grip the ball right. I was worried, but hopeful that I'd just strained something. The doctors tried a series of treatments. No response, no improvement. My emotions ranged from mild concern to fear and back again. This was no big deal; I'd be fine. Or had I wrecked my arm and my career? I couldn't believe that my arm, my security, my ultimate hedge against all catastrophes, would fail me when I needed it most. Maybe I wasn't as indestructible as I'd thought.

I went back to L.A., where I was greeted by a skeptical Al Campanis. I'm sure Al thought I was faking and just wanted to come home. "Just rest it, Steve," said Dr. Al. "Just rest it and it'll be all right. There's nothing wrong with it."

I wasn't convinced, and I wasn't handling my insecurity well. Not long after I got home, I had a date with a pile of coke and got fried. Cindy, apparently hoping to avoid a repeat of Christmas Wars '83, immediately hustled me off to CareUnit for some abbreviated counseling and treatment.

When that was over, Cindy resumed her never-ending salvage operation on our marriage. Between Thanksgiving and Christmas, she took me on a weekend marriage retreat sponsored by the Church on the Way. We talked through our problems with two pastors and other participants in the retreat. It helped keep me straight for a couple of weeks, and, more important, it had a permanent healing effect on our relationship.

The Campanis prescription wasn't helping my elbow, so Dr. Frank Jobe proposed a nerve test. This is a grim procedure in which doctors stick metal rods into different areas of your arm to find out if the nerves are working properly. If it hurts like hell and you scream in pain, the nerves are fine. When they stuck the rods in my hand and forearm, it hurt like hell. But when they jabbed the rods into my elbow, I didn't feel a thing. Jobe now had a fix on the problem.

It was mid-December, and spring training was only ten weeks away. Jobe tried some new treatments, hoping the nerve would heal without surgery. No luck. On January 9 Jobe spent more than two hours in surgery, repositioning my ulnar nerve.

The cast stayed on my elbow for a week or so. When Jobe took it off, the muscles had contracted and atrophied, and my arm had assumed what looked and felt like a permanent L-shape. The doc, a nationally renowned orthopedic guru, took my sickeningly skinny arm in his hands and studied this phenomenon.

"You know, Steve," he said, "you've got really long muscles, and I wouldn't do this to anybody else. But you're really flexible and strong enough to take it." Then, before I could protest, with one deft motion he straightened my arm.

Three huge beads of sweat formed on my forehead and ran straight down my face. "If you weren't such a good doctor," I said, "I would have punched you right in the mouth. That was a dirty trick."

Therapy began immediately. For the first week I had to soak my elbow in a bowl of warm water while I tried to squeeze water out of a sponge. For two days I couldn't squeeze a drop out. Part of the problem was weakness in muscles that hadn't recovered from surgery. I was also afraid that if I strained too hard, my elbow might fall apart again. Soon I stopped babying the elbow and began working with weights and squeezing rubber balls to rebuild the arm.

Uncertainty and doubt gnawed at me, and I found refuge, or at least a good time, in some rampaging binges in the weeks before and after surgery. Unfortunately, some of those good times turned into life-threatening disasters.

It was right after my release from the hospital that I snorted some bad stuff. I began to feel queasy at the end of a two-day binge, and I called Cindy and told her I'd be home in 20 minutes. My truck was making bizarre noises. I was feeling sicker all the time, and the ride seemed like it took hours. I parked in the driveway, but I was too sick to go inside. Cindy found me in the backyard, puking uncontrollably.

Cindy brought me into the house and got a blanket and pillow. "I'd appreciate it if you'd sleep downstairs tonight," she said. "I can't sleep with you in the bed upstairs, the way you are now." I spent the night on the living room floor.

That should have been enough to slow me down, but a few days later I had my close encounter with the gun-toting freebaser on Sherman Way. When I got home from that, I was a mess. My shirt was torn, and I was still pretty high. I had no muscle control and was twitching badly. I just lay in bed in a fetal position, staring off into space. Cindy called our friend Tony Hart, and he arranged to have me admitted into Palmdale Hospital, a Christian chemical dependency counseling center. To protect my career, they admitted me for a nervous breakdown.

The sessions at Palmdale were some of the most useful I'd experienced. The counselors understood that I had internalized a lot of anger toward my parents, and they helped me bring that anger out in the open and deal with it. When I left Palmdale, it seemed as if part of the huge malignancy of resentment inside my head had been removed, I felt better about myself, and I looked great.

My self-esteem got another boost in Vero Beach, about three weeks after I began spring training with the Dodgers. My early attempts to throw, less than two months after major elbow surgery, had not gone well. I woke up every morning wondering when my arm would be ready to go to work.

After our exhibition game on my 27th birthday, March 10, 1985, I decided to go shoot some pool with several other ballplayers in the complex where Cindy, Chelsi and I were living. One of the guys stopped me. "You don't want to go play pool," he said. "We've got better stuff to do."

Stubborn to a fault, I said, "Yes I do want to play pool, and if you guys don't want to play, I'll go play by myself."

I started to go down to the pool room, and the guys went along, shuffling ahead of me. Cindy stopped me on the way with some contrived question that annoyed me, and by the time I got to the room, everyone else had arrived. As I opened the door, someone yelled, "Surprise!"

In college and throughout my pro career, I'd always been away from home playing ball on my birthday, so no one had ever made a big deal about it. It was wonderful to know that my teammates cared enough about me to throw a surprise party. Maybe I was a worthwhile human being after all.

12

Trip, Stumble and Fall

He had never failed before. For the first time in his career, OK, he was going to fail. He was going to have a tough time because he was just not physically ready to go out there and perform at the same level that he had before.

So he was trying to handle that, and not doing a very good job of handling it, and then trying to handle his addiction problem. There was just too much expected of him in too short a period of time. I certainly knew that, before long, something was going to happen.

Now, on the road he never had any problems. There was never any problem on the road because he had a good support system. What happened was he didn't have a good support system at home. He could get away, and he knew that if he needed to escape, he could do that. That's where the problems manifested themselves—at home.

I'm not going to mention names, but there were still a couple of players on [the Dodgers] who, if they didn't have a problem, I was certainly very suspicious of them. There were constant calls, all the time, at really bad times of the night, from players on the team who wanted to see Steve. You know what I mean? You don't call at 3:30 in the morning and say, "How you doin', Steve?"

I'll tell you how bad it was. I roomed with him on the road from the day the season started until he left. It's June or July, and these people on the team still did not realize that I was rooming with him.

They would call and I would answer the phone, and they couldn't understand why I was answering the phone. They'd say, "Well, what are you doing there?" And I'd say, "Don't worry what I'm doing here, just get your ass to bed and shut up. And don't call the room anymore." They'd call again.

—Joe Ferguson
Coach, Los Angeles Dodgers, 1985
Coach, Texas Rangers, 1987
September 1987

Through the worst of times, baseball had been my safe harbor. I believed that no matter how often I got loaded, ran away from responsibility and treated my family like dirt, I'd always be able to take pride in my talent and accomplishments on the field. If I was a worthless fool away from the ballpark, I was master of all situations at the office. Tell me to stop poisoning myself with drugs or be considerate of my wife, and I'd expect to screw up. Tell me to retire Mike Schmidt with the tying run on base, and I was confident I'd do it. My view of my life was completely out of balance.

While CareUnit, Palmdale and later St. Mary's were slowly building my self-esteem as a human being and family man, my elbow was having the opposite effect on my perception of my career. Suddenly, when I couldn't throw without pain and the hitters began catching up with me, I saw for the first time that my career wouldn't always pay the bills and make me look good. Through much of 1985, I wondered if my stardom was already past. I even lost some of my cockiness, but not for long. No one would have recognized me without it.

Slowly, directed by events I couldn't control, my view of my world was moving toward a healthier balance. Eventually, I would no longer view baseball as my only arena of competence, and I wouldn't see the rest of my life as a mistake. I was creating an environment that, according to the therapists, is best for recovery from chemical dependency.

If I'd known that between March and September of 1985, it might have relieved some of the torture of dealing with the elbow problem. I was trying to come back in a few months from surgery that sometimes requires a year of rehabilitation. Maybe I should have spent most of the season on the disabled list and in baseball rehabilitation, resting until the elbow had healed and then going to

Albuquerque to work my arm back into shape at a leisurely pace. Instead, I threw myself back into a pressure cooker I hadn't handled well in the past. I'd just sat out an entire season, and I couldn't stand to miss another one. I also thought I owed it to the Dodgers, who had taken care of me while I was suspended, to come back and contribute as soon as possible.

From the moment I woke up after surgery, my elbow hurt. For weeks, whenever I closed my hand, I could feel something grinding near the incision. When I first started throwing, my arm was stiff and sore because the elbow joint was dry, a common problem created by surgery. I tried to help the healing process by working with weights every day. I was driven to return my arm to full strength.

One day during our daily stretching exercises at spring training, I was lying on my back, pulling a knee up to my chest with both hands, when I felt something pop in the elbow. An incredibly sharp pain shot through my arm and exploded in my head. Jerry Reuss, who was stretching next to me, heard the pop. "What the hell was that?" he asked.

"I don't know, but I'm done, that's it," I said, and I got up and walked into the clubhouse sweating. Everyone was looking at me with a sense of dread, but no one could have been more scared than I was.

Dr. Jobe quickly appeared in the clubhouse and began twisting and yanking my arm with his customary vigor. "Oh, that was nothing," he said when he was satisfied that my elbow wasn't going to disintegrate before his eyes. "That was just an adhesion breaking loose."

"Gosh," I said, "I gotta look forward to that all year?"

"No, that's probably all the scar tissue that needed to break loose." I wasn't convinced. It wasn't until after the regular season started that I was able to overcome my fears and cut the ball loose.

In March there was an incident that added to my nervousness about my elbow. We were playing the Red Sox in Winter Haven, and I was throwing batting practice without a screen. Sure enough, I got nailed by a line drive, right in the left elbow. The pain was overpowering, but it turned out to be nothing more than a bruise.

Meanwhile, I developed another physical problem that was really a recurrence of an old injury. Back in high school, when I'd played a lot of ice hockey, I'd been hit so often with sticks that I'd developed a bone chip in my right ankle. The problem flared up for no apparent reason during spring training of 1985. My ankle swelled up every time I pitched, and it hurt like hell. I didn't want Lasorda to know I was hurt because I wanted to keep pitching, so I consulted doctors who weren't connected with the team. The doctors tried without surgery to dissolve the bone chip, but it didn't work. The pain was so bad that by the time the season started, there were days I could pitch only if the pain was deadened by a shot of novocaine. I must have had 30 novocaine shots in my ankle during the season.

Given my physical limitations and anxiety, it was no surprise that I wasn't blowing hitters away. My first appearance under game conditions was on April 1 in an exhibition against the Detroit Tigers. I worked two-thirds of an inning, threw 36 pitches and gave up three hits, two walks and four runs.

Jobe had advised me not to throw as hard as I could, so my radar clockings never exceeded 88 miles per hour. I was nervous, my control wasn't very good, my pitching mechanics were atrocious, and the Tigers pounded me when I got the ball over. Otherwise, I was great. My arm was sore on the days after I pitched, but at least I was able to pick it up far enough to brush my hair with my left hand. But the pain told me I wasn't ready to pitch on consecutive days.

Things got better, at least for a while. I threw an inning against the Angels on April 7 in one of our last exhibitions, and retired the side on only six pitches. Lasorda was talking about bringing me back slowly, but he must have forgotten all about that when we got into a tight spot in Houston on April 10, the second day of the season.

We led 5–3 entering the bottom of the ninth, but Ken Howell and Tom Niedenfuer were having trouble holding off the Astros. A walk, a single and a sacrifice fly brought the Astros within a run with two outs. Jose Cruz, still tough, was the next hitter. Lasorda started for the mound and signaled with his left hand. I was out the bullpen door and on my way before he could lower his arm. For the first time in almost 19 months, it was Howe to the rescue.

I'd started warming up in the seventh, and my arm didn't feel great, but I wouldn't let my head play 20 questions. On my way to the mound, I said a quick prayer and fought off the butterflies while I thought about Cruz and his free-swinging affection for high pitches. By the time I'd thrown my first warm-up pitch, my nerves had vanished and it was like old times. Good old times.

I threw a fastball. Cruz let it go for a strike. I tried a slider and wanted to recall it as soon as I let it go. It was chest high and didn't break, and Cruz smoked it to center. Luckily, Kenny Landreaux didn't have far to run. He almost lost it in the lights and fell down when he caught it, but I had a save. It felt like I'd just won another championship. The guys told me it shouldn't count because I got Cruz with a hanging slider, but I didn't care.

Unfortunately, that save was not the start of a successful campaign for Comeback Player of the Year. When the Astros came to L.A. six days later, they nicked me for a couple of runs. Not long after that, I gave up a cheap run to San Diego in the eighth inning of a lost cause. Lasorda started using me for mop-up duty earlier in games. I hated that role, but I wasn't pitching well enough to justify a demand for my old job.

For no apparent reason, Tommy started to rely on me again in early May. I had about five strong appearances in a row, and I think I gave up only one unearned run the entire month. I wasn't the Howe of old, and my elbow usually throbbed and ached, but somehow I was getting the job done. In early June I picked up my first win and a save in three days against the Mets.

The pitcher's mound became an unfriendly place for me again on June 9 in Atlanta. We trailed 5–3 when I came in for the bottom of the seventh. My arm was killing me and I had nothing on the ball. In two innings I gave up five hits, a walk and five runs, but only one of the runs was earned because shortstop Mariano Duncan committed four errors.

I understood that I couldn't hand in coke-laden urine specimens if I wanted to keep pitching in 1985. The Dodgers kept those little sample containers coming at me at regular intervals, and the world hadn't yet discovered mail-order urine samples, so I couldn't snort for a while.

Of course, I didn't have many opportunities to step out for a blast. When the Dodgers were at home, Cindy watched me constantly. When we were on the road, Tommy Lasorda assigned me a roommate, Joe Ferguson, a former Dodger player who had become a coach. Joe was a good guy and one hell of a good babysitter. If Joe wasn't around, one or more of my teammates went everywhere with me. They wouldn't even let me stay in the hotel by myself and go to sleep. It was nice to know they cared, but I had no privacy at all. Big Brother was watching.

In almost every city we visited, Lasorda had friends who invited him out to dinner, usually to four-star restaurants. When Tommy and his friends sat down to chow, they didn't just eat. They feasted for hours. Tommy took me with him often, so I was eating like a prize hog and still pocketing my meal money.

We arrived in Chicago one night in early May at about dinner time, and Tommy immediately hustled a group of us outside the city for a major feed. I knew it would last for hours so I tried to stay behind to sleep, but they dragged me along. We ate and drank forever, while Tommy and his hosts chattered away, pausing only long enough to stoke some more food. On the way back to town, at about midnight, the car broke down. We finally got in at 2:00 a.m., exhausted and half drunk, facing an early wake-up call so we could get to Wrigley Field for our afternoon game. Under those circumstances, how was I supposed to rest and rehabilitate a sore elbow? Fortunately, I didn't have to pitch the next day.

The Dodgers' plan to keep me off coke may have angered me, but it was effective. Joe and I were in our room in Houston one night when some guys we knew came by and offered to get me high. In the past I'd have sneaked off down the hall and buried a straw in the baggie. In fact, that's what I wanted to do this time, but I was learning to fight my urges.

"Hey, Joe," I told Fergie, "these people have got some stuff."

"Hey, we don't want any of it," Joe said to the guys. "You people do what you wanna do, but don't do it around us." I was really proud of myself.

Don't get the idea that I'd become a disciple of clean living. There were a lot of things bothering me, and I hadn't yet learned to deal with them without mind-altering medication. My arm hurt, I wasn't pitching worth a damn, and I didn't feel like Steve Howe. From the time the season began, I drank heavily. I was eating and drinking so much that my weight ballooned to a hefty 204 pounds, about 14 over my best playing weight, and it stayed there because I wasn't snorting coke and frying my system.

Although probably half the Dodgers were into substances other than liquor, alcohol was still the team's universally accepted tribal method of blowing off steam. Bobby Welch was about the only guy who abstained. Sometimes after a tough win, but more often after a brutal loss, we'd hit the bars in groups, pour down a few and try to forget what had happened. I was pouring down more than a few.

I'm sure Dodger management knew my drinking was reaching problem levels, but no one ever said anything about it to me. I guess they accepted it because at least I wasn't doing coke, and I wasn't coming to the ballpark drunk. If I got tanked at night, all they had to do was carry me back to my room and put me to sleep, not check me into a rehab center and risk losing me.

As it had done in high school, liquor turned me into an irritable and aggressive person I didn't like. It didn't take much to set me off, and I got into some embarrassing scrapes.

Once I was with several players in a bar in Atlanta after a game, and I was blitzed. As I was walking out, someone made what I interpreted as a smartass remark. In my condition anything beyond "hello" probably would have qualified as smartass. I was ready to grab the guy and pinch his head off when Steve Yeager pushed me away and said, "Come on, let's get outta here."

Yeager's basically OK. He wasn't one of my best friends, but we'd always gotten along fairly well. But it's never a wise move to push me, and the way I was feeling at that moment, I didn't much care who was friend and who was foe. I pushed Yeager back, hard. Our teammates got us out of there fast, but it was an ugly spectacle, two Dodgers going after each other in a public bar. It's a good thing the press wasn't on hand.

Yeager and the other guys wanted to forget the whole thing, but old pighead Howe was still drunk and mad. I felt like the whole world was against me. I stomped off and walked around town for a couple of hours, looking for cocaine. I couldn't find any, so I finally went back to my room.

I suppose it was inevitable that things would unravel. It began to happen in late May.

On the morning of a Sunday game at home, Cindy took Chelsi and went to the Magic Mountain amusement park in her car. When it was time for me to leave for the ballpark in midmorning, I couldn't find the keys to my car. I figured I'd left my entire key ring, including my sets of keys to both cars, in Cindy's car, which I had driven the night before.

I was frantic. I knew what the Dodgers, not to mention the media, would think if I showed up late for a game. I was especially afraid because I had been using the night before and I knew if I was late, they would test me. But there was no way I was going to get to Dodger Stadium on schedule. I called a cab, but getting a cab to pick you up in Agoura is like waiting for the smog to blow out of L.A. in August.

I called Al Campanis and told him what had happened. "What the hell am I gonna do?" I asked him. "I don't have my car keys, Al. I'm paranoid. I need to get there because I know what you people are thinking."

"No, no, we're not thinking that," said Al, not quite succeeding in reassuring me. "Just get a cab and get to the park."

I didn't get there until after the game had started. I warmed up, but I wasn't called in to pitch. I dreaded going back to the clubhouse after the game. I knew the vultures were waiting. About a dozen of them were camped in front of my locker, hatchets ready. The first drug question was asked before I even reached my locker.

The Dodgers gave me a drug test, and I passed, but that didn't matter to the media. They spent the next few days ripping my butt, questioning whether the Dodgers should keep a player whose behavior was so unpredictable. When the media had come after me in previous years—no problem. I'd just kept doing my job and ignored them. Now, for the first time, I couldn't look at a string of impressive pitching performances to fortify my belief in my value to the team. The press was getting to me.

Early in the season, Cindy and I saw a movie called *Eddie and the Cruisers* about a rock'n'roll singer who disappears and is never heard from again, but continues to influence the lives of his old friends. As times got tougher for me, I thought about Eddie more and more. Maybe Eddie had the right idea. Maybe I should just disappear one day, fly to South America and lose myself in a jungle. At least then my family would no longer have to put up with all the public embarrassment that came with being related to me. I wondered if the media and the public would think of me more favorably after I was gone.

Lasorda didn't use me very often in June. After Mariano Duncan's virtuoso fielding exhibition in Atlanta, I pitched only twice in 17 days, and I was respectable both times. My elbow would have let me pitch a little more often than that, but not much.

Then, on June 26 in San Diego, Tommy trusted me in a "hold" situation and I fell apart. We trailed 6–4 with the Padres coming to bat in the seventh, but with Pedro Guerrero in the middle of an awesome power streak (10 homers in the previous 18 days), the game was winnable. I changed that in a hurry.

My pitches weren't doing anything, but it didn't matter because I had no idea where they were going. The greatest insult was the first: LaMarr Hoyt, a pitcher who had just come over from the American League and got hits only by accident, singled. I hit Tim Flannery with a pitch, although it looked like he cleverly walked into the ball. After Tony Gwynn bounced into a force, my old buddy Steve Garvey ripped a meatball over the wall for three runs, and the game was out of reach. I got tagged for another run before Lasorda brought in Bobby Castillo, who'd returned to the team, to close out the inning. We lost 10–4.

After the game, I found Tommy in his office in the visitors' clubhouse. I sat down in front of him and started to cry. "Tommy," I said, "nothing against you or anyone else, but the media is killing me and I'm not pitching worth shit. Would you please try to trade me?"

"C'mon, Steve, you don't really want that and neither do we. Things aren't really that bad. I know your arm's not right yet, but when it comes back, things'll be fine. You'll see."

"I mean it, Tommy. I want to be traded. I mean it. See what you can do."

Tommy Lasorda had always been wonderful to me, but I could never talk to him about my cocaine problem and what it was doing to me. Tommy just didn't understand. He'd quit smoking a few years before on sheer willpower, so he thought all I had to do was wake up one day and say, "No more." Tommy was disappointed that I couldn't accomplish what seemed so simple to him. He never sat down with me and asked what was going through my head.

Tommy delivered my trade request to Campanis, who also told me I could forget about a trade. It felt good to know the Dodgers wanted to keep me, but they didn't understand how much things were bothering me.

Two days later, the Braves were visiting L.A. and Lasorda gave me another shot, this time with no pressure. Castillo had been pounded in relief in the eighth and ninth, and I inherited an 8–2 deficit with two out and two on in the ninth. The first hitter I faced was Terry Harper. Terry looked happy to see me. Boom, another three-run homer. I think that's the first time I ever gave up homers in successive appearances. I had gone almost entire seasons without giving up two homers.

Somewhere in the clubhouse, I found a bottle of whiskey. I took it into Lasorda's office after the game and got trashed. I didn't come out until I was sure the clubhouse had cleared.

The following day, Saturday, we had a day game followed by the Boy Scout dinner I'd organized for Mike Hernandez. After the game, I headed back toward my house, debating whether I should go to the dinner. It was my show, and I was obligated to be there. But I didn't feel much like a hero, so I couldn't face the kids, and I couldn't face my teammates because I'd let them down so often.

I went into Spat's, a bar near my house, for a couple of drinks. I started talking to a guy I'd never met before, and we got seriously drunk together. Somehow, he wound up taking my car that night, and I walked home, hours after the Boy Scout dinner had concluded without me.

I did some deep thinking while drowning my liver that night. I concluded that I could no longer stay in L.A. The town had turned on me. My arm was still weak and I couldn't get anyone out. The media were all over me for poor performances and erratic behavior. People who said they were my friends kept offering me coke. I had to convince the Dodgers I was serious about wanting to leave.

I decided to skip Sunday's game without even contacting the team. Then I'd give the Dodgers a urine sample that would prove I hadn't been snorting coke. I figured the Dodgers would get the point and let me go.

Late Sunday morning, I walked to an open lot in my subdivision and sat under a big tree. I knew the Dodgers would be calling me at home. I had no intention of being there to answer.

I thought for a while about *Eddie and the Cruisers*. The idea of an Eddie-style disappearance was romantic, but it wasn't the solution. I knew God had a plan for me, because he'd kept me alive and reasonably healthy when I easily could have snorted myself to death. I believed it was God's plan for me to continue my career, and I couldn't do that in a South American jungle. I also couldn't leave Chelsi, who was two years old and just developing her personality. I fell asleep under the tree. It was 10:30 p.m. and dark when I woke up and walked home.

On Monday morning, July 1, I went to the stadium and demanded that I be given a urinalysis. The Dodgers were happy to comply. I tested clean. Because I'd missed a game, the Dodgers put me on the restricted list, meaning I couldn't play until the team reinstated me.

Jim Hawkins joined me for talks with Fred Claire and Al Campanis. We repeated my demand to be traded or released. The Dodgers refused at first, but we wore them down. On Wednesday, July 3, the Dodgers gave me my unconditional release.

I cried when I walked out of the stadium that day. For the first time since I left the University of Michigan, I was no longer a Dodger. I felt like an orphan.

I was unemployed for six weeks. It was no secret that I was available, but major league general managers weren't lining up outside Jim Hawkins's office door with open checkbooks in their hands. After the strange events leading to my departure from the Dodgers, most baseball men probably thought I was either hopelessly addicted or mentally deranged. They also had reason to question whether I could still pitch.

I couldn't do much more than hang around L.A. and get into trouble. It was around this time that I fell into another life-threatening situation. I had a friend I'll call Gary who was a biker and a drug dealer. Gary was a good guy, but he liked to mix his chemicals, and when he did he was a monster. During the latter stages of my addiction, I liked to get high at Gary's because it was a good place to hide.

Lots of people owed Gary money. A few of us were snorting at his house one night when one of the deadbeats showed up. After a short exchange of words, Gary took a 9.0 mm handgun out of his belt and fired. The shell went right through the deadbeat's ear and stuck in the door.

My first thought was logical: Get the hell out of here. Then the wired addict in my head said: No, he's got another whole bag of coke here, and if I can pacify him, I'm going to get some. I stayed.

I talked to several teams, but discussions were extended with only two—the Texas Rangers and the Minnesota Twins. The Rangers were desperate for pitchers. Their manager, Bobby Valentine, had grown up in the Dodger system and was close to Lasorda. Tommy told Bobby that I'd be able to help the Rangers once my elbow was fit.

The Twins invited Hawkins and me to fly to Minneapolis for a visit. Ray Miller, the new manager of the sixth-place Twins, had been a successful pitching coach in Baltimore. The inconsistency of the Twins' staff was driving him nuts. I worked out at the Metrodome and threw pretty well.

"What's your objective, Steve?" Ray asked.

"All I want to do is pitch. Just pitch. I want to play ball," I told him. Ray liked that.

A little more than a week later, on August 11, I signed a contract with Minnesota that was the most lucrative of my career. The base salary for 1986 was to be $450,000, and I could have made $750,000 if I satisfied all the incentive clauses. There was no requirement for drug testing.

I was anxious to repay the Twins for their faith and generosity. Miller gave me a chance right away. On August 12, in the second game of a doubleheader against Oakand, Ray threw me out there in the sixth inning. I was a little apprehensive about how the fans would respond, but they greeted me warmly. I closed off an A's rally and kept sending the hitters back to the dugout. I retired the first 11 batters I faced as an American Leaguer. I stayed in the game until there were two out in the ninth, when I gave up a hit and Ron Davis bailed me out. I got the win.

Three and two-thirds innings is a lot of work for a reliever with a shaky elbow who hasn't pitched in six weeks. As usual, I gave it maximum effort. I don't know any other way to pitch. The next day, my elbow let me know it hadn't enjoyed all that work. The pain was a sign of things to come.

The Twins had a solution to my elbow problem: drugs. When I reported the soreness to the team trainer, he put me on Darvocet, a painkiller that was supposed to be nonaddictive. I began taking four to eight 100-milligram pills a day. Darvocet dulled the pain all right, but it also put the brakes on my natural aggressiveness. Half the time when I was on the mound, I had trouble deciding whether I wanted to throw a slider or fall asleep. But I never told the doctor how the painkillers were affecting me.

The team was only about 13 games out and still had a distant chance in the evenly balanced Western Division, so Miller began using me every other day. I hadn't rebuilt enough arm strength to handle the load. Seattle hit me hard twice in a row. Then we went to Milwaukee, where I blew two games in the ninth inning on successive nights, although one of the losses resulted from two errors on one batted ball and wasn't my fault. Miller rested me for six days after that, but I responded with bad outings at home against Toronto and Boston. The team seemed to lose every time I pitched and was gaining no ground in the pennant race. I didn't look like a good investment for the Twins. My confidence was at an all-time low.

In early September the trial of Curtis Strong, a caterer who had sold cocaine to ballplayers, began in Pittsburgh. Players were parading to the witness stand and admitting they'd had long-term coke habits and had purchased the stuff from Strong. The players' stories came as no shock to me because I'd snorted with some of them. I wondered what the commissioner was going to do to players who were coming forward and admitting their use, as I had done.

Drug use in baseball, and in sports generally, was suddenly big news. It was so big that Ted Koppel, the anchor of ABC's "Nightline," devoted an entire show to the subject on the night of September 12. Koppel's producers asked me to be on the show that night. I had become a national symbol of the problem of cocaine abuse in baseball.

The Twins completed a series in Chicago that Thursday night, then flew to Cleveland. With the team's permission, I appeared on the show from a Chicago studio. Then I was to hop an ABC charter, fly to Detroit to visit my family and jump back on the charter on Friday morning to meet the team in Cleveland. I had the charter pilot's phone number. I was supposed to call him whenever I was ready to leave Detroit. Everything was set up for my convenience.

The other guests on "Nightline" were former Dallas Cowboy Pete Gent, former pitcher Dock Ellis and Mark Liebl, a dealer who'd sold cocaine to some of the Kansas City Royals. Koppel directed his first questions to me.

> KOPPEL: Steve, let me begin with a very fundamental question: Why? There are an awful lot of people out there who sit there, see you guys playing baseball, making a lot of money, a great deal of fame, on top of the world—what do you need the artificial stimulant for?
>
> HOWE: Well, first of all, Ted, I don't feel that—cocaine and alcohol and different things that we use as an obsession in

life aren't really the major problems. Life in general and people and places and things and success a lot of times are people's problems. At least it was for me. I had to straighten out my personal life and grow, as they say, mature a little bit. I had no responsibility. I was making a six-figure salary; I was in Hollywood, and you know, so I fell into the crowd. I came from a middle-income family, a very hard-working family, and you know, I just—my life was so unprioritized that I just fell into the trap. And the bad thing—the unfortunate thing about addiction is you don't know that you've become an addict until you cross the line.

For me, my sole existence of what I did in life was what I did on the ballfield. That's what I'm talking about, prioritizing your life. My sole existence was whether I struck out the guy with the bases loaded and, you know, 3-and-2 count and we're winning by one run. That was my sole existence. When nothing else matters, and you don't feel that you're going to be able to perform up to your capabilities, and someone gives you an avenue to deaden that pain, because athletes do play in a lot of pain. You know, with that as your sole existence, you're going to do what you can do so that people are going to like you and accept you.

KOPPEL: Gentlemen, each of you has some experience that we want to tap tonight. . . . One thing, if there were one thing that could be done, what would it, what should it be?

HOWE: Well, the only thing that I could say, Ted, is that there are a lot of good people out there, and it took me a long time to realize that, hey, there are people that care and that you've really got to reach down. And what I had to do for me was just say, hey, the price is too high; do I want to live or do I want to carry on in this form? And it's just a question that each individual has to ask himself.

I wonder if anyone watching "Nightline" that night could tell I was ripe for a major blowout. Koppel asked me how I'd gotten involved with drugs, but I was describing the way I felt at that moment. It's weird how I bared my soul and then, a few hours later, played out the scene I'd described on national TV. I was the one in pain because I wasn't performing to my capabilities, and someone was about to offer me an avenue to deaden that pain.

My life might have taken a different path if Ron Davis had gone to Detroit with me. Ron and I had become close during my month with the Twins. Ron's a big, laid-back, good-natured country boy from Texas, one of the neatest people I've ever known. We found we shared a love of fishing, and we'd escape for hours and fish in lakes around Minneapolis. With my precious career in a state of at least temporary collapse, those fishing sessions with Ron helped preserve my sanity.

I knew my state of mind was dangerous. I wanted to ask Ron to go with me, and he wanted to go. He later told me, "I wanted to go with you because I knew it was going to be hard on you." But we didn't make the connection because I never asked Ron to join me. It was a lot like the night of Chelsi's birth, when I should have called Peter O'Malley as soon as I recognized the warning signals instead of after I got fried. By September 1985 I was even more familiar with those signals, but I still wasn't willing to call for help.

The charter landed in Detroit at about 1:40 a.m. Friday. There wasn't much for me to do at home in the middle of the night. In a few hours both my parents would leave for work. Near the car rental counter, I ran into an old friend, a guy I hadn't seen in years. He suggested we go party. I couldn't come up with a good reason to refuse, although one reason should have jumped out at me: My career was at stake.

The binge lasted two days. I probably did more drinking than snorting, but I inhaled plenty of coke too. I didn't rejoin the world until Sunday morning. By then the media had told the whole country that I was missing and presumed wasted. My parents had been called by reporters who wanted to know where I was. Mom and Dad had to admit they hadn't seen me. When I finally showed up, they were relieved, embarrassed and angry.

I telephoned Andy MacPhail, the personnel director of the Twins. I avoided Andy's questions because I thought the Twins were entitled to hear the truth from me face-to-face. I'm sure the Twins wanted to hear that I'd disappeared because of a family emergency, but I couldn't lie. They'd given me a chance and treated me fairly. If they wanted to let me go, I'd have to face it. Andy told me a plane ticket to Minneapolis would be waiting for me at the airport in Detroit.

I met with MacPhail and Twins President Howard Fox during a Twins game on Monday night. They were shocked and outwardly sad when they heard the story. All I could do was apologize, as I'd done to so many other people so many times before. I couldn't swear it would never happen again.

"We want you to say that you asked for your release," Howard Fox said. "Then we'll release you."

On Tuesday, September 17, the Twins unconditionally released me. Once again, I was on the outside looking in.

Coincidence and fate seemed to hammer me every time. An outstanding example: Just before I went AWOL in Detroit, I missed a chance to meet Dr. George Mann, who was director of the St. Mary's Hospital Rehabilitation Center in Minneapolis and also ran the Twins' employee assistance program. The Twins had begun trying to arrange a casual meeting between us shortly after I signed with the team. Dr. Mann and I had an appointment to get acquainted, but he had to go out of town on short notice, so we postponed it.

The circumstances weren't casual when Dr. Mann and I finally got together. Instead of being a visitor at St. Mary's, I was a patient, a four-time loser watching his career slip away, desperate for a change of direction. I was ready to be helped, but I didn't have much faith in myself. Experience told me I wasn't worth a damn.

I found out right away that my con games weren't going to work at St. Mary's. They gave me no special privileges because I was an athlete. I was just another addict in therapy. Dr. Mann recognized that I liked to take charge of my own rehab program so I could design shortcuts. He wasn't going to let that happen.

During preliminary detox and medical and psychological testing at St. Mary's, I told Dr. Mann how the Twins had fed me Darvocet. No one from the team had asked whether he thought it was a good idea to feed a semiaddictive painkiller to an addict, and he was angry about it. I'm sure ears were burning at the Metrodome after Dr. Mann reviewed the Darvocet fiasco with the Twins' front office.

Dr. Mann believes an addict's only chance to recover is by total abstinence from chemicals. Cocaine wasn't my only poison. I was told I had to stay away from all chemicals on which I could become dependent. Dr. Mann accepts the increasingly popular theory that some people have a genetic predisposition to abuse chemicals. It's especially likely to happen to sons of fathers who are chemically dependent. He made me realize that I'm not going to do myself any good by drinking to replace coke, even if liquor isn't forbidden by the powers of baseball.

My primary therapy counselor, Cal Scheidegger, knew addiction from both sides—10 years as a counselor at St. Mary's and 20 before that as an addict. He noticed right away that I approached therapy like it was spring training and I was trying to make the team. I'd been in therapy before, and I knew how to play the game. I was outgoing and enthusiastic, an eager participant and even a leader in group discussions. I tried hard to create the impression that I was over the hump and on the road to recovery. But Cal knew I wasn't telling the whole story. "Come on, Steve, cut the bullshit," Cal would say. "Tell us what's really on your mind."

It wasn't easy for Cal and the rest of the St. Mary's staff to get me to be completely honest about my feelings and doubts. In fact, I was never completely honest. The macho code of Clarkston still prevailed at times. But St. Mary's brought me closer than I'd ever been to dealing with my emotions and my past.

At first, although I told Dr. Mann and everyone else that I was looking forward to family week, I did what I could to keep my family away from St. Mary's. I didn't want a rerun of the Battle of CareUnit.

Dr. Mann convinced me that unless I faced my parents, my resentment would hinder my recovery. Family week didn't happen during my first stay at St. Mary's, but Mom and Dad met me in Minneapolis in December of 1985, when I returned for follow-up treatment after another relapse. It had to be tough on Mom and Dad. They must have thought I blamed them for everything that happened. I'm grateful that they went through with it to help me. When it was finally over, I was relieved.

Dr. Mann recommended that I spend time in a halfway house in the Twin Cities after my first St. Mary's treatment ended in October. He told me the other addicts with whom I'd live would provide a strong base of support to help me adjust to daily life without drugs. He'd even arranged for me to use the Twins' facilities for workouts while I was in the halfway house.

Again I rejected this alternative. I was afraid reporters would find out and camp on my doorstep. My family and I could do without that kind of harassment and embarrassment. Cindy was also opposed. She wanted me home, at our new place in Montana.

Dr. Mann had worked hard to build my self-confidence, stressing that I had positive qualities as a person that had nothing to do with my status as a professional athlete. I arrived in Montana feeling a lot better about myself, thinking that I was finally ready to put drugs and failure behind me. Between my release from St. Mary's and Christmas of 1985, I got high only once, in early December. For a change, we had a warm, normal family Christmas.

There was just one issue left to be resolved, and it gnawed at me a little more each day. I'd had three well-publicized relapses in two and a half years, and two teams had released me in 1985. Had my baseball career been obliterated by an avalanche of white powder?

13

Two Nomads in Florida

Steve's fragility comes from a number of sources. One is that his self-image is very tenuous, based on some very superficial kinds of things. Looking good externally, performing well. His core—at least at that time—was pretty much missing. That makes you pretty vulnerable, if you don't have a good core inside yourself.

Another thing which is a terrible problem for Steve is that he's very immature, and immaturity was another really significant part of his fragility. In all the work we did with him over the past—seems like five years—the thing that always came to the surface that was outstanding was immature, immature, immature. Every test we gave, every psychological test, Steve came out very immature.

To sort of digress for a second, when you're dealing in chemical dependency, that is not unusual. The reason it's not unusual is that there's pretty good evidence that if someone begins to drink relatively heavily or use other substances in adolescence, the maturation process really stops in adolescence, so you may have someone who is a 40-year-old adolescent. They're chronologically 40 years old, but if you test them, they look like a 15-year-old. That's not unusual, so in that sense Steve's not unusual at all. But the fact is that he is a 29-year-old adolescent. That really makes him very vulnerable, very, very fragile, because he's got all of the vulnerability that all adolescents have.

The other thing that's very closely related is that he's terribly impulsive. The combination of his impulsiveness and his immaturity is what always gets him in trouble. He can't keep his mouth shut; he's gotta talk.

He gets in settings and says stuff that he never should say, sort of loses his judgment, and he will impulsively say something, impulsively do something.

Then, because his self-image is so fragile, he's gotta find ways to protect that. Either "I never said it," "I never did it," or he tries to justify it. It's very hard for Steve to say, "Yup, I did it; I was wrong; I'm sorry; I really screwed up." Very hard for him to say that.

—Dr. George Mann
Director, St. Mary's Hospital
Rehabilitation Center,
Minneapolis
November 1986

———————

I was confident that my physical ailments were behind me. All my elbow needed was rest. I didn't use it from the time I entered St. Mary's until early December, when I started weight training and throwing with high school players in Whitefish. I was surprised that almost right away my velocity was back and the pain was only a bad memory. I knew that by February I'd be ready to go to somebody's spring training camp and prove I could still pitch with the best.

Who would give me that chance? I felt better than ever about my ability to throw a ball, but no amount of throwing from a mound would show a team what was going on inside me. Baseball people are trained to assess physical skills, not psychological health. My track record suggested that I was less than a good risk.

If I was going to get back into baseball, I'd need the most able, aggressive and persuasive agent around, a real pro. Little did I know that the right guy would turn out to be a sawed-off Montana lawyer with no experience as an agent for professional athletes.

Ron Holliday and Benny Bee are successful businessmen in the Kalispell-Whitefish area, and John Lence represents both of them. Lence built his reputation as a business and tax lawyer—he's never lost a tax case—and he'd always wanted to represent ballplayers. Ron and Benny told me to forget that Lence had no experience as an agent. After one long meeting at Lence's office in January, I realized they were right. The little Italian sucker is smart, knows a lot of baseball and negotiates like the Godfather. He may be low to the ground, but he's high profile.

The Lence family is another family that has taken me in and treated me as one of its own. John's wife, Gwen, is a beautiful woman, and the littlest Lences, Mario Valentino and Natalee, are lovely children.

It's hard for me to believe that so many athletes get in trouble or go broke because they've trusted agents who've had no special training and don't have to obey a professional code of ethics. Most agents aren't lawyers. An athlete works too hard for his money, and his career is too short, for him to take risks away from the playing field. He should be represented by a lawyer who has been thoroughly checked out and is both competent and ethical.

Before Lence began to represent me, I tried to mend fences on my own. In late November or early December, I called Commissioner Peter Ueberroth from Benny Bee's office at the KJJR and B-98 studios in Whitefish. Ueberroth had been in office for only a year, following his successful management of the 1984 Olympics. The commissioner had his hands full trying to decide what kind of punitive action to take against 11 players who had been implicated as cocaine abusers during the Pittsburgh drug trials. At that point, Uebie hadn't yet interviewed the players.

In late February he announced one-year suspensions for seven players unless they agreed to pay ten percent of their 1986 salaries to drug prevention programs, undergo random testing and donate 100 hours of community service. Those players were Joaquin Andujar, Dave Parker, Keith Hernandez, Lonnie Smith, Enos Cabell, Jeff Leonard and Dale Berra. All of the players agreed to the conditions in order to keep playing. The other four players—Al Holland, Lee Lacy, Lary Sorensen and Claudell Washington—were suspended for 60 days unless they took the same medicine from Dr. Ueberroth.

The community service and testing penalties turned out to be jokes. From what I've heard, some of those guys—Keith Hernandez of the Mets, for one—paid no attention to the community service requirement. In July 1987 Lonnie Smith revealed he'd been tested only a couple of times in 17 months.

My first conversation with the commissioner lasted 25 minutes. He was cordial. At least he sounded that way. "Sir," I said, in an unusual display of respect, "I'm willing to fly to New York at my expense to meet with you. I want to prove to you that I'm off drugs and I'm working hard every day to stay that way. I'll answer any questions you have and provide any information you want. I want to come back to the major leagues."

"Steve," he said, "I have no problem with you. I'd like to meet with you, but right now I've got to interview all these people from the Pittsburgh trial. I'll get back to you as soon as I'm done with them." He never called back.

Lence's first task was to contact all 26 major league teams to find out if any of them were interested in me. His letters were mailed during the first week of February 1986.

The response wasn't overwhelming. There were no offers, no mention of future possibilities. Most of the teams didn't have the courtesy to reply. The rudest organization was Atlanta's, which didn't respond to letters and didn't return phone calls. Given the Braves' perennial finish at the bottom of the heap, you'd think they'd be looking for all the help they could get. Only the Chicago White Sox and Cubs, the Toronto Blue Jays and the San Francisco Giants were friendly.

All through February, Lence phoned Ueberroth. On each occasion, the commissioner's office told Lence that Uebie was out of town and would call back as soon as he returned. I guess he never made it back to New York because we never heard from him.

Lence started directing his calls to Ed Durso, a lawyer who has a fancy title and serves as house servant and minister of doom in Uebie's office. Baseball executives sometimes refer to Durso as "The Commissionerette." Durso also was too busy to call back. Lence estimates that maybe a handful of his 150 or so calls to the commissioner's office were returned in four months.

In early March Durso agreed to meet us at John Wayne Airport in Orange County, California. "If you tell anyone that you're meeting with me, I won't show up," Durso said.

Durso is a short, impatient guy with no personality. We'd brought documentation of my treatment history, my medical condition and my aftercare program. Durso wasn't interested. He didn't even want to know what had happened in Minnesota.

But he was very interested in quizzing me about cocaine use in baseball. Who were the dirty players and the suppliers? Which towns were the worst drug traps? Where were the drug hangouts in each town? I thought Harry Gibbs had reappeared in Durso's body. That shouldn't have been much of a surprise, though, because Durso is Gibbs's boss.

Durso was trying to tell us that I had no chance to play in the majors again unless I'd snitch on everyone who'd ever had a toot. I wanted to play, but not badly enough to turn commissioner's evidence and ruin a lot of careers. It was a waste of our time and money to meet with Durso.

By the time we got back to Montana, John and I decided to go to spring training camps in Florida and knock on doors to find a job for me. I was sure that once the baseball executives saw me pitch and talked to me face-to-face, they'd be impressed by my physical condition and supposed newfound dedication to sobriety.

Before we could pack and take off, John got a call from Al Rosen, vice president of the Giants, who'd been friendly to us. "I am definitely interested in Steve Howe," he said. "But for reasons I don't want to discuss with you, I cannot make a commitment now, and our rosters are filled."

We offered to stop in Phoenix, where the Giants train, before going to Florida. "I don't want you flying over here, because I can't make you a commitment," Rosen repeated. "Frankly, your persistence impresses me. But I can't make a commitment, and I don't want you to waste your time."

If Rosen really didn't have room for me in his organization, he wouldn't have bothered to call with a message like that. Maybe he'd been told he couldn't have me. We began to get the idea that Ueberroth had a solution to the Howe problem. We were about to find out how chilly Florida can be in the spring.

We lucked into some free lodging in Winter Haven, right down the street from the Red Sox training facility. Norman and Nona Wood, Lence's clients from Great Falls, Montana, owned a Comfort Inn there and comped the rooms for us. The location couldn't have been better. We wanted to visit the Red Sox, who'd encouraged us to stop by if we were in the neighborhood.

The Sox opened camp on February 20 and we showed up at 9:00 a.m. Lou Gorman, the general manager, was greeting visitors in the press area. We asked someone to tell him we were there. Two hours later, Gorman came by. As soon as he saw us, he hustled us into his office and closed the door to get me out of sight.

"Good to see you, Steve," Gorman said, looking at me as if I had the plague. "Jeez, boy, you look like you're in great shape."

I was offering to sign a contract for the major league minimum salary, without a guarantee, with a 30-day spring training option. In other words, the Sox could cut me for any contrived reason after 30 days with no further obligation. Gorman wasn't encouraging. He didn't offer me a chance to work out. He wouldn't even make eye contact. It was obvious that he wanted the meeting to be as short and as unproductive as possible.

Lence went back that afternoon to see if Gorman would tell him more without me around. "I think you're wasting your time," Gorman told Lence. "We just don't have a place on the team. We have a guy named Zambito—"

"You mean Sambito," Lence said.

"Zambito, whatever. He's gonna be our left-handed stopper."

Joe Sambito had been a hard-throwing, successful reliever for Houston for about six years, but he'd blown out his arm in 1982 and hadn't been the same since. "What about his arm?" Lence asked Gorman.

"We clocked his fastball at 87 in winter ball," Gorman said proudly.

"Howe warms up at 87," Lence said.

Gorman still wouldn't permit a workout, even after we offered to do it late in the day with no one around. "I can't really tell you why exactly," Gorman told Lence the next day. "I'm really sorry. My answer's still no."

Lence was calling other general managers throughout Florida, but the answer was always the same: No thanks, our rosters are full. Syd Thrift of Pittsburgh and Bobby Cox of Atlanta turned us down. So did Dick Wagner, who was still GM for Houston. Wagner added the same phrase we'd heard from Rosen and Gorman: "I can't tell you why."

Several days later, we drove to Tampa for a meeting with Gord Ash and Pat Gillick of Toronto. The Blue Jays wanted me, and they later proved it by following me around for most of 1986 and making an offer before I signed with Texas in 1987. But in February of 1986, Gillick and Ash might as well have been bound and gagged. They were unable to do much more than wish me luck.

Bill Lajoie of the Tigers was downright rude when we visited him in Lakeland. He was haggling over a minor league contract and didn't even say hello. Lajoie walked into his office, slammed the door and waited us out. We got the message and left. That hurt the worst, because since college days I have considered Bill Lajoie a good friend.

A couple of days after we arrived in Florida, when we were still talking with Gorman, I started worrying that my arm would suffer if I didn't work out. Nona Wood said she knew former major leaguers Denny, Blake and Brian Doyle, who operated the Doyle Baseball School out of an office in Winter Haven. One of the Doyles—not Denny, who was out of town—offered to let me work out with one of their young instructors. We had to drive 90 miles so I could throw for 20 minutes on a sandlot field to a catcher who'd played AAA ball in the Twins' system.

Denny Doyle called Lence the next day. "I just talked to our legal counsel," Denny said, "and he said it isn't a good idea to let Steve Howe work out at our school."

Lence got hot. "Come on, Denny, give us a break. Why don't you just level with us and tell us what the problem is? I'm a lawyer and I know there's no problem with liability. What is it? Are you afraid Howe's going to be out there snorting and beaning people? All he wants to do is go out on the side of the field and play catch with somebody."

"Well," said Doyle, "I just don't want to take the chance."

What chance? The chance that Peter Ueberroth would revoke Major League Baseball's endorsement of the Doyles' school, an endorsement upon which the Doyles depend for survival. Ueberroth never had to lift a tanned, manicured finger from his recliner by the pool in Newport Beach to let Doyle know he was on dangerous ground. The implied threat could have been delivered by one of Uebie's lackeys in New York. Something like, "Hey, Denny, we don't think Howe will be a positive influence on the kids who are working out at your school." Doyle got the message from someone.

The commissioner's signature was all over the closed-door reception Lence and I got in Florida. Teams needed relief help but wouldn't let me throw a pitch anywhere near their spring training complexes. General managers avoided meeting with us. When we did meet, the conversations were quick, hushed, secluded and aimless. It all could have been a coincidence of disinterest in an addict who had fallen off the wagon a few times too many—except for one thing. At least three GMs used the same apologetic yet ominous phrase: "I can't tell you why." You don't need a lot of imagination to conclude that a higher authority was jerking the strings of the team executives.

There were a lot of other admitted drug users rattling around spring training camps that spring, but guys like Dave Parker, Keith Hernandez, Joaquin Andujar and Jeff Leonard got their usual hefty paychecks instead of the cold shoulder. They'd been under contract before their publicized involvement in the Pittsburgh drug trial, so their teams went to bat for them and the commissioner did nothing more than slap their wrists.

Parker and Hernandez and the rest of the drug trial celebrities had been addicted to coke or had snorted their way through several baseball seasons, just like me. The difference was that I'd been caught more than once after I'd admitted my problem.

I was still "The Example." Ueberroth couldn't fine me or order community service because I didn't have a contract. But it was easy for him to secretly hit me with the ultimate penalty: banishment from major league organizations. I had no ballclub to protect me.

In telephone conversations with Lence in early March, a couple of which took place when I was in Lence's office, Durso let us know I was not going to be welcomed back anytime soon. When Lence asked what the commissioner wanted me to do, Durso said, "I want assurances that you client isn't going to get back on drugs and isn't going to embarrass Major League Baseball. And I want that documented with medical evidence."

Those conditions were not only unique, they were impossible to satisfy, and Durso knew it. Dr. Mann couldn't pledge with medical certainty that I would never snort coke again. Dr. Mann couldn't even say that he wouldn't try the stuff. Chemical dependency is principally a disease of the mind, not a physical injury. You can't relieve the pain with a cortisone shot or repair the damage with surgery. The most definite report Dr. Mann could make was that, based on the medical evidence before him, I was progressing toward recovery.

It looked to Lence and me that I had two choices: bring legal action to clarify my eligibility, or sit around—probably for a year—until the commissioner decided I was no longer a menace to society. Neither alternative was appealing. But we hadn't thought about the independents.

14

The San Jose Shuffle

Oh, I knew Steve Howe could still pitch. I really had nothing to lose on this. Steve Howe's problems to me weren't physical at all. You know, maybe at one point he had an arm problem, but I wasn't even worried about that end of it. That was the furthest thing from my mind.

Any doubts were removed when I saw him his first day. Then as we got into the season, I knew it was just a matter of him staying clean and passing the tests, and it would only be a matter of time before he got back up there. Everything was going fine until he flunked that first test.

He was always early to practice. There were occasional times, like everybody else, when he would be late, but most of the time he was here real early and worked hard when he was here. He was a professional in all respects once he got to the park. And he had the kind of personality where he was a big part of the club; he was well-liked by everybody.

—Harry Steve
President, San Jose Bees
October 1986

Nearly all of the dozens of minor league teams in organized baseball are affiliated with major league teams. But there are a handful

214

of minor league clubs that have no affiliation. Most of them are owned by dreamers who love the game enough (or are crazy enough) to endure a lot of financial punishment, betting against the odds that they'll be able to cut a deal with a major league organization before they go broke. If they make the major league connection, they can count on a steady flow of promising young players whose salaries are paid by the major league club. If they can't affiliate, they scramble for money and bodies.

In early March Lence was contacted by a guy from Miami who wanted to serve as our contact with the Miami Marlins, an independent team playing in the Class A Florida State League. Lence checked the guy out and found he was just a sleazebag without solid connections to the Marlins. Then Lence got a call from Harry Steve, president of the San Jose Bees of the California League.

Harry was about 30, a fidgety little operator who'd gone west from Youngstown, Ohio, to seek his fortune. Instead he found the Bees. In 1985 he'd averaged about 600 fans a game and lost a pile of money. But Harry wasn't going to accept the poverty that usually dogs an independent owner. He had a plan to improve his attendance, and I was the central figure in the plan.

San Jose is a big, growing city where the media competition is intense. Harry figured if he could attract media attention by signing well-known ballplayers, he could draw enough fans to survive. He'd already signed Mike Norris, Ken Reitz and Derrel Thomas and was pursuing Daryl Sconiers. He also wanted me.

Harry flew to Montana during the first week of March. He wanted to sign me to a contract on the spot, but we were still talking to Toronto and put him off. "When I call you and tell you I'm on my way, I'll join the team and sign the contract," I told Harry.

Nothing happened with Toronto or any other big league club, so I took off for San Jose. Cindy stayed in Montana with Chelsi. I didn't expect to be in San Jose for long, so it seemed senseless to uproot my family until I was signed by a major league team. Besides, I wouldn't be making enough money to pay for respectable lodging for all three of us.

On March 21 I signed with Harry and the Bees for all of $2,000 a month, a fraction of the major league minimum. I couldn't complain because I was the highest-paid player on the team. Most of the guys were making about $500 a month.

Our deal with Harry was that I owned 75 percent of my contract. If a major league club purchased the contract, Harry would get a quarter of the purchase price. He'd also get extra revenue from the additional fans he'd draw when I pitched. In order to take full advantage of my notoriety, Harry needed to announce when I'd pitch, so I became a starter.

Harry's marquee names were more likely to be appointed to the FBI's most wanted list than to the boards of their local Rotary Clubs. Mike Norris had won 22 games for Oakland in 1980, but had hardly pitched since 1983 because of injuries and cocaine dependency. He'd also been arrested twice for drug possession. Ken Reitz, the former Cardinal and Giant third baseman, had a history of amphetamine abuse and was near the end of a long career. Derrel Thomas, my old Dodger teammate, had run into difficulties too numerous to mention, but Harry had signed him. Daryl Sconiers, the former Angel first baseman, had also undergone rehabilitation for cocaine dependency. I fit right in.

A couple of other Bees had served in major league organizations, but had left after disagreements with management. Darryl Cias, a catcher, hit .333 in 19 games with Oakland in 1983, but was released at his request after bickering with A's General Manager Karl Kuehl during spring training in 1984. Mike Bigusiak was pitching for Clinton, Iowa, in the Dodger organization in 1976 when his manager, Bob Hartsfield, called him a "dumb Polack." Bigusiak decked him with one punch. His payoff for that KO was a pink slip.

Most of the rest of the players had never been successful, so we weren't loaded with talent. The Seibu Lions, a Japanese major league team, helped out by loaning the Bees five young players from their organization. Harry's connection with the Lions was Hank Wada, a former catcher in Japan who also served as the Bees' acupuncturist and pitching coach.

This collection of rejects got along well with one another. The guys with the checkered pasts weren't bad people—they were good people who'd made mistakes. They were a great bunch, and Harry Steve, the Greek tycoon, was a fun guy to work for.

As he'd hoped, Harry's act played well with the media. His collection of derelicts, misfits and rejects drew national attention. Even *Rolling Stone* magazine sent a writer to follow us, and he aptly nicknamed us the "Bad Nose Bees."

My first two weeks of spring training consisted of throwing and running with Reitz and a couple of other players until the rest of the team showed up. As a team, we worked out together for only a week before the season started. There was one training camp casualty. Derrel Thomas decided he should be the manager. Harry, who planned to manage the team himself, disagreed. Derrel wouldn't back down, and Harry released him on April 9.

Norris was still popular in the nearby Bay Area, so Harry selected him to start the opener. Nearly 5,000 fans filled our little ballpark. Harry was ecstatic until shortly before game time, when he noticed that Norris was missing. Harry tried to call him. No luck. Harry was frantic. "Can you go, Howzer?" he asked. I was ready.

Always the showman, Harry introduced each Bee individually over the PA system before the game, as though we were defending world champions. He saved me for last. When I was announced as the starter, the crowd went bananas, singing and screaming and blowing horns. It was wild.

Pitching to Class A hitters was tougher than you might think. We had no scouting reports, and I knew the kids on the other side would be flailing away at everything, hoping to impress their manager by ripping one against a pitcher with major league stuff. I couldn't try to set them up. My arm was fully recovered and felt great, so I let it rip and had some fun. I was hoping I'd be in San Jose only a month, until a major league team saw I was healthy and grabbed me. This was going to be an extended but important spring training for me.

I struck out the first hitter on four pitches, the last one a nasty curve the kid swung at long before the ball arrived. I worked five innings, giving up two hits and no runs. Norris arrived after a few innings. Car trouble, he said.

Although we continued to draw great crowds at home when Norris and I pitched, things went downhill for the Bees on the field after a good start. There wasn't enough talent, and we hadn't played together much. Fielders were colliding and missing cutoff men, and baserunners were making hilarious blunders. When I was on the bench watching, I averaged 10 to 15 big league chuckles a game.

When I was pitching I wasn't chuckling much, maybe because I was working hard and the team seemed to play better behind me. There were scouts in the stands, and I wanted to impress them. By

May 1 I'd thrown 15 and two-thirds innings, rung up 13 strikeouts, and allowed only nine hits, no walks and one earned run.

Even before the California League season started, Toronto scout Gerry Sobeck was hanging around the ballpark, watching me work out. Gerry and I became friends. We'd hang around together and go out for food. "Toronto could sure use you," he said. "You know, I send them my reports on you, and those reports are the best I've ever done. I'm recommending that they sign you."

Gerry soon had plenty of professional company in the stands. Every time I pitched, there were six or seven scouts on hand. Scouts from San Francisco, Oakland and Pittsburgh were regulars.

I had to keep plugging. Several weeks into the major league season, team executives had abandoned their spring training dreams and were coldly evaluating their weaknesses. Lots of teams needed left-handed relievers. There seemed to be plenty of interest in me. I sensed that something was about to break.

When the Bees' season started, Harry Steve tested me regularly for drug use. The tests were for my benefit as much as for the Bees' protection. Unless I could offer substantial evidence that I was clean, no major league team was going to take a chance on me. By the end of April, I'd handed in several clean samples. I was on a hot streak.

Years from now, when I reflect on my baseball career, the dominant and most consistent image in my mind probably will be a plastic specimen bottle. Since 1983 the teams, teammates, cities and even leagues have changed frequently, but the plastic bottles and cups have always been there.

On Monday, April 28, 1986, Durso told Lence that the commissioner's office was going to start testing me. "If he tests clean, we'll need some kind of solution for him," Durso said.

We had to cooperate. Maybe Ueberroth didn't trust the reliability of the Bees' test results. Maybe a few teams had inquired about my eligibility and Ueberroth wanted his own investigation. Maybe a combination of the two. I think Uebie was looking for a positive test so he could declare me ineligible. That's just my opinion. The only basis for my opinion is the facts.

The Giants' interest in me had intensified, and Cleveland had checked in with Lence. Oakland was still in the picture, but the A's didn't want anyone to know about it. "We're going to send somebody from our front office over there to watch Howe," A's GM Sandy Alderson told Lence. "But don't leak it to the press or we won't show up."

Alderson must have borrowed his script from Durso. That's the kind of garbage I had to put up with all year. Most teams treated me like a Jew in wartime Germany, a Jew they hoped to disguise as an Aryan and hide in their bullpen.

I expected the commissioner's representative to test me within two or three days. I refused to leave my room at the Holiday Inn by myself, except to go to the ballpark. I wasn't going to give the commissioner any ammunition.

I spent almost all day Wednesday with Toronto's Sobeck. We went to dinner that night and to lunch on Thursday. When we got back to San Jose Municipal Stadium after lunch, Tony Rogers, the commissioner's testing representative, had been waiting more than an hour in an office. Mike Verdi, a Bees coach, was the only other person in the room. Rogers gave me a plastic container. I filled it halfway, right in front of him. It's embarrassing, even dehumanizing to urinate in a container in front of a total stranger, but I was used to it. "That's not enough," Rogers said.

I was no rookie in the testing league, and I knew Rogers had enough to run a test. "That's all I got," I said.

"Well, why don't you go drink some water until you can pee again?"

Without thinking about it, I walked out of the room to find water, leaving Rogers with my unsealed sample. Verdi left with me. I went back 15 or 20 minutes later and finished the job. Rogers sealed the sample and left the stadium.

The procedure of testing a urine sample is not complicated, and it rarely takes longer than three days for a test result to come back. Sometimes the results of the Bees' tests were available the same day. When I heard nothing from the commissioner's office for several days, I figured all was well. I had no reason to worry about it.

On May 5 Lence called Durso. "Can we go make a deal?" Lence asked.

"Yeah, I don't see any problem. Go make a deal," Durso said.

Until early May major league teams had sent scouts to see me pitch. Now the front office executives, the guys with the power to sign contracts, started coming to San Jose to find out if there was any truth to the rave scouting reports they'd been reading. Al Rosen of the Giants and Toronto's Pat Gillick told Lence they would personally attend my May 14 start. Cleveland and possibly Oakland would also be represented. It was show time.

On May 12 Lence got calls from several teams. "Give Ed Durso a little nudge," Gillick told Lence. "I think he's ready."

Instead, Durso and Ueberroth nudged me. Durso called Lence on May 13 and told him that the commissioner's office had just received the result of a preliminary (and often inaccurate) EMIT screen run on my May 1 urine sample. According to Durso, the result was positive.

"Does it take you guys two weeks to run a test through a screen?" Lence asked.

Durso didn't answer. Instead, he asked permission to run a more sophisticated and usually reliable gas chromatography/mass spectrometry (GCMS) test, which can actually measure and report the levels of chemicals in a sample when you tell the machine what chemicals you want it to look for. Lence agreed to the GCMS. On the afternoon of the 14th, Durso called back and said the GCMS result was positive. He demanded that Lence call me and tell me not to pitch. "Why would I pull my player off the field?" Lence yelled. "If you want to call, you call. You're making a hell of a mistake."

I was happy and excited when I walked into the stadium that afternoon. Harry Steve came into the clubhouse and told me Lence was on the phone. I took the call in Harry's office.

"You're not going to believe this," Lence said. "They told us there's a problem with the test. They don't want you to pitch tonight."

Durso didn't have the guts to call me himself. The late John Johnson, who was then president of the National Association that controls the minor leagues, called and told both Harry and me that I couldn't pitch. He also suggested that Harry announce I was unable to pitch because my arm was sore.

Bedlam reigned at the stadium. Harry was off the wall. I was so angry and frustrated that I thought my head was going to blow up. Still in uniform, I stormed out of the stadium and returned to the Holiday Inn.

As soon as I got there, I called the stadium and got Al Rosen on the phone. "Al, I don't know what's going on," I said. "They said I had a dirty test, or there's a problem with the test, and that's bullshit. I want you to know that. I'm really embarrassed by this. I can't believe this is happening to me."

"Hey, just hang in there," said Rosen. "Everything is going to be all right. They'll clear it up."

Two minutes after I hung up, Harry called. He was scared to death that if he disobeyed the commissioner and let me pitch, he'd lose his franchise. But Harry also had a ballpark full of people who'd paid to see me pitch, he was mad as hell at the commissioner, and he had a lot of guts.

"You wanna pitch?" he asked.

"That's right."

"Then come on and pitch."

First I called Johnny Johnson in Florida. "I'm letting you know right now that I'm defying your order and the commissioner's order and Harry Steve's order not to pitch," I said, trying to protect Harry. "It's on the record. I'm pitching."

"This will have grave implications for your baseball career," Johnson threatened.

"What have you done for my baseball career in the last six months? I've got nothing to lose."

I got to the stadium ten minutes before game time and threw a few warm-ups. I was in outer space. Jumbled thoughts whirled through my head at 1,000 miles an hour. They couldn't stop me from pitching this game. I wasn't going to quit. Then it occurred to me that this might be my last game as a professional ballplayer. My sweat turned cold. My hands shook from dread as well as anger.

I wasn't a craftsman that night. I gave up three runs and my first two walks of the year, but we won.

Rosen came up to me after the game. "That showed a lot of guts, for you to go out there and pitch," he said.

"If I'd have done something wrong, I'd have packed my bags and left," I said. "But I didn't, and I'm not walking away from this."

Punishment came swiftly. The next morning Joe Gagliardi, president of the California League, suspended me for defying a direct order from Johnson. He also suspended Harry Steve indefinitely.

No one in San Jose could believe what had happened. "If you were doing any of that stuff," Sobeck said later, "I have to give it to you. I was in contact with you every day, talking on the phone, taking you out to lunch and dinner. There is no way you could have used coke any time that I was associated with you in San Jose. I saw you too much."

On the day I was suspended, Mike Verdi, who'd been there when Rogers took my urine sample, came up to me. "Why did you ever leave that guy in the office by himself with your urine unsealed?" he asked. "You know you're not supposed to do that."

The commissioner's office asked me to go to Los Angeles to meet with Dr. Anthony Daly, Major League Baseball's drug consultant and a Ueberroth crony from the 1984 Olympics. I flew to L.A. at my expense on May 16.

I talked to a psychiatrist for an hour, then met with Daly for 15 minutes. "We think you should go into inpatient therapy," said Daly.

I saw the trap. If I went into the tank again at their suggestion, I'd be admitting that I'd failed the May 1 test and needed help. I told Daly I wouldn't do it. "For what?" I asked him. "I'm not using cocaine. How can I go in for therapy when I'm not doing something?"

Instead of running home to Montana, I went back to San Jose. Even after meeting with Daly, I was sure the test incident was just another bureaucratic fiasco that Lence and I would straighten out with the commissioner's office in no time. Why go all the way home when my return to the mound was only a few days away?

When Harry Steve and I refused to lie and say that a sore arm had kept me off the mound on May 14, Durso, Johnny Johnson and Joe Gagliardi passed the word that there had been a "discrepancy" on my drug test. The choice of explanations they forced on me was really no choice at all. Either way, the major league teams were going to retreat and deny they'd ever considered signing me. And that's what happened.

Not for the first time in my life, my alleged test failure caused widespread controversy. Some major league players, including several Dodgers, complained that the commissioner's office should not have violated the pledge of confidentiality that is the implied exchange for a player's agreement to be tested. Ueberroth's office never responded to this point, and the Players Association didn't pick up the issue and run with it. Technically, my problem was outside the jurisdiction of the Players Association, which represents only major league players. Still, I felt abandoned by the union at a time when I most needed its help.

With my major league hopes temporarily on the shelf, Lence and I began investigating what had happened and plotting my reinstatement with the Bees. Not long after my suspension, we learned through our sources that the commissioner's office actually knew the result of the May 1 test on May 5. This scenario makes sense—a sample taken on a Thursday should be tested and analyzed by Monday. If that's true, and if Durso really received a positive reading on the test, Durso sat on it for eight days, hoping he'd never have to use such a tainted result. Then he heard who would be attending my May 14 start and recognized that several teams were hot to sign me, so he trotted out the test to nuke my chances. I doubt that Durso would have enacted such a plan without Ueberroth's approval.

If our inside information turned out to be bogus and my urine sample was not tested until May 12 or 13, the test was suspect for that reason alone. Where was my urine specimen, and who was tinkering with it during the holding period? But Durso's story doesn't add up. Why would the commissioner's office, which was so intent on catching me with a straw up my nose, hold my sample for 11 or 12 days before running it through a machine? It couldn't have happened that way.

Despite the numerous blatant flaws in the procedure for the May 1 test, no one in the offices of Major League Baseball, the National Association or the California League was anxious to reinstate me. Thinking we might have to sue to restore my eligibility, Lence and I retained Topel & Goodman, a small but nasty San Francisco law firm. During strategy sessions with Bill Goodman, we decided in early June that I should return to St. Mary's, not for therapy but for an evaluation that would establish my continuing recovery to the satisfaction of organized baseball. It was our last hope for working things out, short of litigation.

I checked into St. Mary's on June 9. For five days Dr. George Dorsey and the rest of Dr. Mann's staff ran me through a battery of physical and psychological examinations. They sampled my blood and tested it for any signs of drug use. They checked to see if drugs had diminished the concentrations of vitamins in my blood. I participated in group sessions and individual counseling so the doctors could see whether I would get nervous and lie like an addict trying to conceal a relapse.

The report signed by Dr. Mann and Dr. Dorsey contained a glowing diagnosis of "cocaine abuse in remission." They found that I was still somewhat immature and impulsive—nothing new there—but I was maturing. The doctors reported "no evidence of a relapse or cocaine use," and all of the St. Mary's staff involved in my evaluation were "strongly convinced" that I hadn't snorted coke during the period that the commissioner tested me. The prognosis: "There is no medical reason why this individual cannot return to the occupation of playing baseball."

Bill Goodman sent the report to Lou Hoynes, who was representing Major League Baseball (when the going got tough, Durso dialed outside counsel), by Federal Express on June 18. We had a deal two days later, probably because the commissioner's office knew it could save face by using the St. Mary's report to reinstate me. Goodman had made it clear that if I was not reinstated, litigation would surely follow and the commissioner's office would be embarrassed by public revelations about the May 1 test.

The conditions of my reinstatement were to follow a seven-point St. Mary's program that included drug testing twice a week, Alcoholics Anonymous/Narcotics Anonymous meetings twice a week, continued contact with my AA sponsor, return visits to St. Mary's at least once every three months, work to improve my relationships with Cindy and my parents, workouts and diets to stay in shape and telephone calls to Dr. Mann at least once a month. The deal also made me eligible to sign a major league contract during or after the All-Star break, which would begin July 14. We got the commissioner's office to agree that Tony Rogers would not be taking my urine samples.

I was also told to refrain from making any public comment about the circumstances of my suspension. Oops, I guess I just violated that order. There are two good reasons for my disobedience. One is that everyone should know how this commissioner of baseball, who hollered long and loud about the "integrity of the game," really operated. The other reason is that Johnny Johnson gave false information to the public about my visit to St. Mary's when my reinstatement was announced. I wonder who put him up to that.

When the announcement was made on June 24, the day my suspension officially ended, neither Ueberroth nor Durso wanted to be in the neighborhood. They hid behind the tinted glass in their offices on Park Avenue in New York and got someone else to do their dirty work for them. Once again they chose Johnny Johnson, a good man and solid baseball executive, who deserved a better fate than being the doormat under Peter Ueberroth's feet.

Johnson made the following statement: "Since his suspension last May, Howe has undergone additional drug rehabilitation therapy, and shown a positive and constructive attitude in addressing the concerns which gave rise to my action [the suspension]."

The statement can be interpreted only one way: I had recognized that I was still a drug abuser and, like a good citizen, had sought help. I wouldn't agree to Dr. Daly's request that I undergo therapy, so Johnson used my St. Mary's evaluation as a confession that I'd failed the May 1 test.

I was at St. Mary's for only five days, and no one who relapses and undergoes rehabilitation therapy gets away from Dr. Mann in less than three weeks. More to the point, Ueberroth and Durso had seen the report by St. Mary's, which clearly said there was "no evidence of a relapse."

I had to pass my drug tests and lure the scouts and big-league executives back to San Jose by showing that six weeks off hadn't hurt my stuff. I'd been so busy visiting lawyers and bouncing around between Minnesota and the West Coast that I'd thrown only three times during the suspension.

I started pitching well right away. Between June 24 and the end of my season, I pitched poorly only once. That outing and my stressed-out May 14 start were my only two ineffective performances while I was in San Jose. As a Bee I allowed only eight earned runs in 50 innings.

The first major league teams to shadow me after my reinstatement were Toronto and the Chicago White Sox. The Sox's general manager was Tom Haller, who began the season as the Giants' general manager. He hadn't forgotten me.

I worked five innings in my first start. Haller wanted to find out how strong my arm was, so Harry Steve brought me back two days later. I pitched three innings, gave up only one hit and struck out six.

Haller was interviewed on TV and said he was definitely interested in me. Then he disappeared. We never heard from him again.

Lence's discussions with the Blue Jays seemed more serious. Jays Player Personnel Director Gordon Ash was saying nice things about me and implying that he was about to make me an offer. On Monday, July 7, eight days before the All-Star Game, Ash drove to Kalispell by way of Calgary and Medicine Hat, Alberta, where he'd been checking out minor league players. Ash and his wife took a suite at the Outlaw Inn for three nights. That night Ash and Lence had dinner.

"There's still some question whether or not he can throw to a major league batter," Ash told Lence. "I don't have that question, but you always run into that. I am one who happens to believe that Steve Howe rises to the occasion. You put Babe Ruth up against him, he'll strike out Babe Ruth or get him out if he has to. But if you go up against him, he'll pitch to your level."

Ash and Lence agreed to meet in Lence's office at 11:00 a.m. Tuesday to talk contract. But at 10:30 Ash called and canceled. Lence immediately called Ash back at the Outlaw. "We have a real emergency," Ash said. "My wife's sister's husband's mother is ill up in Lethbridge (Alberta). We're gonna have to drive up there."

Ash was in Lence's office at 9:00 a.m. Wednesday. Ash sat and talked for two hours without ever opening his briefcase. "We're not ready to make an offer," Ash finally said, "but I want you to know we're very serious about Steve Howe."

"You could have told me that by telephone," Lence said. "Look, Peter Ueberroth pulled you off this thing, didn't he?"

"I can't say," Ash replied. "I don't want to talk about it." Then Ash left town.

Lence called me and told me what had happened. We figured Ueberroth was keeping everyone away from me until July 14, when I became eligible to sign. We also anticipated a final drug test at about that time. Lence said, "Trying to get you a major league offer is like trying to get Attila the Hun a job in a nursery."

The following weekend, the Bees traveled to Modesto. Knowing I was facing a drug test and possible negotiations with major league clubs, Harry let me stay in San Jose. I wish he'd insisted that I ride the bus to Modesto.

In any town where professional baseball is played, from Boston to Bellingham, there are people who hang around the team just because they like to be in the company of pro athletes. Maybe they hope the ballplayers' celebrity will rub off on them. I got to know a few of San Jose's baseball junkies through chance conversations around the ballpark. On July 13 one of them invited me to a party at his house that evening. He seemed like a regular, harmless guy. I should have chained myself to my hotel bed, but impulse took over.

The party was wilder than I'd expected. My acquaintance from the ballpark was laying out lines of coke on mirrors and table tops all over the house. Voices in my head urged me to leave, or at least sit in a corner and politely decline. You're so close, and now you're going to blow all these months of hard work, the voices said. Think how you'll hurt Cindy, Chelsi, Lence, Harry and all the others who've stuck with you for so long, they said. But with each passing minute the voices grew weak and the lure of the white powder, so long forbidden and so close at hand, grew powerful. I wasn't yet strong enough to resist.

A line or two won't hurt, I told myself. A line or two became a dozen, and by the time I escaped, I knew I was in deep trouble.

The commissioner's representative called me the next morning, and I agreed to drive to San Francisco to provide a urine sample. I couldn't hide, couldn't refuse. Disappearance would be judged as harshly as a positive test result.

I took three tests that day: one for the commissioner, one for the Bees and one on my own as insurance. As proof that the tests are not always accurate, the test I took on my own came back negative the next day. The other two results were positive.

This time Harry suspended me before the commissioner or Johnny Johnson could act. I lied to Harry, told him I was clean and urged him to wait. Harry said he had to protect his franchise. Later Joe Gagliardi suspended me from the California League.

I spent the next couple of months lying to everyone about what had happened. I'd been so close, and so many people had counted on me to make it. I couldn't tell them I'd let them down.

Since the spring, Ueberroth had searched for evidence that I was still a dirtball. This time the commissioner didn't have to manufacture his proof. I handed it to him.

15

Fear and Loathing in the Fuhrer's Office

July 3rd. We had traveled to L.A., Tom Grieve and Sandy Johnson and I, and we hooked up with John Young, who's our West Coast scouting director. The purpose of that visit was really twofold. One, to look at Steve Howe as a pitcher and to have him throw for us, and that's certainly not my area of expertise. Sandy and Tom and John Young were there for that reason. Sam McDowell, our employee assistance program counsel and I were along to look at Steve Howe as a human being.

He threw first, out at UCLA, and he was very impressive. Then we went back to the hotel, and for close to two hours Sam and I really put him through what has to be regarded as a stress interview. I was very impressed with a couple of things. One was the apparent resolve that Steve has had in the commitment he seems to have made, on a very personal basis, to his own sobriety.

You know, when asked to provide a description of himself, I think he's pretty accurate. He describes himself as a high-energy, sometimes impulsive individual, who can even be immature in his judgment and foresight. An individual like that who recognizes his own dynamics is in a position to modify them, or at least not to let them lead him to self-defeating behavior.

And I sensed in him a kind of maturity that comes from going through a lot of pain. Growing is painful.

—Mike Stone
President, Texas Rangers
September 1987

229

Once a weather front arrives in the Flathead Valley of Montana, it's reluctant to leave. During July and August you'd call the weather monotonous if it weren't so nice: long, warm, dry days under a strong but never overpowering sun, giving way to cool, starry nights.

When I returned home from San Jose in mid-July 1986, suspended for the second time in nine weeks from the California League, the upbeat nature of my surroundings helped me mask my disappointment. I assumed a positive, happy-go-lucky attitude for the benefit of my friends and family, but I was hurting inside. I'd climbed the wall, inch by inch, only to lose my grip and fall to the ground just as I was reaching the top. It seemed that my goal was determined to elude me. I questioned whether I had the stamina or even the desire to start over.

As usual, the whole world knew I'd fallen. The media hounded me for days after I reached Montana, and a few reporters visited me there. I told them that maybe the time had come to give up "kids' games."

As the steady downpours of September gave way to October's Indian summer, I devoted most of my time to my family and my snowmobile. I went back to work for Benny Bee, helping Bee Broadcasting construct a new transmitting tower on Big Mountain.

One warm day in October, while I was painting the tower building, a bear strolled out of the woods and past the tower. October is not the best time of year for a close encounter with 800 pounds of barely controlled fury. The bears know winter is coming. Their dispositions turn nastier than usual as their huckleberry supply wanes and they try to fill their bellies for the long sleep ahead.

Aware that I'd be working in bear country, I'd brought a gun with me, but it was on the dashboard of my truck, 30 feet away. The bear's path took him directly between the truck and me. All I could do was flatten myself against the tower building and pray. I didn't breathe for about a minute. Maybe I was downwind from the big guy, but if he knew I was there, he didn't let on. He just moved along nonchalantly and disappeared into the woods. I wasn't surprised to find that my legs were a little unsteady as I jogged to the truck to grab the gun.

Chelsi was three and a half that fall and full of energy. Her boundless enthusiasm and curiosity were exciting and difficult at the same time. It was wonderful to watch her grow and learn, but she was into everything. She was testing Cindy and me, finding out how far she could push us before we would discipline her. Chelsi needed my attention and direction more than ever. For once, I was there for her.

Passion for snowmobiling is so great in the northwest that people grass-drag their machines in summer and fall. That doesn't sound like such a big deal until you've gone 100 miles per hour on a sled through a field. I first tried grass-dragging in September 1986. With the help of Ted Jenkins and his crew at T & S Racing, a motor sports dealership in Kalispell in which I later purchased an interest, I upgraded my Polaris Indy 600 into a three-cylinder, 140-horsepower racer. After only about seven miles of breaking it in, I entered the drags in Kalispell under the sponsorship of Bee Broadcasting.

In both heats I was running at nearly 100 miles per hour by the time I reached the end of the 600-foot strip. I lost them both by a total of five feet. I hated to lose those races as much as I hated to give up a home run.

Generous dumpings of snow began to fall on Montana in November. Finally, I was able to break in my snowmobile by running it up and down mountains and through woods. The extra trail work and some fine tuning paid off the following January when I won a Flathead Valley championship on snow.

Maybe when my ballplaying days are over, I'll race cars and snowmobiles for a living. I love the competition of racing, and I'm good at it. Speed thrills me, and the risk is part of that thrill. Like every good racer, I appreciate the danger and I prepare my machines to minimize the risk. But I guess I'm too cocky, thickheaded or foolhardy—maybe all three—to be afraid. I have complete confidence in my ability to prepare and handle vehicles. I'm in control, so there's no reason for me to be apprehensive. It's not like running into a bear on a mountaintop when you're unarmed.

During the fall of 1986, I thought my full-time racing career might have begun before I was ready for it. Still, despite all the times I'd screwed up, I clung to the hope that I could salvage my baseball career. I was only 28 and my arm was strong. My best four or five years might be right in front of me. The trip back to the majors would be long and difficult, and Peter Ueberroth would throw up roadblocks whenever he had the chance. But I couldn't let him win. I was going to beat him.

Although I knew I was principally responsible for wrecking my career, I focused my natural aggressiveness on Ueberroth, Durso, Johnny Johnson and Joe Gagliardi, using them as motivational targets. They are the bad guys, I told myself. I'm going to show them. When I thought that I might have wasted my talent, I wanted to pitch more than ever before. The thought that others had interrupted my career drove me that much harder to reclaim it.

I'd been suspended only by the California League, on the basis of the Bees' July 14 test. Lence and I decided to begin the comeback process by asking Joe Gagliardi to reinstate me. Then we'd climb the power ladder and try to get clearance from Johnson and, ultimately, the commissioner. In October Lence began talking with Gagliardi by phone.

Gagliardi played Mr. Big Shot at first. He let us know that he, and only he, had the power to restore my eligibility. He asked for information on my aftercare program, my contacts with Dr. Mann and the results of any drug tests I might have taken (none since I'd left California). Lence played along with Gagliardi, telling him what a wonderful, fair-minded baseball executive we thought he was.

It soon became clear that Gagliardi really had no authority. On November 6 Lence sent him a letter formally requesting my reinstatement. At about that time, Gagliardi told us, "I'm sending in my recommendation that Steve be reinstated immediately. John, just give me through the weekend and I'll have it Monday or Tuesday."

"Through the weekend" turned into long weeks of no action. Gagliardi hemmed and hawed, he delayed, he waffled. "I've really got to maneuver Johnny Johnson on this one," he said. "I've gotta be careful too." Finally, on December 31, Gagliardi sent a telegram to Lence terminating my suspension.

I was free to pursue the limited employment options available to me in baseball. I had no interest in a repeat excursion to Florida to be insulted and rejected by a legion of major league general managers. I had a better idea. I was going to play for the Seibu Lions in the Japanese Pacific League.

In San Jose I'd become friendly with Hank Wada, who'd been sent by the Lions to monitor the play of Seibu prospects playing for the Bees. More than once Hank and I discussed the possibility that I might play for the Lions.

The talk became serious in November 1986. Harry Steve was anxious to put together a deal between the Lions and me, because he'd get a piece of the action. The Lions sent a draft contract for my consideration. It was decided in January that I'd go to Tokyo to try out for the Lions. It was expected by all parties that I'd make the team and sign a lucrative contract in March.

I went to San Jose in mid-January to work out for a couple of weeks. Harry Steve let me stay at his place. I was supposed to leave for Japan on February 1. On short notice the Lions pushed my trip back about ten days. It didn't take me long to find out why.

In January the Dodgers sent Ben Hines, a hitting instructor, to conduct clinics for the Japanese. Joining Hines was Ike Ikuhara, a Dodger front-office executive who acted as interpreter. I'd told Fred Claire about the Seibu possibility, and Fred must have innocently mentioned it to Ikuhara.

Ikuhara's comments about me started appearing in the Japanese newspapers almost immediately. He reminded the media that the Dodgers had given me three chances, and he asked whether the Japanese should give me yet another chance. The negative publicity may have made the Lions nervous. They probably held me off for ten days so they could gauge public reaction.

I was treated like royalty from the minute I landed in Tokyo. The Seibu Corporation is one of the wealthiest in the world. It owns, among many other things, the Prince chain of hotels in Japan and Hawaii. The Lions provided me with a suite on the 36th floor of the Sunshine Prince Hotel, from which I had a panoramic view of the city. Every night I could order American movies to play on my video recorder. I could telephone the United States whenever I wanted at the team's expense.

After a couple of days, the team called a press conference. It was a long one. The media wanted to know about everything that had happened to me. I told them the whole sorry story, without lies or excuses. I admitted I'd made a mistake. The reviews of my performance were favorable. The Japanese appreciate honesty and forthrightness.

The only time I didn't feel at home was when the Lions assigned me a uniform. It was a practice uniform without Seibu markings. I understood that all players who try out receive practice uniforms, but for a while it made me feel like I was different and unworthy, even though I knew I was one of the two or three best pitchers in Japan.

My teammates and the fans quickly made me forget my feelings of alienation. They made it clear that they respected my past accomplishments and my ability. When I threw, everyone watched. Fans lined up for autographs when I was free for a few minutes at the ballpark. The Lions organization acted as though my signing a contract and joining the pitching staff were mere formalities.

When the Seibu Lions weren't giving me everything I wanted, they were whipping me into great physical condition. They knew how to get 150 percent out of me every day. Japanese "spring training" begins outdoors in the middle of the winter and lasts much longer than the American version, which is a cakewalk through a few drills and exhibition games in the warm sunshine of Arizona and Florida.

The Japanese accomplish more in a single training season than American pros achieve in three such seasons. The pitchers are constantly running, drilling or throwing. They don't stand around and soak up the sun or shag flies during batting practice. No one gets a day off because the weather's bad. One morning I looked out my window, saw rain and snow, and thought, thank God, no practice. I wasn't completely wrong. We didn't drill or throw. All we did was a little outdoor running. For two and a half hours.

No wonder I fell in love with a Japanese bath. It was the only way I could relieve the pain and exhaustion I felt after every day of training.

When a player was injured, the Lions put red tape on the injury. If he was really hurting, sporting a couple of rolls of tape on various injuries, they assigned him a hat with a white cross. That way the coaches knew who was hurt. But an injured player still worked with everyone else.

The Japanese training regimen built mental toughness and showed the coaches who wanted to play. My teammates were impressed that I was able to jump in and stay with them. They didn't know how much it hurt me to do it those first couple of weeks. There was a quick payoff for all the hard work. By early March I was a lean and mean 190 pounds, in the best condition of my pro career.

In early March I was sure I'd be part of that system for the next seven months. I'd trained well and passed three random drug tests. The Lions were preparing to trade other pitchers to make room for me. They first sent a telex, then an actual contract (similar to the November contract) to Harry Steve, confirming I'd be paid $400,000 for 1987.

I was scheduled for an interview in early March with the Japanese commissioner of baseball, but the Lions' general manager, Yasuyuki Sakai, thought it best that he talk with the commissioner alone. Mr. Sakai made a pitch to the skeptical commissioner. He told him about my rehabilitation and gave him the results of the tests I'd taken in Japan. He told him I'd agreed to help set up one of the first drug rehab programs in Japan. He let the commissioner know that a scandal magazine had sent a reporter to follow me around and the reporter had found nothing.

On March 10, my 29th birthday, I told the Lions they had a deal. But there were forces working against me—some old, some new.

For a generation, the Yomiuri Giants of Tokyo, led by Sadaharu Oh as star player and then as manager, had been the greats of Japanese baseball. The Giants feared that the Seibu Lions with Steve Howe would be too powerful a rival. The Giants lobbied hard with the Japanese commissioner to keep me out.

Perhaps coincidentally, but probably not, an American All-Star team was touring Japan in early March, accompanied by Ueberroth. The Japanese desperately want the American commissioner to push for a real World Series, one in which the winner of the major league series meets the Japanese champion.

Later in the day on March 10, after I'd told the Lions I'd accept their offer, I was called to a meeting in the team's offices. I knew something was wrong because Mr. Sakai, Mr. Namoto, who was director of scouting and player personnel for the Lions, and Shin Kusatani, my interpreter, were in tears. In a few minutes, so was I.

"We must withdraw the offer," said Mr. Kusatani. "We cannot sign the contract because we have a problem."

"What is the problem?" I asked.

"Commissioner."

"Japanese commissioner?"

"No. Commissioner."

Like damaged goods, I was shipped back to the United States.

Officially, the Japanese commissioner had declared me ineligible because no one in the United States had let me play for them since my last suspension. Unofficially, the Japanese commissioner told Seibu that I was so good that there must be something wrong because no American team wanted me. A twist on the "I won't join any club that would have me for a member" bit.

Seibu said all I'd have to do was throw a single competitive pitch for any American professional team, and I'd be approved by the Japanese commissioner to play for the Lions. That gave me no cause for optimism. I'd gone to Japan in the first place because I'd been de facto expelled from American baseball. If I signed a contract with an American team, I wasn't going to be able to jump back to Japan anytime soon.

I wanted to sue Peter Ueberroth and Major League Baseball immediately. Lence calmed me down and said that since I was still out of baseball, the time wasn't ripe for litigation. We decided that I'd have to build a record of sobriety, stay in shape and keep pushing for a chance to play.

Before I left Tokyo, the Lions gave me a Japanese board that advised patience. That quality has never been my strong suit, but I realized it was my only way to return to baseball.

Now that I look back, the Japanese experience was a turning point in my maturing process. Although I'd suffered a crushing defeat, I'd become a stronger person. The Lions' management had taken a personal interest in me and bolstered my confidence. Their honesty and integrity had set a good example for me. I learned that when a man lives honestly and ethically, he never has to explain his behavior. I wanted to live that way. I was also more determined than ever to come back.

I didn't have many options. We decided to contact the Bees, who had released me at my request several weeks before. Harry Steve wasn't as enthusiastic as he'd been a year before, but he would have given me another shot. The problem with San Jose was Joe Gagliardi.

I called Joe and tried to be cordial. Joe was arrogant right out of the gate. "I don't even want to talk to you," he said. "I'm not going to let you play in the California League."

"Why? Give me a reason why."

"I don't have to give you a reason."

"Oh yes you do. I'm off suspension and you can't stop me from playing anywhere."

"I do not want you in this league, and the reason is that I said so. As far as I'm concerned, I'm not going to talk to you anymore."

"You will have to talk to me if I don't play baseball," I said ominously.

"What's that mean? Are you threatening me?"

"No, I'm promising you. You will talk to me again." I slammed down the phone.

I returned to southern California, where I could work out every day in good weather. I was out of money and had no place to live, but Mike Hernandez, Sr. intervened. Mike let me live rent-free in a condo he owns in Rosemead, and he gave me a job at the auto dealership. Mike must be my patron saint. Whenever I flounder and seem lost, he's there to throw me a line and give me a gentle, fatherly push. Cindy, nearly six months pregnant with Brian, had flown from Montana with Chelsi to visit her parents in Hemet, about 35 miles southeast of Riverside. Cindy and Chelsi joined me at the condo. Dave Culbert, a family friend, drove Cindy's car down from Montana.

I began working out every other day with Bob Boone, the 39-year-old catcher who was still one of the best in the game but had no job. Unable to agree on a contract with the California Angels after the 1986 season, Boone declared free agency. For the second straight winter, major league owners were conspiring not to sign free agents. By the time Bob and I began training together, he'd decided to return to the Angels, but he couldn't sign with his old team until May 1.

On several occasions Boone and I were joined by Dave Kingman, the slugger who, at age 38, was trying to catch on with someone for one more year. Before long, the media found out about the workouts. Kingman told a few people that he couldn't hit me at all. Boonie went on camera and compared me favorably to

Steve Carlton at his best. Pretty heady stuff. Major league scouts began to drop by and watch.

Trying to take advantage of the publicity, I began contacting major league teams. I started with teams that had shown interest in '86. Whenever possible, I enlisted inside help. Boone and my old buddy Don Sutton urged Angels General Manager Mike Port to take a hard look at me. Port didn't share their enthusiasm. No one else expressed much interest either.

"You're gonna have one heck of a time getting back in this game, fella," Sutton told me. "Right now you're poison to the general managers." He hesitated. "You're fighting something bigger than the teams."

"What's that?" I asked.

"I don't know. Mum's the word."

In late March I heard that another independent California League team was going to play in San Bernardino, just down the freeway from Rosemead. I called Barry Axelrod, an attorney and sports agent who was involved with the franchise. Axelrod was ecstatic. "It would be great if you could play for San Bernardino," he said. "Everybody in L.A. knows you. It would be great for us."

Axelrod told me to talk to Bill Shanahan, the team's general manager. Apparently I didn't get to the spineless Shanahan before someone else did, because when I called him, he said, "I've got a full roster."

Within ten days after I set up temporary headquarters in Rosemead, I began pursuing a program to prove I was off coke. I went to see Joan Elvidge, one of my favorite people and one of the few drug therapists with whom I've been comfortable. Joan's office was conveniently located in West Covina, only 15 minutes east of Rosemead on the San Bernardino Freeway.

Joan's boss at Community Health Projects was Dr. Forest Tennant, who had treated me in 1984 and told me more than once that I might never recover from addiction because I was uncooperative. I wasn't looking forward to working with Dr. Tennant. But I didn't much care who the supervising medical professional was as long as he was reputable, because I wasn't going to make a mistake this time. Besides, I couldn't hold Dr. Tennant's 1984 views against him. He'd been right about my attitude.

Three or four times a week, at my expense, I presented Dr. Tennant with a urine specimen for testing. Dr. Tennant's lab, using new machines that can detect the presence of substances in urine up to five days after ingestion, tested my samples for cocaine, alcohol, marijuana and amphetamines. All my tests came back negative.

From time to time, I dropped in at Dodger Stadium to visit with Fred Claire. I repeatedly envisioned a storybook ending to my odyssey that put me back in a Dodger uniform, mowing down National League hitters, leading the Dodgers back to the World Series. Part of my heart stubbornly remained Dodger blue.

Fred did nothing to discourage my dreams. In fact, he encouraged them. He told me on several occasions that he was delighted by the way I was conducting my life, and he made it clear that a pitching job with the Dodgers was not an impossibility.

When Fred called me in early April, just after the season had started, I knew by his carefully chosen words that he had cleared his approach with the commissioner's office. "Just talking as your friend, Steve," Fred said, "I think it would be in your best interest to test every day for 30 days."

I was elated by the positive implications of Fred's suggestion, but its substance angered me. Daily testing was medically and technologically unnecessary and would be doubly expensive. A test every other day would have been more than adequate to prove I was clean. But if the Dodgers wanted daily tests, perhaps to present to the commissioner, I'd jump through that hoop too.

Every day for a month, I had to arrange my intimate moment with a plastic cup. It wasn't easy. My workouts, family, counseling sessions and job at Camino Real Chevrolet were more than enough to keep me busy. Sometimes I had to drive an hour from another commitment so I could perform the familiar ritual. On Sunday mornings I raced over to West Covina and peed before I took my family to church. I never missed a test.

On May 1, as expected, Bob Boone signed with the Angels. I recruited my old San Jose buddy, Darryl Cias, to work out with me. The most mutually convenient workout location we could find was in Burbank, an hour away. The extra commuting time left so little play in my schedule that I had to take drug tests at 8:00 a.m., before workouts.

I tried to find out what the Dodgers thought of the new Citizen Howe. The reaction I got was silence. Fred Claire and Peter O'Malley both said they'd get back to me. The last time I heard that was from O'Malley's secretary in early May, on about the 28th day of the 30-day testing frenzy requested by the Dodgers. The message she left with Mike Hernandez, Jr. was, "We haven't forgotten about you. We're working some things out." Until after I signed with the Rangers, I did not personally hear from the Dodgers again.

As May wore on and my testing and training continued, it made me queasy to think of the Dodgers. They'd hinted at job prospects and encouraged me to build a record of sobriety. It's fair to say that they led me on. Now they wouldn't even talk to me. I felt like a jilted lover. I wondered who would give me a chance if the Dodgers wouldn't.

Fred Claire did answer letters from Cindy and from Jim Greenfield, who is a litigator with the Philadelphia law firm of Dilworth, Paxson, Kalish & Kauffman, and who had been working with me on this book. In a letter dated June 3, Claire told Greenfield that the Dodgers were trying to do "what we feel is in the best interest of Steve as an individual."

I'm not sure that keeping me out of the game was in my best interest, but I'd bet that the Dodgers' decision was not Fred's. I believe Fred sincerely wanted to bring me back to the Dodgers. He'd always battled for me, but he didn't always win.

I suffered a mild psychological setback at about the time the Dodgers rejected me. The wild side of my personality threatened to take over. I stayed out and drank a couple of nights, and I was mean to Cindy. I wasn't being honest with myself about my feelings, and I turned inward. I was ripe for a blowout that would have finished me professionally.

Mike Hernandez, Sr. saw what was happening. He sat me down in his office. "I think you're getting away from things that are important to you again," he said. "You want something, but you're afraid to do it. You can make it. You've shown me that you can be different." Mike had turned me around again. His encouragement meant a lot.

On June 1 Dr. Tennant issued his report on me, which took the form of a long letter to John Lence. Dr. Tennant said he was satisfied with my continuing recovery, recommended that I resume my baseball career and lamented that my employment situation was unsettled.

The Dodgers' reaction to the report was odd. Dr. Tennant, a Dodger fan, had hoped that my return to the Dodgers would be possible, but he said that my "past history with the team makes it difficult for the organization to make rapid decisions." Dr. Tennant recommended that I "find a baseball team unrelated to the ones that he has previously played for." Before the report was sent to Lence, but after I'd received a copy of it, Dr. Tennant informed me that the Dodgers tried to get him to change that section.

Maybe the Dodgers really were interested in me and just had a funny way of showing their wayward son how much they loved him. Maybe they wanted to use the report to stake a claim on me, scaring off other teams, while they made up their minds. Beats me. I only know that I didn't appreciate the interference.

Dr. Tennant's report was the major turning point in my comeback. I had satisfied a recognized expert and true skeptic that my recovery was real and I was a good risk. Lence and his hardworking, tolerant secretary, Janet Hagel, immediately packaged the report and sent it to all 26 major league teams.

———————

Just before Dr. Tennant announced to the world that I was no longer hopeless, Harry Steve got a call from some guy who said he could hook me up with a team in the Mexican League. It had been a long time since I'd seen live hitters. I was interested.

Umberto Tapia of the Tabasco Gonaderos told me I could pitch for him without a contract. "Steve, you want to become a starter?" he asked.

"Hey, I just want to pitch."

"Well, I got a guy in the bullpen doing a real good job."

I caught a plane to the Gonaderos' home in Villahermosa, 45 miles from the Bay of Campeche in the Gulf of Mexico, and about 150 miles from the Guatemalan border. I was a Gonadero for a month and three days.

I was neither the only American nor the only former major leaguer on the team. Manny Castillo, who had played for Seattle, and Al Woods, who had been with Minnesota and Toronto, became my best friends in town. Castillo, a Dominican who spoke English and Spanish and was able to bridge the communications gap between the American and Mexican players, was a natural team leader. When Castillo wasn't around, the Anglos and Mexicans didn't communicate much orally, but we all shared the common language of pranks and good times. It was a close-knit and relaxed team that liked a good practical joke, so I fit right in.

Tabasco was the minor leagues all over again, with some added attractions. The team gave the players $1.25 a day meal money on the road. It rained almost every day, and temperatures hovered in the high 90s. Lots of games were interrupted by cloudbursts, and when the downpours stopped, we scraped some dirt around and kept playing. There were bus rides for 15 hours without air conditioning. Clubhouse facilities were either dilapidated or nonexistent. Players who had to relieve themselves during a game discreetly used the water trough or the far corner of the dugout.

Umberto Tapia, a wonderful and honorable man, found a spot for me in the bullpen after all. I busted my butt for him. I had great stuff the entire time I was down there, and I dominated the hitters. In 29 and a third innings, I gave up only four hits, seven walks and no runs, and I struck out 26. I had seven saves.

The people of economically depressed southern Mexico don't have much to get excited about, but they love their Gonaderos. They adopted me as a favorite son. They called me "Juero," which means "Blondie." When I came in to pitch, 15,000 fans stood and chanted, "Jue-ro! Jue-ro!"

While I was taking Villahermosa by storm, Lence and Greenfield were trying to clarify my eligibility to play in the United States. We felt that an official declaration of my eligibility, or even just a clarification of my status, combined with Dr. Tennant's report, would result in contract offers. A copy of the report was sent to Ueberroth, but the commissioner didn't immediately call a press conference and pronounce me medically and morally fit for prime-time play. In fact, he didn't react at all.

Jim personally took responsibility for eliciting some response from the commissioner's office. In case there was none, Greenfield began considering arbitration and other potential litigation strategies.

Greenfield called Durso repeatedly, but Durso didn't return the calls. On June 16 Greenfield went to New York and dropped in (without invitation) at the commissioner's office. Durso's secretary reported that her boss was "in a meeting" and unavailable. Greenfield walked two blocks to the office of Lou Hoynes, the commissioner's outside counsel. "I haven't been asked to get involved in this," Hoynes said. "At this point I'm an attorney without authorization from his client to act."

Greenfield went back to Philadelphia and telecopied a letter to Durso that got an immediate response. One thing in the letter apparently got the attention of Ueberroth and Durso: Greenfield's threat to invoke the arbitrator's July 1984 ruling in the Vida Blue case.

Despite Blue's conviction and stretch in prison for a drug-related offense, the Giants wanted to sign him in June 1984. The Giants asked the commissioner's office about Blue's status. The commissioner repeatedly told the Giants that they couldn't sign Blue because his status was under review. The arbitrator ruled that the commissioner couldn't use the pretense of an investigation to prevent Blue from signing, and he ordered the commissioner to rule on Blue's eligibility in a matter of days. Greenfield's letter told Durso that the Blue decision permitted me to sign a contract immediately, regardless of the commissioner's refusal to clarify my status.

The commissioner has been hammered by arbitrators when he's tried to discipline drug-troubled players such as Blue and LaMarr Hoyt. The thought that he could lose again to me—with Dr. Tennant's report, we had a sure winner—may have made Uebie decide it was best not to ban me and force arbitration.

Maybe Ueberroth and Durso noticed that Greenfield sent a copy of his letter to The Honorable Jim Bunning. Bunning, one of baseball's best pitchers for the Tigers and Phillies in the 1960s, is a congressman from northern Kentucky. Bunning used to be a players' agent. He had a tough time getting Lonnie Smith back into baseball in 1986 after Smith had drug problems.

Congress is a force that truly frightens Ueberroth and the team owners, because Congress can radically change baseball. In 1922 the Supreme Court ruled that baseball was exempt from the nation's antitrust laws, giving organized baseball unlimited power to run the game, restrict competition and discipline players and member teams. (For reasons that are unclear, the courts have refused to give the same protection to football and other sports.) Only the collective bargaining process and arbitration now prevent Ueberroth from being an absolute dictator. The Supreme Court had an opportunity to rescind the exemption as recently as 1972, but passed the hot potato to Congress, which can legislate the exemption out of existence.

Jim Bunning has said he doesn't like the antitrust exemption and the unbridled power it gives the baseball establishment. If Bunning persuades his colleagues to take action, baseball could face financially disastrous competition and government interference. The commissioner would rather cooperate with me than make Jim Bunning mad.

For whatever reason, Hoynes called Greenfield within a couple of hours after Durso received Greenfield's letter on June 17. Now Hoynes was authorized to speak for the commissioner's office. Hoynes made it clear that his client was annoyed that I wouldn't go away and leave baseball alone. He said the commissioner's office had a "sense of here we go again," was "worn down about this" and was "putting on a wet bathing suit here."

The commissioner had ruled that since the National Association had the most recent jurisdiction over me, Johnny Johnson would decide on my eligibility. Hoynes said I'd have to spend a "significant time"—meaning the rest of the season—in the minors to prove I could pitch and stay drug-free at the same time. Hoynes said Ueberroth had never considered the possibility that a major league team would want to put me on its roster immediately. That notion was "preposterous" because I'd been gone so long that nobody knew whether I could still pitch. Hoynes doubted that Ueberroth would approve a major league contract.

We'd already begun to follow the commissioner's orders. Lence had spoken to Johnson and was supplying medical records and other information demanded by Charley Crist, general counsel of the National Association.

It was around June 20 when Umberto Tapia came to me and said, "We have a problem, a big problem. The president of the Mexico City Diablos wants to know if you signed a contract. I told him you did. And he wants to see it."

My immediate reaction was: What business is it of his? Then I started thinking it through. The Mexican League is affiliated with the National Association, supervised by my old friend Johnny Johnson. Had the president of the Diablos called Johnson and asked if I'd signed a contract? Or vice versa?

A contract was no big deal in Mexico. Plenty of Americans had played there without contracts. Why were Johnson and the Diablos making a big deal about me? The Diablos hoped to make the Gonaderos forfeit all the games in which I'd pitched. My guess is that Johnson was involved for one of two reasons. He may have been trying to egg me into signing a contract in Mexico that I couldn't break, so he wouldn't have to worry about my American eligibility for the rest of the year. Or Johnson was just jerking my chain, letting me know he was watching and could reach me even though I was far away.

I told Umberto I'd sign a contract as long as I could walk away from it at any time. As it turned out, though, we never had to worry about it, because Cindy needed me in California.

After I left for Mexico, Cindy and Chelsi moved into Cindy's parents' home in Hemet. Cindy was due to have the baby any day. I knew she had gone into the hospital on June 25, but I couldn't reach anyone to get an update. Finally, the next day, I got my father-in-law on the phone. "What's happening? How's she doing?" I asked.

"You don't know?"

"No, I don't know."

"Well, you've got a boy."

I caught the next plane home and saw my son for the first time shortly after I arrived. Cindy and I thought of naming him after me, but Cindy didn't want him to have to fight his way through school, so we named him Brian Steven Raphael Howe. The Hebrew "Raphael" means "God has healed." It seemed a hopeful, positive name for our son and God had revealed that name to Cindy even before she was pregnant.

Lence had some news. He'd had telephone conversations with several teams, but Tom Grieve, general manager of the Texas Rangers, had called a number of times. Lence thought the Rangers' interest was serious. They wanted to talk to me and watch me work out.

We met in Los Angeles on Friday, July 3. I was impressed that the Rangers sent a committee of five, including Grieve, Rangers President Mike Stone and Employee Assistance Program Director

Sam McDowell. "Sudden" Sam McDowell had been one of maybe half a dozen pitchers in history who could throw a baseball more than 100 miles per hour, but he wasn't there to study my pitching mechanics. McDowell had kicked away much of his enormous talent by drinking to excess. He's a professional substance abuse counselor, and he'd come to L.A. in his professional capacity.

My workout at UCLA lasted all of ten minutes before Grieve said, "I've seen enough." The Rangers were more concerned about what was going on inside my head. The interview that followed the workout was more difficult for me. McDowell and Stone, a clinical psychologist by training, wanted to look into my eyes and hear me talk about my past, my personality and my progress toward recovery. I talked for close to two hours, and I spared neither detail nor emotion. I readily admitted past mistakes, but I didn't avoid placing blame on others. I let them know how angry I was at the commissioner and Durso for what they'd done to me.

The Rangers already knew a lot about me. McDowell had inquired into my background and had interviewed more than a dozen people. They were ready to make a move immediately. But first Johnny Johnson and the commissioner had to take their last ounce of flesh.

Lence had supplied Johnson with every insignificant scrap of information that Johnson claimed he needed to make a decision. Don Hossack, the assistant chief of police in Kalispell, had written directly to Johnson, telling him I'd been a model citizen since I got to Montana. Lence was calling General Counsel Crist every day, demanding an answer. Crist always had an original excuse for Johnson's inaction.

Finally, on Tuesday, July 7, Johnson declared me eligible to play in the National Association as long as I agreed to a closely supervised aftercare program, including testing. But I still couldn't sign a Rangers contract. Ueberroth was barring the door to the home clubhouse at Arlington Stadium. The commissioner wanted to give other teams an opportunity to make offers now that I was officially eligible, so I couldn't sign before July 12. Uebie seemed to be telling the Rangers that because they should have had the good sense not to sign me, we both deserved to suffer for another five days.

Ueberroth probably didn't realize how painful the extra five days were for me. Cindy, Chelsi, Brian and I were still staying at Cindy's parents' small house in Hemet, and the arrangement was straining everyone's tolerance. Cindy's parents wanted to close their house to take their annual summer trip to Montana, but that would have forced four Howes—one of them a week-old infant—into a hotel. We didn't want to impose any longer on Cindy's parents, but we couldn't pick up and leave until we had somewhere to go. Finally, Cindy's parents left and let us stay in the house until I signed.

I played along with the commissioner's hazing period. Toronto and the Yankees wanted to work me out, and I obliged. The Yankees sent Bob Lemon, who'd seen me up close when he managed the Yanks in the 1981 World Series, to check me out. Lemon was nearly an hour late. My workout was about over, but I agreed to throw a few more for him. "Right now," Bob Lemon said, "you look better than anything we've got."

The Rangers offered me $175,000 for the rest of 1987, and they retained the option to drop me or pay me even more generous sums in 1988–89. Kansas City, Toronto and the Yankees also made contract offers. Toronto's was the best of the three, and it was very close to the Rangers' offer.

I was flattered by the attention, but there was never much doubt that I would become a Ranger, even if another team had offered more money. I felt a strong sense of loyalty to the Rangers. They'd taken an interest in me not just as a body that could throw a baseball, but as a person. The Rangers had taken a risk and pursued me long before the commissioner declared open season. I wanted to help this young and unusually humanistic organization win a pennant. Cindy, the kids and I flew to Arlington on July 12 for a press conference that officially made me a Ranger.

16

Crashing the Party

No, the commissioner never came out and told us, "Don't sign Steve Howe." It was my impression that he was not totally behind our signing of Steve. There were many baseball people who didn't have the same confidence that the Rangers did in Steve Howe, that he could be a good pitcher and stay clean. If we were to canvass a lot of major league people on whether they thought we should sign Steve, I think the majority would say it would be a bad thing to do.

One of the things the critics of Steve Howe would have everybody believe was that he could be a very disruptive and bad influence on a major league team, and that he had no business being in the big leagues because of the influence he would have on the team. High-ranking baseball officials told us that.

We didn't believe it for one minute, and our belief has been reinforced since we've seen Steve here. He's a great influence on the team because we don't have anybody on the team who wants to win more than Steve does. I think what allowed him to be accepted so fast was that he showed the team right off the bat that he was an unselfish player, that the only thing that mattered to him was how well the team did. He showed that in Oklahoma City with our AAA team.

It would've been very easy for him to talk only about the big leagues and how long he was going to have to stay in Oklahoma City, but all he talked about was what he could do to help the Oklahoma City 89ers win ballgames. I think he gained a great deal of respect from the minor league players, and I think he's gained a great deal of respect from the big league players.

He's been a very positive influence on some of the players who may have had some minor problems off the field, whether it's minor drug problems or minor alcohol problems. We know that he's clean, and we're confident he'll stay clean.

—Tom Grieve
General Manager, Texas Rangers
September 1987

Reaction to my signing in the Dallas-Fort Worth metroplex, as they call it, was positive. Fans and sports columnists praised the Rangers for having the moral courage and baseball savvy to give me a chance. I've always gotten along well with fans, but I hadn't enjoyed the pleasant experience of media support since 1982.

Congratulatory phone calls came from Fred Claire and the Seibu Lions. Dale McReynolds, the scout who'd signed me for the Dodgers, also called, and we made arrangements to have lunch when I got to Indianapolis in a couple of weeks. The Rangers took care of our living arrangements. They found an apartment for us in The Enclave, a secure complex only a couple of hundred yards from the edge of the Arlington Stadium parking lot. When the Rangers called me up, I'd be able to walk to work.

For the time being, I was going to work 200 miles away in Oklahoma City, where the 89ers of the American Association play. The Rangers sent me to their top farm team to comply with Ueberroth's order that I "demonstrate compliance with a drug testing program over a reasonable period of time."

The commissioner had no grounds on which to keep me out of the majors. If the experts said I was drug-free and a good candidate to stay that way, why should I be eligible to play at one competitive level but not at another? I was too much of a dirtball to play in the majors, but it was all right to let me associate with younger, more impressionable minor league players.

My minor league term was Ueberroth's way of tweaking me one last time before I got what I wanted. He's not a graceful loser. His vague "reasonable time" ruling had the same purpose. A "reasonable time" would be whatever he said it was. He wanted to control my fate as long as possible.

The Rangers were in sixth place in the American League West but still within striking distance at the All-Star break, which began after the games of July 12. The team and I were determined not to tolerate the commissioner's interference for long. There was still time for me to make a difference.

Although I'd been a reliever since I'd made the Dodgers' roster in 1980, the Rangers wanted to convert me into a starter. At that time they didn't have a left-handed starter on their major league roster. Grieve asked what I thought of the idea. "If you want me to start, I'll give it a try," I said. "But don't expect great things right away because I haven't really started in eight years."

To become a starter, I'd have to change both my mental and physical approach to pitching. Mentally, a relief pitcher has no rest. He must be prepared to pitch every day. When called upon, he is expected to challenge hitters, using his best stuff and holding nothing back, for as long as he can, rarely more than three innings. For me—mindful of the teachings of Sandy Koufax never to get beaten throwing less than one's best—that meant using fastballs and sliders almost exclusively.

A starter knows he's going to pitch every fourth or fifth day, so he doesn't have to be mentally ready all the time. On days between starts, a starter can run, throw in the bullpen, work with weights or study opposing hitters. When he gets to the mound, the starter knows he's supposed to stay there at least five to seven innings. He has to pace himself instead of letting it all hang out on every pitch.

Starters and relievers also set up hitters differently. The reliever knows he'll see a hitter once, maybe twice. He need not come up with a wide variety of approaches to exploit the hitter's weaknesses—he can simply attack the holes in the hitter's strike zone with his best pitches. A starter, on the other hand, must prepare to pitch to each hitter four times. He has to be more concerned with changing speeds and selecting pitches to keep the hitter off balance. Throwing off-speed stuff to mess up a hitter's timing has never been my strong suit. I had to dust off my slow curve and work on a straight change if I was to survive as a starter.

When working out, starters run distances and long sprints to train for endurance, while relievers run shorter sprints to build strength for short power bursts. Relievers should spend more time in the weight room to rebuild muscles that are used constantly and torn down.

On most summer days in Oklahoma City, the temperature exceeds 90 degrees. Not infrequently, it climbs above 100. It's hard to breathe comfortably when you're standing still, let alone when you're running. The weather added a higher dimension of pain to the training program for my new starting role.

First I had to run 16 long-distance sprints across the outfield, from foul pole to foul pole. Then I took a turn around the entire fairgrounds complex in which All Sports Stadium is located, a distance of three and a half miles.

That wasn't all. The stadium sits in a bowl, flanked on two sides by a hill that ascends at about a 60-degree angle. Once during each home stand, pitching coach Gary "Wheels" Wheelock ordered us to run the hill. Go up, run part way down, then back up, then all the way down. Ten cycles in about 15 minutes. It was murder. After the final cycle, I felt like I'd just climbed Mount Everest. The first time I did it, I lost two and a half pounds in sweat.

My first game for the 89ers was in relief at home against Iowa on Tuesday, July 14. The Rangers wanted me to make a couple of appearances in relief before trying to start. Nearly 7,500 fans, almost double the average, were on hand. I was whipped from throwing for scouts the previous week and then from collecting my family and moving to Arlington. I'd also thrown in the Ranger bullpen at Arlington Stadium for about 15 minutes on Monday before driving to Oke City. But before the game, one of the coaches said, "Don't expect too much right away." That was all the motivation I needed.

Beginning in the seventh, I worked three hitless innings, striking out two and not walking anyone. Only two balls were hit out of the infield. I also picked up a win. I didn't have good stuff, but I located it well, so I wasn't disappointed. Even in my state of semiexhaustion, the slower "ray" gun clocked my fastest pitches at 92 miles per hour.

After another relief outing, in which I was wild and ineffective, I made my first start on July 20 against Buffalo. The Bisons got two runs on ten hits in five innings. I noticed the home plate ump wasn't giving me much of a strike zone to work with. The plate is 17 inches wide, and for most hitters the vertical strike zone distance from the knees to the belly button is at least two feet. The ump gave me about one square foot. I practically had to throw the ball right down the middle to get a strike called. I guess the hitters noticed too.

My next start, on July 25 in Indianapolis, should have been billed as the Battle of the Exile Druggies. I opposed Pascual Perez, another pitcher who'd had drug problems and was playing in the minors at Ueberroth's direction. The Expos dutifully kept Perez at Indianapolis for about three months. When they finally called him up, he went 7–0 down the stretch. If they had called Perez up earlier, the Expos might have won the National League East.

This time I was sure something was up. Again the strike zone was a tiny box, and the ump was itching for me to say something about it. After some especially bad calls, I began saying to him, "You're better than that."

Finally, during my warm-ups in the third inning, the ump said, "I'm not squeezing the plate on you."

"Bull," I said, "you're better than that."

"Well, goddammit—"

"Oh, you're going to cuss me now?"

"I'm not cussing you, goddammit."

"Well, good," I said. "You're better than that. I've already seen it." The strike zone suddenly expanded to normal proportions.

With one out in the Indianapolis fifth, second baseman Johnny Paredes stood in to face me. Paredes, from Venezuela, is a hot dog. My teammates told me that Paredes liked to push bunt. I decided to pitch him high and inside so he'd pop up if he tried a bunt.

He was diving across the plate before I let my first pitch go, and it missed his chin by about two inches. Paredes came out in front of the plate and swore at me in Spanish. Hey, I was fresh out of Mexico, so he didn't confuse me. "You want to go?" I hollered. "I'm here. Come on."

Paredes charged and we started duking it out in front of the mound. I belted him a couple of good shots before teammates from both sides jumped in and created a huge pileup. The brawl went on for about 30 minutes. Toward the end, 89ers Manager Toby Harrah and I went down under the weight of about four Indianapolis guys. While I was lying there, Dallas Williams of Indianapolis sneaked up and kicked me in the ribs.

Five guys, including Paredes and me, were ejected. Before I left, I invited Paredes and Williams to meet me outside the stadium to settle our dispute.

"Look at it this way," Harrah said in the clubhouse. "You got your 70 pitches and 30 punches in. You're right on schedule."

I had a solid start on July 30 against Buffalo, working five shut-out innings and giving up four hits. I finally felt ready to start, both mentally and physically. But a funny thing happened on my way to the Rangers' rotation.

At about the time they signed me, the Rangers brought left-hander Paul Kilgus up from Oklahoma City and put him in the rotation. Killer—who became my road roommate when I joined the Rangers—pitched better than the Rangers expected. He changes speeds well and has good control, and when he's on he's good for at least six or seven innings. The Rangers wanted to leave Killer in the rotation along with Charlie Hough, Jose Guzman, Bobby Witt and Greg Harris. I was going back to the bullpen.

Whoa, there! Shift gears. Suddenly I was back into speed work-outs and daily mental preparation. The mental part of it was no problem—I'd done it for five previous major league seasons. But physically it was difficult. I was only 29, but my body didn't change direction quite as readily as it had at 22, when I first became a reliever.

The Rangers were going to ask for Ueberroth's approval to bring me up after my last start for the 89ers, but the commissioner was in seclusion in California and the great ship of baseball was rudder-less. There would be another delay.

On August 5, after I'd pitched two straight nights in relief, Tom Grieve told me to fly down to Arlington to see my family. The Rangers were hoping to put me in uniform that night and let the home folks see me pitch against the Red Sox before the team took off on a road trip.

Mike Stone and Rangers owner H. Eddie Chiles flew to New York that morning to personally meet with the commissioner and let him know the Rangers were calling me up. They met for several hours and had a luncheon that I heard was stormy, during which some harsh words apparently were exchanged.

Ueberroth asked Stone and Chiles to wait until September 1. I don't know what was magical about September 1. Maybe Ueberroth was trying to delay my access to pension and free agency benefits that are based on length of service. Who knows?

Stone and Chiles, whose team was still a factor in a pennant race, couldn't get the commissioner to tell them why they should wait. They told him they were going to call me up immediately. Stone and Chiles swear that Peter Ueberroth never directly ordered them not to put me in a major league uniform.

Stone and Chiles flew back to Texas that night. Late that afternoon, Grieve called me at The Enclave and said, "I can't get you a uniform tonight. I don't know what happened. Mike and Eddie are on their way back. We'll meet with you Thursday morning."

Chiles could be described as an oil baron. He is the former chairman of the board of The Western Company, a Fort Worth oil concern. He made his reputation as a tough, aggressive, independent businessman. He and his lovely wife, Fran, are in their box for every Rangers game. Chiles is getting on in years, but he doesn't miss much.

On Thursday morning, August 6, Rangers Manager Bobby Valentine, Stone, Grieve and I sat in Stone's office, waiting for Chiles. Rumors were flying around Arlington that Eddie was going to knuckle under and keep me in the minors until he got the commissioner's approval to bring me up.

Then Chiles walked in. I stood up to shake his hand. "Welcome to the Texas Rangers, son," he said. "I've made my decision. I prayed this morning on the way to the park, and God told me to sign this young man. I thought about it, and it just wouldn't be right to turn you down."

There was a moment of stunned silence. Then I thanked Chiles and everyone else congratulated him. For the first time in 23 months, I was a big leaguer.

After a press conference to announce my return to the majors, I boarded the Rangers' flight to Baltimore to begin a ten-day road trip. We were only four and a half games behind Minnesota. All I wanted was to contribute to a pennant charge by the Rangers over the final third of the season.

I hadn't pitched in the majors since I threw a fraction of an inning of mop-up behind Bert Blyleven in a Twins loss in Chicago on September 10, 1985. Bobby Valentine wanted to use me in the same kind of pressure-free situation my first time out as a Ranger. In the first game of the Oriole series, we fell behind 7–0 in the fifth.

Some unruly fans near the bullpen let me know I was back. As I started to loosen up, they chanted, "Just say no! Just say no!" That didn't bother me much. They'd had quite a few beers by then.

I was nervous. What if I got shelled? I desperately wanted to do well my first time out, to build my confidence in myself and the Rangers' in me. Just before I left for the mound, I said a little prayer. I thanked God for bringing me back and asked him to give me the strength not to make a fool of myself.

By the time I got to the mound, I was probably the calmest guy in the ballpark, totally focused on a task I'd faced about 1,500 times before. A major league hitter named Larry Sheets was standing in the batter's box. I had to get him out.

Sheets had hit four home runs off us in the last eight days. I introduced myself by throwing my first fastball up and way in, and Sheets took a tumble in the dirt. Then I retired him, as I did six of the seven hitters I saw. I gave up one infield single and threw 15 of my 20 pitches for strikes. I was throwing hard. If we hadn't lost, I would have been satisfied.

I didn't fare as well the next day. I surrendered a couple of runs, but I didn't entirely blow our big lead, and we won easily.

The inevitable controversy over my recall kicked into high gear as soon as we left Baltimore for Milwaukee. On August 10 USA Today reported that by bringing me up, the Rangers had violated a commissioner's policy that players with a history of drug abuse must spend 60 to 90 days in the minors before they could play in the majors. Player agents and team executives scurried to check their rule books and all recent correspondence from the commissioner. When had this policy been approved? How did that sly fox Uebie sneak it past us? No one had ever heard of it.

In fact, no such rule or policy existed until Ueberroth invented it just before publishing it in his personal public relations sheet, USA Today. The alleged policy was actually in conflict with Ueberroth's expressed wishes during his August 5 meeting with Chiles and Stone, when he asked that I be kept at Oklahoma City until September 1. That would have meant 50 days in the minors, less than the 60-to-90-day period he was now promoting.

The media speculated that the commissioner would do one of two things: suspend me or fine the Rangers. I never thought he would suspend me. I'd just been declared eligible, and I'd been a good boy ever since. We would have filed for arbitration and won. The commissioner's office could not tolerate another arbitration ruling that it had improperly disciplined a player for past drug use.

It seemed more likely that the commissioner would fine the Rangers. Under the Major League Agreement among the teams that set his powers, Ueberroth could fine a team up to $250,000 for conduct that he decided was contrary to the "best interests of baseball." A ballclub could appeal such a fine, but the appeal would be ruled on by Ueberroth. The owners waived their rights to challenge his rulings in the courts. The owners had literally made Ueberroth a dictator over their teams. In fact, he had a lot more power to impose decisions on the owners than on the players, who had arbitration available to them.

For several weeks Ueberroth did nothing. But on September 10, at major league meetings in Toronto, the commissioner told Chiles he was fining the Rangers $250,000, the maximum allowed. I hope the Rangers didn't pay. They were accused of violating a rule that didn't exist when they supposedly violated it, a rule that made no practical sense anyway. The real reason the commissioner fined the Rangers is because they challenged him. His ego couldn't handle it.

We opened the Milwaukee series with a 12-inning loss that dropped us seven and a half games behind the Twins. I threw two fairly strong innings in my first pressure test, but Jeff Russell had to bail me out of a jam in the ninth. Russell pitched brilliantly until the Brewers put together a couple of singles in the 12th.

The Rangers were a young team with lots of talent. Outfielder Ruben Sierra was starting to assert himself as one of the game's great all-around stars. Pete O'Brien, Pete Incaviglia and Larry Parrish were reliable run producers. Oddibe McDowell, Bob Brower and Jerry Browne were solid young players with speed. Scott Fletcher was an excellent shortstop and a consistent offensive contributor. Charlie Hough was the only starting pitcher over 30, but with his knuckleballing style, his age was irrelevant. Among my mates in the bullpen, Dale ("The Horse") Mohorcic was an effective, steady, right-handed stopper, and lefty Mitch Williams was an awesome talent who was still finding out how good he could be. The team was also close, with no overbearing egos and no serious attitude problems.

Young teams are sometimes inconsistent. During the 1987 stretch run, we had trouble putting things together in neat packages. When the pitching was good, our offense came up short. On other days we bombed enemy pitchers, but we turned around and gave up a pile of runs. We also got into the annoying habit of doing whatever the Twins did for weeks at a time. You can't gain ground that way. We stayed tantalizingly close, but we couldn't make the big run that might have been decisive.

I didn't help matters any on my second weekend with the team, when I blew two straight save opportunities in Boston. We'd lost Mohorcic, who'd suffered mysterious intestinal bleeding in Milwaukee. Bobby Valentine was counting on me to assume the closer's role.

I wasn't sharp coming into the Boston series. My control was lousy. Pitches that I was trying to stick on the corners sailed over the middle. I'd also developed bicep tendonitis, commonly called "spring training arm" because pitchers typically develop it in the spring when their arms aren't used to the stress of constant throwing. I might have gotten it during the quick transition from starter to reliever just before the Rangers called me up.

In the first game of a twi-night doubleheader on Friday, August 14, Bobby Witt was wild but overpowering for six innings, and we led 3–2 in the bottom of the seventh. Bobby ran a 2–0 count on Marty Barrett, one of my old Glacier Pilots teammates. Valentine waved me in. In about five minutes he wished he hadn't.

I finished the walk to Barrett. Then I got a fastball up and over the plate to Wade Boggs, the best hitter in the game. Boggs could have hit it almost anywhere he wanted. He lofted it off the Green Monster in left center for a double to tie the game. Then Mike Greenwell, a left-handed hitting rookie with power, untied it with a triple that landed near the base of the wall in center. I was gone. Jeff Russell came in and only made matters worse. We lost 9–3. We took the nightcap 9–4 behind Hough and a storm of hits.

I had a chance to redeem myself the following afternoon on national TV. We'd knocked Roger Clemens out in the seventh and taken a 6–3 lead, which shrunk to 6–5 when Greenwell hit a two-run homer off Russell. I was asked to protect that lead with no one out and one on in the eighth. After a sacrifice, I gave up a game-tying single to Spike Owen and another hit to John Marzano, on which Oddibe McDowell threw Owen out at third. Mitch Williams relieved me and walked three guys in a row to force in the winning run.

We lost again to the Sox on Sunday, then went home to face Kansas City. In the first game of the K.C. series, Kilgus was sharp and took a 5–1 lead into the seventh. Russell came in and the lead vanished, but we went ahead in the eighth. With two out in the ninth, Russell surrendered doubles to Danny Tartabull and Frank White to create another tie. Valentine summoned me to pitch to pinch hitter Thad Bosley, a lefty. He hit my second pitch for what turned out to be a game-winning single.

If I'd done my job, we could have won four out of five instead of losing four out of five. Now we were nine and a half games behind the red-hot Twins. We never recovered, although we were not mathematically eliminated until the last two weeks.

When it became public in September that the team had been fined for bringing me up, I felt even worse about my failure to contribute. We were still treading water in sixth place, and I couldn't help thinking that things might have been different if I'd given the team a lift against Boston and Kansas City. The debt that I owed the Rangers seemed to be growing.

My initial inconsistency didn't seem to upset the Ranger fans, who greeted me with unusual warmth and affection. During our first home stand after I joined the team, management announced that I would sign autographs in the picnic grounds outside the stadium before a night game. Thousands of fans showed up to wish me well. I signed my name to all kinds of documents and objects for half an hour before I had to go into the clubhouse to dress. The experience made me feel wanted in Texas, and I realized how hungry the Ranger fans are for a winner. They deserve one.

My pitching began to improve after the K.C. series. When I got my first win as a Ranger, against the Royals on August 25, we had moved within five and a half games of first place. That was about as close as we got. I picked up two other wins and a save before the season ended. In my last eight-plus innings, I gave up only two hits, two walks (which forced in a run and cost us a game) and no runs. For almost that entire stretch, I was overpowering, pitching like I did in 1983. In terms of my strength, orientation and control, I felt at the end of the season that I had finally worked out my spring training kinks and was ready to pitch my best.

I nearly incited a riot in Oakland on September 9 when I unintentionally hit Carney Lansford with an 0-and-2 pitch. We were losing by three runs at the time. Lansford crowds the plate and often dives into the ball. He had just hit a hard foul, and I wanted to back him off the plate a little to set him up. I threw a tad too far inside and caught Lansford on the left knee. There's no way I wanted to hit him in that situation.

Tony LaRussa, the mouth who manages the A's, charged out and told our catcher, Darrell Porter, that one of his pitchers was going to nail one of our hitters in the head. "Well," said Porter, gesturing toward me, "he's got better control than any of your pitchers, and if we even think you're going to hit one of ours, he'll get three of yours first."

LaRussa started yelling at me. I invited him out to the mound for further discussion. Guys shuffled out of both dugouts and milled around without much enthusiasm. LaRussa was ejected.

Reggie Jackson strolled over to me. "Steve, you're throwing the ball great," Reggie said. "I know you didn't try to hit him. No matter what you do, everyone's going to think it's wrong anyway. So you just go and throw the baseball. Piss on the rest of them."

17

Totally Honest

Steve is real different in the last month. He's open and loving and caring, he's honest, he's trustworthy. He does what he says he's gonna do. He says what he means, whether I like it or not. And I don't always like it—it's an adjustment for me.

He's taking a real interest in the children and in providing a loving, nurturing relationship with Chelsi, especially right now, and he just adores Brian.

I see him really trying to show me that he loves me and cares for me. He affirms me, he tells me I'm special. He hugs me, he kisses me, he teases me relentlessly. I just love it.

We're really starting to rebuild our life together. We're dreaming about building a home in the country, which is something we've wanted to do for a long time.

He's the spiritual leader in our home now, and I am learning to trust him. I am starting to feel safe with him. He's just real special.

—Cindy Howe
October 1988

After the 1987 season was over, Tom Grieve, Mike Stone and Sam McDowell arranged for me to go to the Instructional League in

Florida to talk to the minor leaguers about the evils of drug abuse. The players were young, with their lives and careers in front of them. I was supposed to share my experiences, strengths and hopes with them. I told them that drugs give only a temporary high, but their destructive impact can be permanent.

I had a good story to tell, and I am good at speaking in public, but I probably wasn't persuasive, because I was unwilling to share the embarrassment and hurt that chemical abuse had caused in every area of my life. Although I had admitted that I was a chemical dependent, I had never been able to accept that fact. I was still in denial of my own chemical dependency. I was powerless against drugs, but I still thought I was in control. For that reason, I was not moving toward recovery. My pride was getting in the way.

It was no surprise, then, that when I returned home to Montana, the insanity started all over again. My first night in town, I failed to come home or call my wife. Cindy did me a favor. She decided that she would not "enable" me to use drugs anymore, so she called Sam and told him what I was up to.

Sam flew up to Montana immediately and told me he was going to recommend that Texas not sign me to a new contract until I showed them I was serious. That scared me, so I decided to agree to whatever Sam wanted me to do.

My first assignment was to join Sam at Freedom '87, a chemical dependency conference at the Adams Mark Hotel in Philadelphia. My head still wasn't straight. I knew intellectually that I didn't want to fall back into addiction, but I had begun to question who I was and whether I was missing any fun. I wasn't comfortable with my recovery.

Many times, in countless rehab center therapy sessions, I had said I was powerless against drugs and alcohol. I had said it because I knew that was the only way they would let me leave. It was part of the game.

On Thursday, October 22, I went to Sam's room late at night. I told him how I felt. Sam knew why I was uncomfortable. "You haven't truly surrendered to addiction," he said. I returned to my room and turned it over in my mind a hundred times. I still thought I could defeat addiction as though it were a hitter trying to drive in the tying run in the ninth. Trouble was, I had tried every way I knew to retire my addiction, but I had failed every time. My breakthrough came at a spirituality lecture given by Father Leo the following evening.

I'd been a Christian since 1980, but I was still a spiritual fence-jumper. On one side of the fence, the "fun" side, I was a practicing, card-carrying drug addict. On the other side was my faith. When I slipped to the fun side, I told myself that drugs were fun and I was persecuted because I was misunderstood.

But, from time to time, the misery of addiction made me jump back to the Christian side of the fence. I asked God to rescue me from addiction. When it happened, instead of embracing faith, I thought about how I'd been able to use drugs without catastrophe. I'd gotten away with it so easily. Then I'd jump back to the fun side again. I'd used God like aspirin, for temporary pain relief.

My faith had failed to hold me because deep down I believed I wasn't worthy of God's love and forgiveness. I didn't understand that God gives us freedom of choice and makes us responsible for our actions. I didn't see that, through prayer, I could draw from God and Christ the power to take affirmative action to make my life turn out as I wanted.

Father Leo, a priest and an alcoholic, helped me understand. He was a man who had followed a godly course all his life, yet he too had believed himself unworthy of forgiveness. I thought he was speaking directly to me. He told me I was worthy and should be entitled to take what I wanted from life. If Father Leo could forgive himself for sinning while professing to do the work of the Lord, then I too could accept forgiveness. At that moment, my faith became real, a living thing.

Only a few days later, Cindy and I attended the Professional Athletes Outreach Conference in San Diego. PAO is a Christian fellowship group. Compelled by a strange sense of urgency I didn't understand, I stood and spoke before 60 couples at a PAO session. I told about all the things I'd done, the people I'd hurt, the remorse I felt. I told it all, and I broke into tears.

A remarkable thing happened. Twenty minutes after I finished speaking, Andy Van Slyke, an outfielder for the Pittsburgh Pirates, stood before the group and spoke to me. "I have judged you," he said. "I need to apologize to you. I judged you and thought you should never be back in the game, from what I read in the paper. I believed you had slandered the name of baseball. I judged you because I didn't understand." Andy started to cry.

Three more players, Dave Dravecky, Brian Harper and Brett Butler, stood up one by one and said the same thing. Here I was, the greatest sinner, the most unworthy person in the room, and these Christians were apologizing to me. I felt and accepted forgiveness from them and from God. It was an incredible healing experience.

By early January I felt better—physically, emotionally and spiritually—than at any time since 1980. I'd turned my life almost completely around, and I knew that if I kept moving in the same direction, I'd remain sober and regain my lost prominence as a top relief pitcher.

How, then, could I have allowed the events of January 11–17 in Arlington to happen? I thank Sam and Cindy for the insight they have given me as I've considered this nagging question. The answer is that I didn't yet realize that I had to change my old ways of living and thinking to stay sober. Among my teammates for the first time in three months, anticipating the beginning of a new season under a great contract, on a roll after an impressive workout at the stadium, I felt so good that I forgot I'm powerless against chemicals and tempting situations. God and the AA program gave baseball back to me time and again, but because of my fear and unwillingness to make permanent changes, my chances of long-term recovery were nil.

After I lost the contract in Texas, I came back home and started going to AA meetings again, but my commitment to sobriety had no real substance. I was still lying and denying that it was my chemical dependency that had taken away my self-respect and baseball career. I was minimizing the grief and humiliation I felt and ignoring the plain truth that I had plotted and planned one more high. I was unable to accept myself without baseball. So while I was staying clean and sober and going to meetings and church, I still wasn't honest.

My feelings of fear and worthlessness led up to what I call the "St. Patrick's Day Massacre." It began on a Thursday afternoon when one of my friends suggested we go to his condominium for a while. Another friend decided to ride with us, and we picked up a beer for each of us to drink during the 20-minute ride to Columbia Falls. Each beer, however, was quart-sized, and by the time we got to Columbia Falls, I had a good buzz.

We stopped at a bar to have one more beer before going to the condo. I asked the bartender where I could get some coke, and he gave me a telephone number. I purchased two grams of coke to add to our celebration of St. Patrick's Day, and then we left for the condo, taking the bartender with us. The celebration was about to turn into a nightmare.

Once we reached the condo, we all got high, but it wasn't a good experience for any of us. One of my friends spent the entire time pacing up and down the stairs in total paranoia. I was in equally bad shape, because all I could do was follow him around. My other friend was so paranoid that he started doubling up on drinks so he could come down more rapidly.

I was so high that I didn't want to drive my truck home, so I let one of my friends drive it to his house. Real clever. Here I was, giving my $25,000 truck to someone who was as high as I was.

I knew I would be in trouble with Cindy if I went home high. My solution was to stay away and get even higher, so the bartender and I headed to his house to party some more. The friend who had my truck didn't come to get me until Sunday. I had him take me down to his ranch in Bigfork.

I was worried. Sam McDowell had told Cindy that if I stayed clean and sober, I could possibly get another baseball job. I knew that opportunity would be in jeopardy if Sam and Cindy found out I'd gotten high (as if they didn't already know, when I failed to come home that first night), so I did what any addict in denial would do: I lied. My two friends thought of a good cover story for me. One of them had another friend in Philipsburg who had an excavation business. We would contact him to see if he'd go along with the lie and give me a check for two weeks of work in Philipsburg to prove I'd been there. Then I could go home, tell Cindy and Sam I was working off a gambling debt, provide the check, give a clean urine sample and be off the hook. It didn't work out that way. God intervened.

I believe that up to this point, God had been showing me that I was going to be responsible for my actions one way or another, whether I liked it or not. I went home on Thursday, a week after I left, and submitted a urine sample on Friday. Somehow I knew the test would be positive, even though I hadn't used in over three days.

As it turned out, it didn't matter whether I gave a positive or a negative, because Sam had called Cindy on Monday while I was AWOL. Cindy as usual told Sam the truth—that she had not seen me in four days. That was enough for Sam. He told Cindy he was really sorry because he had called to offer me a job, but under the circumstances he was unable to make that offer. I was devastated. I took it out on Cindy, blaming her for telling Sam. I even blamed my friends for covering for me. The truth is I hated myself so much that I couldn't stand it. I left again, and it was to be a full month before I would talk to Sam or see my family.

When I finally talked to Sam, I asked him if he thought I should go to treatment. He said no, that if I followed AA's program, I might have a chance. He also said that without complete and total surrender, I would never make it.

I moved back home and went to work building decks on our neighbors' townhouses. Although I was going to a few AA meetings, I was still using coke on occasion after Cindy went to bed. But she had an uncanny way of waking up, looking at me and knowing I'd been using. It made me mad that I kept getting caught. I felt more and more trapped. My lies were no longer effective, and I couldn't give up drugs. I hated myself. When an opportunity arose for me to play minor league ball in Cancun, Mexico, I jumped at it. I had to get away. I left immediately and told Cindy that she and the kids could come down four days later.

I didn't call Cindy for two weeks. I was drinking heavily and the only reason I wasn't doing cocaine was that I couldn't find any. I was sitting on my balcony one day, feeling miserable as memories of my family, my childhood and my major league baseball career flashed before me. Although I was drunk, I clearly perceived that I had only two choices. I was either going to kill myself, or I was going to give myself a real chance.

Later that afternoon, I went to pick up a rental car, and an attendant at Budget noticed the AA medallion I wear around my neck. He must have recognized me, because he asked when I was really going to give AA a try. His words had such an effect on me that I went to a meeting that day and have been sober ever since. I believe that again God placed a significant person in my life to show me how to get my life in order.

When I finally called Cindy, she was angry and refused to come to Mexico. I tried threats, including divorce, but Cindy held her ground. Today I think that God was allowing me to see how badly I wanted to straighten out my life. As I stayed in Mexico and continued to go to AA meetings, I realized how lonely I was and how much I missed my family.

Once again, God came to the rescue. Dale McReynolds had recommended me to a semipro team, the Madison (Wisconsin) A's, for the National Baseball Congress Tournament in Wichita, Kansas in August. Gene Barrett, the owner of the A's, made all the arrangements and called Cindy in Montana. Sensing a change in me, she agreed to bring the kids and meet me in Wichita.

I hadn't seen my family in months, and the meeting in Wichita was a special time of reconciliation. It also marked the beginning of a new era, as God began reassembling the scattered pieces of my life.

I hoped to win a major league contract by pitching well in Wichita, but God had other plans. I developed bicep tendonitis and was unable to pitch in the tournament. Once again, I had to postpone my dream of returning to the majors. For the first time in my life, I accepted the disappointment without anguish. I finally understood that baseball is not all that matters.

Immediately after returning to Montana, I enrolled in a counselor internship at Glacier View Hospital. I spent two weeks there and gained more insight into my addiction. I also learned what I had to do to continue to recover. For me, it's simple: be totally honest and admit I don't have all the answers. In striving for honesty, I had to admit that my principal motivation to recover was baseball. I was using the counseling internship to convince Sam and the baseball authorities that I was fit to return to the game. I've left the hospital program for now. Maybe in the future I'll decide to become a counselor, but if I do, it will be to help others, not to further my career.

Cindy and I were scheduled to leave on October 7, 1988 for Last Days Ministries in Lindale, Texas, to attend Intensive Christian Training School for ten weeks. We were packed and ready to go, but we didn't have any money. Cindy felt sure that God would provide, and within a week Last Days called and told us they would cover the cost of the school and our living expenses for the next couple of months.

Cindy thought that was God's answer to our needs, but God had taught me otherwise. For so long, I had let other people be responsible for me and pay my way, and I now felt God testing the strength of my recovery. Was I finally willing to take responsibility for my life, even if it meant that I couldn't go to Texas, knowing how disappointed Cindy would be? I was afraid to take responsibility for myself, and the prospect of going to Texas was very attractive. I had a choice: escape or become responsible. I decided to stay home, work and allow God to mold me through everyday circumstances.

I've been severely wounded by drugs, but my health is good. I still have my family, and I have no criminal record of drug-related offenses. I've fallen down often, but thanks to all the loving people who didn't give up on me, I've been able to let God guide me in the right direction. He's already recorded the most important save of all—my life.

Appendix I

ADMINISTRATIVE OFFICES: 336½ South Glendora Ave., West Covina, California 91790 • (818) 919-1879 • (818) 919-1870

BOARD:

Rev. Lawrence F. Cole
William Crawford, J.D.
Carmel Marti Day, M.A.M., Ph.D.
Ross Figgins, Ph.D.
Seymour E. Lichtman, C.L.U.
William C. Maslow, M.D.
Craig Meacham
Howard Pertulla
Louis Petrie, Jr.
Ben Ruiz

EXECUTIVE DIRECTOR:

Forest S. Tennant, Jr. M.D., Dr. P.H.

COMMUNITIES WE SERVE:

Baldwin Park
El Monte
Fresno
Glendora
La Puente
Ontario
Oxnard
Pasadena
Pinedale
Phelan
Pomona
Santa Barbara
Santa Maria
West Covina
Whittier

June 1, 1987

John A. Lence
Attorney at Law
745 So. Main
Kalispell, MT 59901

RE: Summary of case of Steve Howe

Dear Mr. Lence,

This extended letter summarizes the current clinical condition of Steve as well as some of my recommendations and opinions as to what his future course should be relative to employment and particularly whether he should play baseball.

CURRENT SUMMARY OF STEVE HOWE

When Steve returned to Los Angeles in March of this year (1987), he asked if he could be under the care of me and one of my chief therapists, Joan Elvidge. Since we have a long-standing policy in my facilities that we always take our former patients back and since we know that drug dependency is a chronic-relapsing condition, we do this routinely for patients. I point this out since Steve sought our care voluntarily and independent of any employment with the Los Angeles Dodgers. To me this voluntary effort was a great step forward for Steve since he has, in the past, reluctantly accepted the advice and counsel of professionals like myself and he has particularly resisted urine testing. Since March Steve has taken approximately 50 urine tests including one 30 day period where he tested every day. He has been observed each time and his urine has not contained any cocaine, alcohol, marijuana, or amphetamines. His appearance is excellent, physical health is good, and more

269

importantly, his attitudes towards recovery are much more positive and objective. Put another way, I never get the opportunity to see a person who appears in a better recovery state and able to resume employment than Steve now appears. To this end, I highly encourage you, Steve, and all parties concerned to develop a course of employment and pursue it. I am aware that Steve has not only been successful but enjoys his automobile business and this factor definitely needs to be taken into account.

SHOULD STEVE ATTEMPT TO AGAIN PLAY BASEBALL?

The question as to whether Steve should attempt to play professional baseball again is one that I believe should primarily rest with Steve. He informs me that he definitely wants to return to professional baseball and that the barriers in his way are primarily the lack of a solid offer from a professional team and the Commissioner's approval. First, from a clinical point of view he is certainly capable and should pursue his chosen occupation. Second, however, baseball is so public and has to set such a public image that I am well aware of the dilemmas that the Commissioner and individual teams have in deciding whether Steve should again be a professional baseball player and set an image for young people in this country. Although I personally would like to see Steve again be a Dodger, his past history with the team makes it difficult for the organization to make rapid decisions. After some reflection I suspect that Steve's best hope would be to find a baseball team unrelated to the ones that he has previously played for and one which will accept his medical condition which is that of a chronic, relapsing condition.

It seems to me that the problem now is to convince a professional team that Steve is worth the risk. In this regard you should be aware that Steve has never been a cocaine addict or dependent upon cocaine to the extent of many persons I have treated and not near as dependent as many professional ballplayers that I have treated. A great deal of Steve's difficulty is that his case became public. Naturally being in Los Angeles helped that a great deal! Even Steve's relapses were of a minor nature as drug dependence goes since he was usually detected before he became very dependent again.

Naturally, neither I or anyone else, including Steve, can really tell us whether he will relapse in the future. Employers throughout the country as well as professional sports

is now having to deal with the dilemma as to whether they want
to employ someone who has relapsed one, two or even more times.
Unfortunately, professional baseball and other professional
sports don't give a person a lot of flexibility relative to
employment so I believe that you and Steve should pursue
employment in baseball if this is a desire of yours. In
addition, I am very hopeful one of the teams and the
Commissioner will see fit to again give him an opportunity to
play. If they don't I suspect it will be because they are very
concerned about the image that is given to young people when
they accept a player who has relapsed multiple times.

SOME GUIDELINES FOR FUTURE DECISIONS AND EMPLOYMENT

At this time Steve now appears to be more than willing to
participate in a program that I believe would protect the
employer and Steve against future relapse. He is willing to
undergo as much urine testing and any other type of examination
as is needed to keep him clean and functioning. This is a
considerable attitude change of Steve's, and he has obviously
learned that recovery is based on setting up a monitoring system
for oneself that guarantees abstinence and the detection of
early relapse. Whatever happens in the future or wherever he is
employed, I will be glad to give any records or assistance that
I can to help any physician or other involved parties relative
to my information, urine test results, and advice for future
treatment.

You should recommend to Steve and to any team that he might play
with that he needs to urine test two to three times per week.
In addition, the urine tests need to be analyzed by the new
urine testing technology which is described below.

LET'S MAKE A DECISION

I am very uncomfortable and unhappy with the limbo that Steve
now finds himself in. I would like to see you and Steve, as
well as any parties in baseball that you should communicate to
set up some kind of plan which has some time points in it to
make some decisions. For example, perhaps the baseball commissioner
or a prospective team will be willing to accept Steve if he can
remain abstinent for a certain period of time. Please count on
me to provide any and all records and test results that I have
in this regard.

NEW URINE TESTING TECHNOLOGY TO DETECT EARLY RELAPSE

Please be aware that I ahve been monitoring Steve with a new
urine screening technology that is less than 90 days old and
which is far better than anything we have had in the past to
detect early relapse. I am quite confident that I would have

271

been able to detect Steve's relapses in past years much earlier and could have saved him and all of us a lot of grief. As pointed out, the technology is less than 90 days old. This technology will detect on a screening basis the use of cocaine at very low levels in the urine and it will detect it for several days after it has been used. Unfortunately, the urine screening technology of the past has been quite good at eliminating what we call false positives but very poor at detecting low levels of cocaine in the urine which we often call false negatives. This new testing capability which is commercially made by Abbott Laboratories should be a "must" for monitoring Steve in the future. This information can be passed on to appropriate parties.

In summary, I empathize with the agony and position that you and Steve now find yourselves in. He has relapsed on a number of occasions, become very public and becomes a financial and public relations risk to any future employer including a professional baseball team and the Commissioner. Not withstanding, however, is the fact that employers throughout this country are going to have to now face the fact that we have many young persons who are in need of employment and who have relapsed multiple times. Furthermore, there is no guarantee that they will remain totally abstinent when they are employed. The only way out of this dilemma, as I see it, for a public employer like baseball is for the player to be urine tested a minimum of two or three times per week so that early relapse can be detected and also that it can be kept confidential and dealt with behind the scenes.

I hope this information is helpful and I am forwarding a copy of this to Commissioner Ueberroth who I know will give Steve and all other ball players every consideration that he can after he weighs all of the facts.

Best Regards,

Forest Tennant

Forest Tennant, M.D., Dr. P.H.

cc: Peter Ueberroth
    John Johnson

FST:cm

272

Appendix II

1.   TERM OF PLAYER CONTRACT. The term of this Player Contract ("Term") shall be for a period of two (2) years representing the 1988 and 1989 major league baseball championship seasons ("Championship Season[s]"), including all play-off and World Series games.

2.   SALARY. The 1988 Salary shall be $425,000 (Four Hundred and Twenty Five Thousand Dollars) for the Championship Season. The 1989 Salary shall be $500,000 (Five Hundred Thousand Dollars) for the Championship Season. (The 1988 and 1989 Salaries will be collectively referred to herein sometimes as "Salary".) For purposes of payment of Salary, this Player Contract shall be divided into two (2) contract years: the 1988 Salary to be paid in equal semi-monthly installments over the course of the regular 1988 Championship Season and the 1989 Salary to be paid in equal semi-monthly installments over the course of the regular 1989 Championship Season.

3.   BONUSES. If earned, and only if earned, the Club shall pay the Player for each Championship Season in which the Player meets the following performance levels in 1988 and/or 1989:

a) $25,000 (twenty five thousand dollars) if the Player earns fifty (50) points. The point system entitles the Player to one (1) point for each relief appearance and two (2) points for each start; plus

b) $50,000 (fifty thousand dollars) if the Player is voted first through fifth in the official voting for the Cy Young Award or first through third under the former rules for the Rolaids Fireman of the Year Award; plus

c) $50,.000 (fifty thousand dollars) if the Player is voted the most Valuable Player in the League Championship Series; plus

d) $50,000 (fifty thousand dollars) if the Player is voted the Most Valuable Player in the World Series.

Any performance bonus earned hereunder shall be payable within thirty (30) days of the conclusion of the season in which it is earned.

4. <u>GUARANTEE PROVISION AND EXCEPTIONS</u>. So long as this Player Contract is not terminated, the Club only agrees to pay the Player in full the 1988 and 1989 Salaries and no other compensation including but not limited to Performance Bonuses, unless and only if earned; provided, however, that the Club shall be released of its obligation to pay any Salary during any period during the Term that Player fails to render his services to the Club pursuant to this Player Contract due to:

a) The Player and Club recognize that Player's participation in certain sports or activities may impair or destroy the Player's ability and skills as a professional baseball player. Accordingly, during the Term of the Player Contract, the Player agrees that if he engages in automobile or motorcycle racing, piloting of aircraft, fencing, parachuting or skydiving, organized softball, weight-lifting, organized basketball, skiing, hockey, karate, judo, organized football, tug-of-war, boxing, wrestling, superstar or super team competition ("Non-Permitted Sports"), and if he suffers any incapacity, injury, sickness, disability or death which impairs his ability to play major league professional baseball as a result of same, then such occurence will release the Club from all of its obligations, liabilities, and responsibilities hereunder, from the date of such incapacity, injury, sickness, disability or death unless the Player has previously requested and received in writing permission from the Board of Directors of the Managing General Partner of the Club to participate in the Non-Permitted Sports, in which event such Board must give its decision in writing to the Player within ten (10) days after the receipt of such request. Player also agrees that except with the prior written consent of such Board, he will not participate in any other sport or activity involving substantial risk of incapacity, injury, sickness, disability or death to him.

b) If any incapacity, injury, sickness, disability or death of the Player is caused by: (i) suicide or attempted suicide; (ii) intentional self-inflicted injury; (iii) committing or attempting to commit a criminal or feloneous act in which the Player pleads or is found guilty by a court of last resort; or (iv) drug abuse, alcohol abuse, drug addiction or alcoholism ("Non-Permitted Activities"), then the Club shall be relieved from all of its obligations, liabilities, and responsibilities hereunder from the date of such incapacity, injury, sickness, disability or death.

c) If the Player refuses to render his professional services to the Club, or if the Player voluntarily retires as an active player from major league baseball, then such refusal or retirement will release the Club from all of its obligations, liabilities, and responsibilities hereunder from the date of such refusal or retirement.

d) It is further understood that the Salary and Performance Bonus specified in Paragraphs 2 and 3 of this Addendum shall not be paid:

> (i) During any period or periods of strike by the members of the Major League Baseball Players' Association;

> (ii) During any period or periods that the Player is unable to play by virtue of being suspended pursuant to Major League Rule 13; or

> (iii) During any period or periods that the Player is on the Restricted List, the Ineligible List or the Disqualified List specified in Major League Rule 15, or is unable to play by action of the League President or the Commissioner of Baseball.

e) The Player and the Club ratify, adopt and incorporate herein by reference as Exhibit A all of the terms and conditions of that certain "Texas Rangers After Care Program for Steve Howe" (the "Program") attached hereto, and in the event of a breach, violation, or transgression of any of the covenants contained in the Program, the remedies set out in the Program (including but not limited to suspension and/or termination of this contract) shall be fully enforceable in all respects in accordance with their terms and supersede any and all other covenants or remedies contained in this Contract that relate to the subject matter of the Program.

5. Incapacity, injury, sickness, disability or death directly resulting from injury sustained in the course and within the scope of the Player's employment under the Player Contract, or incapacity, injury, sickness, disability or death occuring during the Term of the Player Contract not as a result of the Player engaging in Non-Permitted Sports or Non-Permitted Activities shall not impair the right:

a) of the Player to receive his Salary, including any deferred compensation, if any, for the period of such incapacity, injury, sickness or disability during the unexpired Term of the Player Contract, but only upon the express condition that written notice of same, including the time, place, cause and nature of same, is served upon and received by the Club within ten (10) days of the sustaining of said incapacity, injury, sickness or disability; or

b) of his estate or designated beneficiary, upon his death, to receive the unpaid portion, if any, of his Salary during the unexpired Term of the Player Contract in accordance with the payment schedule in the Player Contract.

6.   The Club agrees that if this Player Contract is terminated because the Player fails, in the opinion of the Club's management, to exhibit sufficient skill or competitive ability to qualify or continue as a member of the Club's team (Paragraph 7 [b] [2] of this Player Contract), the Player shall continue to receive the unpaid balance of the Salary stipulated in Paragraph 2 of this Addendum for the Term of this Player Contract; provided however, that the foregoing covenant to continue the Player's Salary applies only in those situations where insufficient skill or competitive ability does not result from the Player's misconduct, or the Player's unlawful or contractually prohibited acts, which include the following acts:

a) The Player's failure, refusal or neglect to conform his personal conduct to the standards of good citizenship and good sportsmanship or to keep himself in first-class condition or to obey the Club's training rules (Paragraph 7 [b] [1] of this Player Contract); or

b) The Player's failure, refusal or neglect to render services under this Player Contract or in any other manner materially breach this Player Contract (Paragraph 7 [b] [3] of this Player Contract); or

c) The Player's failure to render his services due to physical or mental incapacity or death directly due to or attributable to participation in any Non-Permitted Sports or any Non-Permitted Activities.

7.   In the event this Player Contract is terminated and during its Term the Player signs a contract with another club or clubs, notwithstanding anything to the contrary in this Addendum, the Club's total obligations to the Player (including the amounts deferred to later years, if any) in any year shall be reduced by the amount(s) which the Player earns during that year from any club or clubs, including the amount(s) deferred to later years, if any, and bonuses.

276

8.   In the event the Player refuses to accept a reasonable Major League contract offered by a club other than the club which released him, the Player shall forfeit that portion of the Salary which would not have been payable had he accepted such other contract.

9.   If the Club terminates this Player Contract pursuant to Paragraph 7 [b] [1] or 7 [b] [3] of this Player Contract, all obligations of both parties hereunder, including the obligation to pay the Player in full the Salary stipulated in Paragraph 2 of this Addendum shall cease on the date of termination, except the obligation to pay the Player compensation earned to said date which will include deferred compensation.

THE TEXAS RANGERS, LTD. by its
Managing General Partner, Rangers
Management, Inc. ("CLUB")

By _Thomas A. Grieve_____

Its _Vice President & General Manager_

Date_____ 11/25/87 _____

_____
STEVEN ROY HOWE ("PLAYER")

x_ 12-08-87 _____
DATE

Appendix III

STEVEN ROY HOWE
Born March 10, 1958 at Pontiac, MI
Height 6.01   Weight 195
Throws and bats left-handed
Attended University of Michigan

Year	Club	League	G	IP	W	L	SV	H	R	ER	SO	BB	ERA
1979	San Antonio	Texas	13	95	6	2	0	78	36	33	57	22	3.13
1980	Los Angeles	National	59	85	7	9	17	83	33	25	39	22	2.65
1981	Los Angeles	National	41	54	5	3	8	51	17	15	32	18	2.50
1982	Los Angeles	National	66	99.1	7	5	13	87	27	23	49	17	2.08
1983	Los Angeles	National	46	68.2	4	7	18	55	15	11	52	12	1.44
1985	Los Angeles	National	19	22	1	1	3	30	17	12	11	5	4.91
1985	Minnesota	American	13	19	2	3	0	28	16	13	10	7	6.16
1986	San Jose	California	14	49	3	2	2	40	14	8	37	5	1.47
1987	Tabasco	Mexican	15	23	2	0	7	4	0	0	28	2	0.00
1987	Oklahoma City	AA	7	21	2	2	0	26	8	8	14	5	3.48
1987	Texas	American	24	31.1	3	3	1	33	15	15	19	8	4.31
	National League Totals		231	329	24	25	59	306	109	86	183	74	2.35
	American League Totals		37	50.1	5	6	1	61	31	28	29	15	5.01
	Major League Totals		286	379.1	29	31	60	367	140	114	212	89	2.70

DIVISION SERIES RECORD

Year	Club	League	G	IP	W	L	SV	H	R	ER	SO	BB	ERA
1981	Los Angeles	National	2	2	0	0	0	1	0	0	2	0	0.00

CHAMPIONSHIP SERIES RECORD

Year	Club	League	G	IP	W	L	SV	H	R	ER	SO	BB	ERA
1981	Los Angeles	National	2	2	0	0	0	1	0	0	2	0	0.00

WORLD SERIES RECORD

Year	Club	League	G	IP	W	L	SV	H	R	ER	SO	BB	ERA
1981	Los Angeles	National	3	7	1	0	1	7	3	3	4	1	3.86

ALL-STAR GAME RECORD

Year	Club	League	G	IP	W	L	SV	H	R	ER	SO	BB	ERA
1982		National		1/3	0	0	0	0	0	0	0	0	0.00